A Year On
The Garden Path

A 52-Week Organic Gardening Guide

Carolyn Herriot

> "Today we are faced with a challenge that calls for a shift in our thinking, so that humanity stops threatening its life-support system. We are called to assist the Earth to heal her wounds and in the process heal our own."
>
> *Dr. Wangari Maathai,*
> *Nobel Peace Prize Laureate, 2004*

Text copyright © 2005 Carolyn Herriot
Photographs copyright © 2005 Carolyn Herriot
Illustrations copyright © 2005 Fang Zhang

Photos: Carolyn Herriot
Cover and interior design and layout: Reber Creative, Victoria BC
Monthly faceplate illustrations: Fang Zhang

Printed and bound in Canada
Second edition

Library and Archives Canada Cataloguing in Publication

Herriot, Carolyn
    A year on the garden path : a 52-week organic gardening
    guide / Carolyn Herriot.

    Includes index.
    ISBN 0-9738058-0-3

    1. Organic gardening – Canada. I. Title.

SB453.5.H465 2005   635'.0484'0971   C2005-902741-X

Published by Earthfuture Publications, Victoria BC

This book is printed on New Leaf Reincarnation Matte, made with 100% recycled fiber, 50% post-consumer waste, processed chlorine free. By using this environmental paper, the following resources were saved on the second print run of this book: 87 fully grown trees; 18,986 gallons water; 40 million BTUs energy; 4,153 pounds solid waste; 7,019 pounds of greenhouse gases.

Calculated based on research done by Environmental Defense and other members of the Paper Task Force.
© New Leaf Paper   www.newleafpaper.com   888.989.5323

Contents

Acknowledgements

To all the Landscape Angels who have overlighted The Garden Path

And with endless gratitude to:

Josie

Guy

Philip and Margot Clegg, my incredible parents, for the strong foundation upon which I grew. Lucy Clegg for her garden of childhood memories. Eileen and Peter Caddy and Dorothy McLean for co-creating the magical Findhorn Garden. Hallie Cameron for her wise guidance and infectious laughter. Chris Edwards for his love and support at the very beginning. Pat Lansdowne for her loving kindness and a safe haven. The Gathright Family for sharing their garden and for giving so many 'coconuts' to The Garden Path.

Jamie

Jolene

Especially to Jolene Billwiller, for moving every plant and sharing every fun minute with me (and lots of great lunches!)

The BIGS Program, Camosun College, David Greig and Laurie Hardy, without whose amazing support The Garden Path would not be what it is today. Carrie and Brian Berglund, the best neighbours a Nursery could ever ask for! Joyce McDonald for her support and generous website skills. Wayne Poohachoff for recycled boxes galore! Amanda Maslany for her special artistic touches. Anne Derrett for wonderful service, wisdom and friendship.

Priscilla

Hiroe

Ann Tasko for counsel, love and lots of laughter! Dan Jason for 'seedy' inspiration and constant friendship. Ilona and Bill Beedie, Christine Lawlor, Ros Thomas, Wendy McVicar and Jacqueline Sutton for being wonderful lifelong friends. Judy Barz, Hilda and Bob Matsuo, Lynda Dowling, Mona Hansen, Karl Koster and Michele and Allan Dickeson, for their friendship and generosity of endless plant donations.

Sandy

Mizue

Jackie and Bill Robson, Angie Darbyson and Kevin, Thelma Chandler, Sandy Faria, Mariel Swann, Diane Needham, Dustin Fields, Paul Spriggs, Shannon Wilson, John Pion, Dean Brenner, Christine England, Lorrie Lancaster, Zita McCallum, Liz Antiller, Lynn Daniel, Dwight Pennell, Sandor Czepregi and Maryse Arnold, who all appeared when I needed them most.

Amber

Tammy

Robyn Burton, Roger Harper, Pamela Charlesworth, Helen Chesnut, Betty Campbell, Mary Mills, John Adams, Jennifer Ireland, Rob Lowrie, Chad Sargeant, Doug Hope, John Ewing and Colin Bowen who helped get me launched as a writer, public speaker and TV personality.

Patricia

Natasha

To all the incredible volunteers over the years, who put their energy into the garden, and all the amazing Garden Path customers who believed in our vision enough to speak up for us, and when we won, followed us too.

John

Ginnie

Sandy Reber for her inspired creative talent and support. Christina Nikolic for proof reading this book. Fang Zhang for capturing the essence of *The Garden Path* in her delightful monthly sketches.

Tonia

To my 'one and only' husband, Guy Dauncey, who patiently endures, listens, supports, builds, shares, contributes and loves me… and all for endless cups of tea and cookies!

In memory of Jill Stewart Bowen, the most cheerful and bravest gardener I ever met.

Dustin

The BIGS students

The Growth of the Organic Gardening Movement

1840   Justus von Liebig, a German chemist, burned plants, analyzed the ashes, and deduced that plants were nourished by three key elements, Nitrogen (N), Phosphorus, (P) and Potassium, (K). He wrote *Law of the Minimum*. Germany was mined for muriate of potash and created superphosphates.

World War 1. Chemical companies relocated to the US. A very profitable American plant food industry began. Chemical agriculture was born. Farmers were told they could bypass nature, while increasing yields significantly and indefinitely. Sir Albert Howard (1873-1948), served as Imperial Botanist to the Raj of India. He discovered soil fertility to be the basis of plant health.

1912   Rudolf Steiner (1861-1925), founded the Anthroposophical Society. (Anthroposophy = wisdom of man). Steiner believed plants had non-physical requirements such as light and warmth, and responded to energies from the sun and moon.

1922   Steiner created the first biodynamic preparations.

1924   Biodynamic farming was established.

1938   Ehrenfried Pfeiffer (1899-1961), wrote *Soil Fertility: its Renewal and Preservation*, the textbook for biodynamic agriculture.

1940   Sir Albert Howard wrote the *Agricultural Testament*, and became known as the founder of the organic movement. One of his followers, Lady Eve Balfour, founded the Soil Association in England, and wrote *The Living Soil*.

1940   Kimberton, Pennsylvania – 838 acres purchased for the farm school of biodynamic agriculture (J.I. Rodale attended).

1942   J.I. Rodale (1898-1971) launched *Organic Gardening and Farming* magazine.

1947   J.I. Rodale founded the Rodale Institute. It recognized the complexity of living systems and regenerative growing methods.

1958   Lawrence Hills founded the Henry DoubleDay Research Association (HDRA) in the UK.

1960   Robert Rodale (1930-1990) took over from his father as editor of *Organic Gardening Magazine*. Distribution one million copies a month.

1963   Rachel Carson wrote *Silent Spring*. The Ecology Movement was born!

1985   HDRA moved onto a 22-acre field in Ryton, Coventry, UK.

1997   Ryton had 50,000 visitors a year. HDRA had 17,500 members and 80 local groups.

2004   The Ontario College of Family Physicians released a report that found consistent positive associations between lawn care pesticides and cancers, reproductive problems, neurotoxic effects and other serious illnesses.

2005   HDRA is Europe's largest organic gardening association.

2005   The manufacture of specialty pesticides, lawn products, as well as indoor pest killers, is a $2.5 billion annual industry in the US.

2005   A survey, sponsored by *Organic Gardening Magazine*, in conjunction with the National Gardening Association, estimated that of 90 million US households, about 5 million exclusively use organic methods.

Foreword

It all started sixteen years ago when I met my husband, Guy. I was a gardener with a business called *Forget-Me-Not Gardening Services*, and lived in a cottage at the end of Windsor Road, in Victoria, where I grew plants in a small 1930s greenhouse, and vegetables over the fence in dear old Margaret Gordon's garden.

Four days after Guy and I bought our first home in Oak Bay, I knocked on the door of 1834 Haultain Street, a few blocks away, to enquire what was happening with the smashed-up greenhouse and quarter acre of weeds on the property. As fate would have it, Joyce Gathright's reply was that her family was moving to Texas for ten years, and I was welcome to use the greenhouse and surrounding land while they were away. This is how *The Garden Path* came to be.

Ten years later Guy and I moved *The Garden Path* onto two and a half rural acres, where everything I'd learnt over the years was put to use. We built a larger greenhouse for the nursery, and created a beautiful garden for display and seed saving.

When I first met Guy I didn't know what a fax machine was, never mind how to send an e-mail – I considered myself technologically impaired! I didn't know it at the time, but we were perfectly suited. Guy taught me to put my brain to work, and I taught him to put his brawn into action! He showed me how to use a computer, and I showed him how to turn a compost pile. A fair exchange when you understand the benefits of compost!

I volunteered to write articles for the Victoria Horticultural Society's newsletter, *Gardenry*, which taught me that I loved writing about plants. I volunteered to do a weekly gardening show on AM900 radio, which taught me I loved talking about plants. One thing led to another, so here I am today, spreading the 'Gospel of Gardening' on a TV show, giving lectures and writing my first book – putting it all down on paper.

This book started a year ago with *Greetings from The Garden Path,* a weekly e-mail newsletter I sent to customers who trusted me enough to give me their e-mail address. Each week I wrote about what we were doing at the nursery, in the garden and in the greenhouse, with seed saving and soil building – everything including strawberry scone recipes! I tried to fill the newsletters with useful information and inspire my readers enough to make them want to rush out into their gardens, flush with newfound knowledge, confidence and eagerness.

That's why I call this book *A Year on the Garden Path: A 52-Week Organic Gardening Guide.* I write with the intention of helping gardeners of all levels realize they can have the most healthy, productive and beautiful garden without resorting to substances harmful to humans, animals, wildlife, plants, worms or the myriad of soil-dwelling organisms. I hope you will find this book both useful and inspiring, and that you can pick it up any day, any year, to help you in your garden – organically!

Why Organic?

I'm an old-fashioned girl at heart, often wishing I could turn the clock back to slower and saner times. I especially feel this when it comes to the modern practices of farming and gardening. So many farmers and gardeners have come to rely

on huge inputs of synthetic chemical substances – herbicides, pesticides and fertilizers – which we now know cause havoc to the environment, our health and the delicate web of soil life.

Seventy years ago people relied on small-scale family farms, local markets and home gardens for fresh fruits, vegetables and livestock. The Victorians were acclaimed for their prowess in their kitchen gardens, where they grew a diversity of nutritious vegetables, herbs, fruits and flowers without synthetic chemicals. Natural source materials, such as horse and cow manure, were the mainstays of small-scale agriculture then.

When I started my first garden maintenance business, I was shocked to discover customers' sheds and garages full of chemical products with names such as Diazinon, Malathion (organophosphates) Methoxychlor and Captan (organochlorines). I was expected to use these products routinely throughout the year, and was even required to pass a pesticide applicator exam just to be a gardener. The belief was that without these products a garden could not thrive. This is what led me to garden organically, and later to an interest in heritage plants and historic gardening practices.

Pesticide Active Ingredient Use
USA in 2001
Agriculture   675 million lbs.
Home and Garden   102 million lbs.

Modern farming depends on chemical products to maximize yields for greater profits. It does not focus on soil health, plant diversity, seed saving or the protection of wildlife. It is only recently that the detrimental impacts of modern farming have even been acknowledged. Referred to as agribusiness, modern farming is clearly disconnected from the natural cycles of life.

Seasonal spraying of millions of gallons of pesticides over fields, into soil and onto food leaves me with a feeling of deep despair. This pales in comparison to the dread I feel about the manipulation of plant genes and, even worse, the exchange of genetic material between species from different kingdoms. Pandora's box has been opened, and there's no going back. Human-created plant mutants have already cross-fertilized with wild plants of the same species, allowing this alien genetic material to establish itself in nature.

After millennia of miraculous evolution, surely Mother Nature knows best? Hers is a power and creation worthy of the utmost respect, but nature's mystical power is not respected by our ceaseless drive to exploit, control and replicate. It is with pure wonder, humility and boundless joy that, as an organic gardener, I try my best to co-create with Mother Nature, not work against her.

"When we kill off the natural enemies of the pest, we inherit their work."
Karl Huffaker, University of California, Dept. of Biological Control

Diversity rules in nature. Whether it is the plants, animals, insects or microbes, or the elements of rock, water and air, all exist in exquisite and vital interdependent relationships with one another. When I interplant vegetables with flowers, herbs and small fruits, plants that attract pollinators and beneficial insects co-exist in perfect balance, taking care of pesky problems as they arise. I love knowing that native bees, butterflies, hoverflies and parasitic wasps are keeping everything in harmony and balance in my garden. My role is to attract them and encourage them to stick around, by providing habitat, drinking water and plants for them to feed on.

The number one priority in my garden is feeding the soil to nurture the myriad microorganisms that dwell in it. It's all about the microbes, which break down organic matter into humus, and make nutrients available to plants. I spend the dormant season from November to March adding natural amendments to the garden so that I can grow healthy plants that are resilient against pests and diseases, which means I have more time to enjoy my beautiful garden.

Carolyn Herriot, May 2005

January

Snow

White are the far-off plains, and white
The fading forests glow;
The wind dies out along the height,
And denser still the snow
A gathering weight on roof and tree,
Falls down scarce audibly.

The meadows and far-sheeted streams
Lie still without a sound;
Like some soft minister of dreams
The snow-fall hoods me round;
In wood and water, earth and air
A silence everywhere.

Save when at lonely intervals
Some farmer's sleigh, urged on,
With rustling runners and sharp bells
Swings by me and is gone;
Or from the empty waste I hear
A sound remote and clear.

The barking of a dog, or call
To cattle, sharply pealed,
Borne echoing from some wayside stall
Or barnyard far afield;
Then all is silent and the snow falls
Settling soft and slow.

The evening deepens and the grey
Folds closer earth and sky.
The world seems shrouded, far away
Its noises sleep, and I, as secret as
Yon buried stream,
Plod dumbly on and dream.

Archibald Lampman (1861-1899)

fang zhang

A Brand New Gardening Year

Cold Snaps

It amazes me how quickly the garden bounces back after a deep freeze. The resilience of nature is astounding, but not always so. In the case of a heavy snowfall, piled up snow can weigh branches down to the ground and tear off limbs, wrecking evergreens and deciduous shrubs alike. If snow falls in your area, remember to knock it off the branches of conifers and shrubs to prevent them from breaking or distorting under its weight. This way, when it freezes at night, there's much less chance of more damage being done. *TIP:* Clear lower branches first, so snow falling from above does not compound the weight on them.

The temperamental month of January offers us a weather palette ranging from cold rain and raging wind storms to mild sunny days followed by snow dumps with sudden freezes. After unexpected cold snaps, gardeners may lose valuable outdoor plants, especially tender perennials, container plants and plants overwintering in greenhouses.

By taking the following measures you can prevent cold snaps from catching you unawares:

- Move container plants to more sheltered spots – under the eaves of the house, under the deck or into the garage.

- Wrap bubblewrap or burlap sacking around container plants left outdoors to prevent the soil inside from freezing. *TIP:* You can also place one pot inside a larger pot, and stuff the space between with an insulating material.

- Cover the crowns of plants that are not totally hardy with straw or a thick mulch of compost or leaf mulch. This stops frost from penetrating and killing roots.

- Check the soil around roots of trees, roses and shrubs that may have been lifted up by frosts and snow. It's surprising how strong winds can uproot even large plant specimens.

- Check that all plant supports, stakes and ties are secure, especially if your area experiences storms and high winds.

About the Birds

There's nothing more adorable in winter than hearing a *phisszzz* sound and spotting an Anna's hummingbird at the feeder outside the window. Once these tiny birds come to expect hospitality, they rely on you to provide food. The onset of very cold weather leaves them vulnerable, so keep the feeder fresh and filled on a regular basis. I use a recipe of one part sugar dissolved in five parts hot water. *TIP:* When in the midst of a deep freeze, thaw out frozen sugar water in the house, and then replace outdoors.

In winter, fill bird feeders with black oiled sunflower seeds, peanuts or wild bird seed regularly. This attracts a host of birds: chickadees, grosbeaks, juncoes, towhees, pine siskins, Stellar's jays, finches and others. Remember, not all birds are nut and seed feeders; some prefer fatty scraps or fruit. *TIP:* Keep a pair of binoculars close at hand for first-class viewing.

To attract hummingbirds to your garden later in the year, plant red and orange flowers such as *Monarda didyma* bee balm, *Lonicera* spp. honeysuckle, *Fuchsia magellanica* hardy fuchsia, *Crocosmia masonorum* 'Lucifer', and *Phygelius* spp. Cape fuchsia.

Birds have five basic needs: food, water, shelter from extreme weather, nesting sites, and protection from predators such as owls, hawks and, most of all, cats. Supply these, and you'll have lots more birds around your home. *TIP:* Be sure to place birdhouses outdoors by early March when birds start searching for nesting sites.

We welcome the swallows who appear each year in April. These two chicks will have fledged by the end of June.

Reading a Seed Catalogue

Gardeners are always eager to plunge into the world of seed catalogues, but glossy pages filled with information can be both tempting and confusing. Knowing how to interpret symbols, abbreviations and classifications will help you get the most from seed catalogues and avoid ordering plants that won't do well in your garden.

If you are an organic gardener, you'll want to be sure that seeds have not been treated or genetically modified (GM), and ideally have been grown organically. Some catalogues clearly state the company does not sell treated or GM seeds. If not, you'll need to note when seed is specified as being treated. This usually means seeds have been coated with a fungicide against soil-borne pathogens to assist with earlier planting. Organic seeds are more readily available now, as seed growers shift their methods of cultivation to meet changing organic standards.

Each year, catalogues are filled with pages of exciting new introductions, the work of plant breeders promoting new hybrid varieties. F1 means 'first filial generation'. F1 hybrids are the first generation produced by crossing unlike parents to create offspring that exhibit hybrid vigour and uniformity. Hybrids are not stable, so seeds saved from F1 plants will not grow true to type, and characteristics may revert back to the parent strains. The original crossing must therefore be repeated each year.

Hybrids are fine unless you want diversity or plan to save your own seeds. Hybrid varieties have been developed for farmers who seek uniformity for harvesting. Home gardeners don't want vegetables that all ripen at the same time, and don't care if they are not all the same size. For greater diversity and seed saving, select open-pollinated vegetable seeds and seeds of flower species only. 'Open-pollinated' indicates that the free agents of nature, the wind and the bees, have pollinated the flowers, and that the resulting seeds will come true.

Many plants are designated as heirloom, heritage or traditional, but the distinction between these terms is confusing. There's no universally accepted definition of these terms, but the following definitions work for me. Heritage or traditional varieties are those that were developed more than fifty years ago, and include many developed commercially. Heirloom varieties have been preserved by home gardeners and private individuals rather than the seed trade, and have been passed down from generation to generation. Heirloom varieties include old varieties developed by seeds growers that have been dropped from commercial trade, and would have become extinct were it not for this grassroots network of seedsavers.

Flower seeds are categorized as HHA, HA, BI, TP and HP. Hardy annuals (HA) are annuals that can stand some frost, and can be sown in early spring as soon as the ground can be worked. Half hardy annuals (HHA) are killed by frost and can be sown outdoors in late spring, or earlier in a greenhouse or under grow lights. They should be transplanted outdoors only after all danger of frost has passed.

Biennials (BI) need to be sown early so they have grown to a good size by fall, when they are planted out to overwinter and flower the following season. Hardy perennials (HP) may flower the first year from seed if started early in a greenhouse or cold frame, and will overwinter if grown in the appropriate climate zone. Tender perennials (TP) need extra winter protection outdoors, and may need to be brought into a greenhouse to get through a severe winter.

Seeds are usually listed alphabetically under their botanical name, followed by their common name. To be sure you get what you want, check the botanical name and don't rely only on the common name, which may vary between catalogues. By knowing the genus, species, and varietal name, you can be sure of what you are ordering.

Quantities of seeds offered vary from sample packets to full ounces; the more you buy, the cheaper the seeds are. Flower seeds often have a viability (shelf life) of several years, so buying larger quantities can be economical, as you can save some seeds to grow in future years. In the case of vegetables, viability varies from one year to five. By taking this 'shelf life' into account, you will not order more than you can grow before the germination rate drops too low.

The days to maturity stated does not always reflect the difference between plants that are direct seeded and those grown from six-week-old transplants. In the case of transplants, you'll need to calculate if your growing season is long enough. To the days of maturity given, add approximately seven days for germination, 42 days for the transplant to develop, and possibly another 21 days for ripening in a cool summer season. This could double the days to maturity from 70 to 140.

There's a big difference between disease resistance and disease tolerance. A designation of tolerance merely indicates that a variety will not suffer from the disease as much as a variety with no tolerance. Disease resistance means that a variety is not likely to get the disease at all. Varieties that have been tested in field trials bear symbols such as BMV (bean mosaic virus), TMV (tomato mosaic virus), or PM (powdery mildew) resistant, which is useful information when ordering.

Check the interpretation of codes and symbols, as different catalogues use different symbols. These can provide you with a wealth of information, such as how easy seeds are to grow, whether they are cold-hardy, or if they are a good greenhouse variety.

Browsing seed catalogues is always fun. Many are full of invaluable cultural information, even recipes, but reading the small print and knowing how to interpret all the information will help you to get the most from them.

First Week of January

New Signs of Growth

In the first week of a brand new gardening year, it's more than encouraging to see signs of growth, and even a few blooms, in the garden. Tiny bead-like, bright red berries on the branches of *Berberis thunbergii* 'Atropurpurea', the red-leafed Japanese barberry, provide dramatic interest in its dormant state. In spring it's covered with pretty yellow flowers, and throughout the year it's a stunning accent plant with dense, purplish-red foliage. *TIP:* Stop *Berberis thunbergii* 'Atropurpurea' from getting straggly by pruning it back hard in fall. It grows back quickly to give a much better show the following season.

Mahonia aquifolium, *tall Oregon grape, is well suited to dry conditions, and is much underrated as a fine garden specimen.*

Even with snow on its branches, *Mahonia aquifolium,* a native west coast shrub, looks glorious. Handsome evergreen, pinnate foliage is topped by dense panicles of golden yellow flowers in the depth of winter. Highlighted against the bark of a Douglas fir, this splash of yellow really lights up the garden.

Jasminum nudiflorum, winter jasmine, is a reliable plant for winter interest. The thought of a jasmine flowering in winter is as cheery as the sight of its tubular, bright yellow flowers. Prune back this evergreen climber hard right after blooming to enhance the floral show on its leafless green stems next year. *TIP:* Pruning makes a world of difference to how shrubs perform. Too many gardeners are reluctant to prune, but I recommend sweeping through the garden with a flash of secateurs as the perfect remedy for straggly plants, and those that are no longer aesthetically pleasing. A prune in time saves mine!

Another winter favourite at *The Garden Path* is *Sarcococca confusa,* sweet box, which I grow in a large terra cotta pot by our front door. It's a glossy green, evergreen shrub that thrives in deep shade and looks splendid, covered in shiny black berries. Tiny white flower buds unfurl in January to fill the air with the most intoxicating fragrance.

Nandina domestica, heavenly bamboo, is a valuable shrub for year-round interest. New foliage emerges pink and bronzy-red, then changes to soft pale green. In fall it lights up the garden with purple-bronze hues, turning fiery crimson in winter. Winter foliage is highlighted by sprays of small red berries, which birds do not eat. In spring it is accented by showy, creamy pink blossoms. Heavenly bamboo is a good shade plant, even growing well in dry shade in competition with tree roots. No wonder it is chosen so often as a feature plant in garden landscapes. *TIP:* Cut the oldest canes down to the ground in spring to encourage new shoots and denser foliage.

Recommended Plants for Winter Interest

Cornus sanguinea 'Midwinter Fire'; *Pernettya mucronata; Corylus avellana* 'Contorta'; *Hamamelis intermedia* 'Jelena', 'Diane' or 'Arnold's Promise'; *Prunus x subhirtella* 'Autumnalis'; *Garrya elliptica* 'James Roof'; *Lonicera fragrantissima; Daphne odora; Viburnum tinus* 'Gwenllian'.

Hurrah for Hellebores

In the winter garden you can rely on hellebores to liven things up. They flower early and become an even better investment over time as clumps establish. Some species set seed so readily you even get lots of freebies!

Helleborus foetidus 'Wester Flisk' adds a good splash of interest to any garden setting. This is a much sought after variety, with showy red stems and smaller, lime-green flowers edged in maroon. I still don't know why they call *H. foetidus* the 'stinking' hellebore. I have never been offended by its odour; in fact I have never even detected one! I also don't know why *Helleborus niger* is called the Christmas rose, as it rarely flowers at Christmas.

H. argutifolius, *Corsican hellebore*

H. argutifolius, Corsican hellebore, creates quite a different effect with its serrated-edged, dark green, leathery leaves and lime-green flowers. It thrives in sunnier, drier places. It has the best foliage of all the hellebores, and provides a long show of chartreuse-green flowers with maroon-flecked centres, lasting well into April.

H. orientalis, the Lenten rose, performs later. The large, cup-shaped flowers come in every shade, from purple-black to rosy pink. *H. orientalis* seed themselves obligingly, so you can become a hellebore breeder by selecting your favourite colours. The time to buy them is when they are flowering, as seed-grown plants will vary widely in colour.

Growing Tips:

- At this time of year, *Helleborus orientalis* look untidy with dying leaves, so trim the leaves away from the emerging flowerbuds. Doing this not only enhances the floral show but also helps prevent *Coniothyrium hellebori,* a disease that blackens the foliage.

- Don't make the mistake of trying to split a prize clump of hellebores. The central part of the plant often dies. Hellebores grow into well-established plants over time, which flower more profusely every year. *TIP:* Choose the site for hellebores with care so they do not have to be transplanted.

- Hellebores prefer fertile, free-draining soils. They don't like being waterlogged but prefer moist soils that don't dry out in summer. Hellebores flourish in lightly shaded positions where they avoid the midday sun. Having said that, however, in my garden *H. orientalis* seem to love being in a border exposed to sun all day.

- An occasional application of slow-release organic fertilizer, forked in round the clump, helps keep hellebores vigorous, but in woodland soil they will thrive without this. Nevertheless, they always appreciate a mulch of manure, leaf mulch and compost.

H. orientalis, *Lenten rose*

Second Week of January

Liming Your Garden

If you live on the west coast in an area of heavy rainfall, soils may need to be adjusted to neutralize an acidic condition on a regular basis. That's because many plants thrive best in a soil with a balanced (neutral) pH of between 6 and 7. A near neutral pH supports the growth of beneficial bacteria in the soil, which make essential nutrients available to plants. Soils with a low pH of less than 5.5 (acidic) foster harmful fungal pathogens, reduce availability of phosphorus to plants, and are generally depleted of calcium, magnesium and sulphur. In spring, if your soil pH is balanced, beneficial bacteria will multiply, making essential soil nutrients available to plants for their new cycle of growth.

I pay particular attention to liming the lawn and vegetable garden yearly, except in beds where I grow ericaceous (acid-loving) plants and vegetables, such as potatoes, strawberries and blueberries. I apply coarse dolomite, a granular form of Dolomitic limestone, which takes longer to break down but is much easier to apply using a broadcast spreader, or even by hand. It's a good source of calcium and magnesium and can be applied anytime, but it's best to apply it in late fall so it will be broken down by spring.

For many gardeners, practising guesswork suffices, but the only way to really know your soil pH is to have a sample tested (see *Taking a Soil Test,* third week of February). If you have soil analysis done and find you need a faster remedy for an acidic condition, choose a fine-mesh dolomite, which breaks down more quickly. Follow directions for application rates, because an over-application of lime can be as harmful as a deficiency. Dolomite lime is inexpensive and often goes on sale in the spring. Plan to have limed your garden beds and lawn by early spring, before you fertilize them. It's best if soil is limed before the application of fertilizer, with at least two weeks between applications.

That Infernal Moss!

How do you get rid of moss in the lawn? Pouring moss killer on the lawn gets rid of the problem temporarily, but if you don't get rid of the underlying cause of the moss, it's only a matter of time before it comes back.

Understanding the reasons why moss thrives is most helpful in getting rid of it, or at the very least reducing its impact on your lawn. Moss thrives when:
- the lawn is mown too short and is stressed
- the lawn has become compacted
- the lawn is shaded
- the lawn is poorly drained
- the lawn is not being properly maintained e.g. thatched, aerated, fertilized, limed
- acidic soil conditions exist that are favourable to the growth of moss, but not grass

Here's what you can do:

- Raise the height of your lawn mower. Give grass a chance!
- Aerate the lawn. *TIP:* Leave the core plugs to rot down on the lawn and feed the soil.
- If possible, create more light in areas of thriving moss by pruning a few branches.
- Provide better drainage to wet lawns.
- Practise better lawn maintenance. If necessary, thatch in early spring, aerate, topdress, fertilize and reseed where needed (see *The Golf Green Lawn,* second week of March).
- Use a mulcher mower. This saves bagging grass clippings and feeds the lawn with nitrogen every time you cut.
- Lime your lawn yearly to neutralize soil pH, as moss thrives in acidic soil conditions.

Third Week of January

Little Pea Secrets

Peas have long been a popular garden vegetable, perhaps because they are one of the earliest vegetables harvested in spring. The Victorians grew over 120 different varieties of garden peas, providing a continuous supply of fresh shelled peas throughout the summer months. The Victorians may have delighted in afternoons spent shelling peas, but these days we're all on the run, so most gardeners grow snow peas or snap peas – no shelling required!

Peas fall into three categories: shelling, snow and snap. Snow peas are edible pod peas harvested when the pods are full-sized and the peas have just begun to swell. With snap peas, also known as 'mangetout', the sweet, tender pods and fully-formed peas are eaten.

Pea varieties vary from two-foot dwarf vines that require no staking, to eight-foot tall climbing vines, which require good support for ease of growth and harvest. *TIP:* Use peasticks for support, for example, long, straight, twiggy branches of pruned apple trees. 'Plant' two rows of peasticks about two feet apart – push them deep into the ground with their tops crossed and tied for extra support.

For the highest yields, grow peas in rows. Moist, well-drained fertile soil in a sunny location, with a pH of 6.0 to 6.5, makes peas happy. Avoid heavy applications of manure, or you'll get lush foliage but few peas. The fastest way to plant peas is to hoe a shallow furrow and drop pea seeds into it, one inch deep and one inch apart. Then just rake over to cover, and water in.

Peas are legumes. Leguminous plants allow bacteria to live on their roots, and in return the bacteria convert nitrogen from the air into usable nitrogen for the peas. When an excess of nitrogen is produced, it goes into the soil where it becomes available to the plants. If sowing peas where no legumes have grown before, you can significantly increase yields by coating the seeds with fresh inoculant when seeding. This provides the bacteria for this mutually beneficial relationship that enhances plant growth. It's as easy as shaking the pea seeds with the black powdery inoculant in a container before sowing.

As long as the soil is moist there's no need to soak pea seeds. In fact, if you grow peas in wet soil, it's best not to soak them at all, as they rot so easily. Germination is fast: peas sprout in six to fourteen days, depending on soil temperature. They will germinate at between 5 and 23°C (40-75°F), but germinate best at between 10 and 20°C (50-70°F). You can expect yields approximately 100 days from sowing, depending on the variety you are growing.

On the west coast we get pea enation disease, spread by green aphids, which causes pea vines to yellow and die. Plant enation-resistant varieties if you are planting peas later in the spring when aphids are at work. Peas perform best in cool growing conditions; the yields drop for sowings later in the year, so it's best to start them as early as possible. Some gardeners plant peas in July and August for a fall crop, but I find the yields never as good as with the spring planting.

Once peas start producing, harvest them every day to keep them producing. Pinching the tips

off will cause the vines to bush out, increasing yields as well as giving you delicious, juicy pea shoots for stirfries and salads. Like corn, peas are sweetest when eaten fresh, as once harvested their sugars turn to starch. If you miss the boat when harvesting, leave the peas on the vines to mature until the pods are brown and dried. Then save the seeds for next year's crop, or keep some as dried peas for hearty winter soups.

TIP: If short of space, try growing a mixed pea patch. Sowing several varieties of peas together that mature at different times will extend your season of harvest.

Peel well-rooted peas out of a gutter for a fast start to a pea patch.

A Big Pea Secret!

All you need is an old gutter or two to get a head start on peas, and avoid problems with pests such as birds, mice, slugs and aphids. Sow peas one inch deep and one inch apart in the gutters, in a sterilized, lightweight potting medium. Keep the gutter in a cold greenhouse or cool garage until the peas have germinated. Harden them off by putting the gutter outside in the day and back under protection at night for two weeks. When the peas are six inches high, 'plant' two rows of peasticks, dig a trench matching the width and length of the gutter around the outside, peel the well-rooted peas out of the gutters, and lay them in the trench,

covering and watering them in. Viola! An instant rows of peas. Now all you have to do is go on a hunt for some used gutters.

The Original Sweet Pea

Have you made the acquaintance of 'Matucana,' the sweet pea from which all modern sweet peas were bred? 'Matucana' was introduced to England in 1699 by a Sicilian monk, Franciscus Cupani. It's close to the original wild species – plain standards but no frills, and two-tone flowers – a maroon-purple keel and deep-purple wings. But the scent! It's rich and fruity, so much headier than the modern varieties. It's also easy to grow and a vigorous climber that flowers over a long period.

Tips for Growing the Best Sweet Peas

- Purchase the best quality seed.
- Sow in early spring, in cool moist soils, directly where they are to flower.
- Plant early, so plants establish before the onset of hot weather, which causes sweet peas to set seed.
- Heavily mulch sweet peas to keep the roots cooler, as this prolongs the flowering season. Use grass clippings or compost for mulch.
- Choosing a site sheltered from direct sun prolongs the blooming season.
- Shade at midday helps maintain the quality of the flowers.
- Sow one inch apart in double rows, at least six inches apart.
- Provide a support system for tall vining plants.
- Watch out for slugs and mice, which can be a problem.
- When seedlings are six inches tall, pinch the tips out to make the plants bushier so you'll get more flowers.
- Cut sweetpeas every few days to encourage continued blooming.

Fourth Week of January

Feed the Soil

Bundle up and enjoy some productive exercise now by feeding the soil during the dormant season. Organic gardeners understand the importance of feeding the soil to maintain healthy populations of microbes and soil-dwelling organisms, which in turn help to feed the plants. Now is a great time to apply mulches of natural materials, which create soils with rich, organic humus, a growing medium plants thrive in. By taking the time to nourish the soil in the dormant season, you will reap the benefits of a healthy, disease-resistant garden for the rest of the year.

Mulches also provide extra insulation against freezing winter conditions, which is especially appreciated by shallow-rooted plants such as pieris, rhododendrons, azaleas, heathers, camellias and hydrangeas. Borderline hardy plants such as fremontias, penstemons, artichokes and prostanthera also benefit from a protective covering of mulch. (See *The Miracle of Mulch*, second week of November.)

Our vegetable garden is flushed with green now. Amidst the rows of winter vegetables, any beds not planted were sown with a green manure crop in late fall. The cold-hardy blend of fall rye, winter wheat, winter barley and field pea holds its own against the winter elements. In spring, as soon the soil warms up, leafy growth shoots up. After cutting this lush top growth back we turn it under; usually a light forking suffices. This provides the soil with plant-based nitrogen, and there's nothing vegetables like better than a ready source of nitrogen at the start of the growing season. (See *Gardening with Green Manures*, first week of November.)

Kales – Nutritious and Delicious

It is said that kale was introduced to North America by Benjamin Franklin after a trip to Scotland two hundred years ago, and it's easy to see why, once you experience the versatility of this prolific and delicious vegetable.

Kale is one of the easiest brassicas to cultivate. It's very cold-tolerant and thrives in temperate winter climates. Kale greens taste even sweeter after hard frosts, because they then have a higher sugar content.

I grow four different cultivars of kale, *Brassica oleracea,* so we never run out of it. After all, it is the most nutritious vegetable you can grow and eat! It contains ten times the vitamin A of an equal weight of lettuce, up to three times the vitamin C as the same amount of oranges, more B vitamins than whole wheat bread and more

Lacinato kale

Redbor kale

Katie's Klassic Kale Salad

1. Chop twelve tender kale leaves into a bowl, avoiding any tough central ribs or older outer leaves.
2. Toss well with a light sprinkle of salt, pepper and 2 tsp. balsamic vinegar.
3. Roughly chop a handful of almonds or hazelnuts.
4. Heat 1/4 cup olive oil in a frying pan or wok and throw in the nuts. Let them sizzle just until they are lightly brown.
5. Immediately pour the hot oil and nuts over the kale. Give it a good toss until the kale wilts, and serve immediately.

calcium than milk. Apart from making delicious steamed greens, the small tender leaves add diversity to salads, and chopped kale makes a fine addition to soups or casseroles and tastes great in mashed potatoes. We've discovered that kale flower buds are superb as a side vegetable when lightly steamed. By harvesting flower buds it delays the setting of seed and prolongs the production of new leaves.

There's much diversity between two distinct groups of kale. The Scotch group has very curly leaves, e.g. 'Winterbor', and the Siberian group has more colourful leaves, e.g. 'Russian Red'. Kale leaves vary from slightly wavy to tightly frilled, and come in a wide range of hues. 'Lacinato' is blue-green, 'Winter Red' is purple-red and 'Redbor' is magenta. This diversity makes kale a visual delight in the garden.

For harvesting throughout the winter, sow kale seed at the end of June or in early July, or transplant established seedlings into the garden in August, but no later than mid-September.

TIP: Add dolomite lime to the soil prior to planting: kale grows better in a soil pH more alkali than acidic. Lime also helps to keep club root, a fungal disease brassicas are prone to, at bay.

Kale is relatively unbothered by insects. Flea beetles make small round holes in the leaves. If you have this problem, you can prevent it by using floating row covers. Cabbage white butterflies lay eggs that develop into cabbage worms, which eat large raggedy holes in the leaves. This problem can be kept under control by removing older kale leaves where masses of grey eggs have been deposited.

In the Greenhouse

In greenhouses the worst problem at this time of year is *botrytis,* a fluffy grey mould that forms on rotted plant parts. You'll know it when you touch it, as puffs of dust fly off, sending spores off to infect other plants. The best way to keep this problem under control is to remove all dead and decaying material, and go easy on watering. Water greenhouse plants sparingly, only as required, and preferably in the morning during winter months. Keeping them on the dry side while in their dormant phase helps them get through cold snaps. In winter, resting plants do not like having their roots in freezing cold water.

The greenhouse in winter.

February

"One month is past, another is begun,
Since merry bells rang out the dying year,
And buds of rarest green began to peer,
As if impatient for a warmer sun;
And though the distant hills are bleak and dun,
The virgin snowdrop, like a lambent fire,
Pierces the cold earth with its green-streaked spire
And in dark woods, the wandering little one
May find a primrose."

Samuel Coleridge (1842)

First Week of February

Carefully Does It!

If you have ever put your back out or suffered from tennis elbow or tendonitis, you may want to read on and take note!

After a long winter it's not surprising that gardeners are bursting to get going, but just like plants, we need to come out of dormancy slowly. Here are a few tips to prevent you from regretting your enthusiasm.

- Keep your posture as upright as possible when working in the garden. Bending too much puts a strain on the spine and back muscles. When digging, keep your body upright, and when pushing in the spade, do not bend your back.

- Restrict your exertions to twenty minutes at a time. Then stretch and take a short break.

- When stretching, place your hands on your hips and bend backwards as far as possible, without overdoing it. This puts the back into its normal upright position.

- When lifting and carrying, keep your feet apart for balance, bend the knees to lower yourself, and lift the object close to your body. Let the legs do the lifting, not the back.

- Invest in some knee pads, or use a padded mat. Knees can take a beating when it comes to hours of hand weeding.

- Wear strong flexible shoes, which puts less strain on calves and heels.

- Invest in padded insoles and wear warm woolen socks in gumboots. This makes 'wellies' more comfortable and will insulate your feet against the cold and damp.

- If your back is aching or your body is protesting, take a break and treat yourself to a lovely cup of tea!

Care of Tools

Nothing is more frustrating for an active gardener than having garden tools fall apart in the middle of a job. After many years I have come to the conclusion that, tempted as I am to save a buck or two, there's no point in buying cheap tools. Quality tools are the only way to go. You pay more to start, but you'll have those trusty tools for a long time.

If you want your tools to last, keep them cleaned and well maintained during the gardening season. Once or twice a year preserve wooden-handled tools by wiping them with a rag soaked in a mix of one part linseed oil and one part turpentine (paint thinner). Allow them to dry in the sun and repeat once more. They not only look and feel great after oiling, but the handles will never dry out, crack or break. My heritage wooden garden tools are my favourites.

An Easy Way to Clean Tools

Take a bucket of clean washed sand and mix the sand with horticultural oil. Every time you finish using your tools, dip them in this bucket of oily sand before you hang them up. This cleans them and stops them from going rusty at the same time.

Proper Pruning Practice

A good pruning can make an amazing difference to how plants perform. Pruning helps maintain a pleasing shape, encourages vibrant new growth and results in more flowers. Here are some useful snippy tips:

- Make sure your pruning equipment is sharp. Use scissor-type pruning shears rather than anvil-type ones to prevent unnecessary injury to plant tissues.
- Never forget: the more you prune, the more it grows.
- The goal is to maintain healthy growth with an aesthetic shape open to sunlight.
- To avoid spreading disease among plants, disinfect pruning tools by spraying them with a 10% solution of bleach between plants.
- Start by pruning out the three Ds: dead, diseased and damaged.
- Remove any one of two crossing branches that are rubbing.
- Remove branches growing into the centre. Keeping an open growth habit is beneficial for good air circulation and the penetration of sunlight.
- Prune no more than 30% at one time. Pruning too heavily will produce water sprouts and an overabundance of soft wood.
- Avoid leaving stubs. Not only are they unsightly, but they also invite disease into the plant as they die back.
- Avoid cutting too close and injuring the main stem/trunk.
- Always prune to an outward facing bud or sideshoot to encourage outward growth.
- Cut immediately above a bud or sideshoot, making a sloped cut away from the bud.
- Allow the plant to heal itself. Nobody uses tar paste over pruning cuts anymore.
- Canopy shaping, or crown raising, should happen early while the tree is young and the branches are thin. Avoid pruning large mature branches unless they have broken after a storm or died from disease.

The general rule of thumb for pruning ornamental shrubs is to do it just after flowering.

Spring flowering ornamentals produce flowers on the previous year's growth, so pruning at the right time is essential! Get to know your plants. If branches have buds on them, pruning now means you will lose all these flowers. Shrubs such as forsythia, philadelphus, weigela and lilac should be pruned in summer, just after they have flowered.

Keep heathers, lavenders, helianthemums and spireas from getting straggly by shearing them back in summer after they bloom. Take a pair of hedge trimmers and give them a rounded or aesthetically pleasing shape, taking care not to cut into old wood. Off with their dead flowerheads – compact, bushy plants for next year! It's rewarding to prune ceanothus (California lilac), escallonias and hebes, as these fast-growing shrubs quickly outgrow their allotted space, and pruning gets them back into scale with the garden.

Early spring is the time to cut back shrubs of *Cornus* (dogwoods) and *Salix* (willows). When you prune a branch, these plants respond by sending out two or three sideshoots. Pruned back now, before bud break, to six inches from the ground, *Cornus* and *Salix* will respond by throwing out lots of colourful new shoots. It's these sideshoots that provide the main feature for the winter garden.

Keep in mind the two Js when it comes to clipping evergreen hedges and shrubs (e.g. cedars, laurels, cypresses). January and July are the best months to perform this activity. Early in the year new growth will soften the shorn appearance of a newly cut hedge. In July, the new growth that results from trimming will still have time to mature before the onset of freezing winter conditions that may damage young shoots.

Yew has the rare capacity of regrowing from mature wood. This means an older hedge can be trimmed back hard by pruning right to the bare trunk. If done now, by midsummer, yews will be covered with a delectable fuzz of new green shoots. To prevent overstressing overgrown yews, do only one side at a time, and wait a season before pruning the other side. Temporary lopsidedness beats complete destruction!

Second Week of February

Welcome the Narcissi

The appearance of narcissus shoots in the garden is a sure sign that the days are lengthening. Such a relief! If you planted early flowering varieties in fall, then you'll be enjoying splashes of cheery yellow blooms in your garden soon. Early daffodils are shorter than the later modern hybrids, a good thing when it comes to wicked weather. High winds and rain flatten displays of 'King Alfreds', whereas flowers that grow nearer the ground will escape this fate.

Trumpet daffodils 'Mount Hood'.

Look out for unusual varieties to tuck around the garden. 'Tête-à-Tête' and 'Jack Snipe', cyclamineus hybrids not more than ten inches high, are adorable with their swept-back petals, exposing trumpets with real attitude. 'February Gold' is another early miniature narcissus that fills rockeries, tubs and planters with masses of early spring heralds.

White narcissi can be captivating. 'Thalia' is a multi-flowering, triandrus narcissus with fragrant, reflexed white petals that perfumes the air with intoxicating fragrance. In my garden 'Thalia' has naturalized to the point where I can pick large bunches of it in spring, which perfume the house beautifully. 'Mount Hood' is a white narcissus that puts on a grand show of large white trumpets. Look for bulbs marked "naturalizing"; over the years these will establish into colonies that give dazzling spring displays.

TIP: Always plant bulbs at least twice the depth of the bulb size and cover well. (Don't forget it's the pointy end up.) Avoid planting bulbs in regimented rows like soldiers. To achieve a natural effect, throw an uneven number of bulbs on the ground and plant them where they land. Bulb planters work great for this.

Classic Camellias

There are two main varieties of camellia, *C. japonica* and *C. williamsii*. The shrubs of this second class are hardier and more free flowering, and dead blooms drop off naturally. Camellias have glossy evergreen foliage and showy blooms from January to May. Little pruning is required to make them one of the best spring garden plants.

Their biggest downfall is hard frost, which turns the flowers brown overnight. Planting them under the protection of buildings or taller plants can alleviate this problem. Flowers can also suffer from petal blight, which causes them to turn brown as well.

Being shallow rooted, camellias prefer moist soils. Gardeners often choose to plant them under the eaves of the house, where the problem of drying out occurs. It's very important to either water regularly or mulch the roots when the weather gets warm and dry. Beware that lack of watering during hot, dry summers will cause buds to drop off the following spring.

Camellias provide showy blooms from January to May.

Camellia Growing Tips

- Camellias are shallow rooted. When planting, the top of the root ball should be at the surface of the soil.
- Camellias prefer to be planted in light shade, as hot sun can scorch their leaves.
- Camellias are ericaceous (acid-loving), so mulch them with an acidic mulch, such as pine needles or coniferous sawdust.
- Group camellias with azaleas and rhododendrons. They all prefer the same acidic growing conditions.
- Plant camellias with an eastern exposure so the early morning sun dries off the flower petals to prevent wet petals turning brown.
- If yellowing occurs on leaves, water with cold black tea, full of tannic acid, or give the camellia a tonic of chelated iron.

Fruit Tree Care

Sunshine, no wind and no sign of rain ahead are the perfect conditions to dormant spray fruit trees. The oil dries faster when the sun is shining. Whatever the weather, do this before the buds open, as dormant sprays burn tender young foliage. Lime sulphur/oil sprays are effective against a host of problems: scale insects, red mite, aphid eggs, twig borer, plum black knot and peach leaf curl.

TIP: Dormant sprays work well for roses too. Spray your trees and rose canes so that all surfaces are well covered. If you are spraying against a house or gardening structure, cover it with a plastic sheet first as copper and sulphur sprays leave stains. If there are foliage plants under trees, cover them with a plastic sheet as well to prevent burning the leaves.

Dormant Lime Sulphur/Oil Spray

In a 3-litre pressure pump sprayer mix:
4 Tbsp. horticultural oil
8 Tbsp. lime/sulphur

Add 3 litres water.

Cankers

Check for canker on fruit trees and prune out any affected areas before infection spreads. Symptoms include a darkened, elliptical shrunken area of the bark that gradually spreads outwards and will eventually girdle the branch. Remove the infected branches by cutting back to healthy wood. If a branch has to be retained, cut out the cankered part with a sharp knife, so that all the diseased bark is removed. Burn the infected prunings to stop reinfection.

Spraying for Canker

- Use a fixed copper spray.
- Apply first at leaf fall.
- Repeat again in December.

Dormant spray your fruit trees now against a host of future problems.

Third Week of February

Rhubarb, Rhubarb, Rhubarb!

One of the earliest plants to stir in the winter garden is rhubarb. How encouraging to see the bright-red, swollen buds pushing their way above ground. Rhubarb is technically a vegetable, but because of its fruity flavour it is most often enjoyed as a dessert, jam or sweet relish.

Rheum rhaponticum, rhubarb, is a member of the Polygonaceae family, first introduced to Canada from Asia. It's a long-lived, hardy perennial that's virtually pest and disease-free, and is easy to grow if you remember one thing – feed it with lots of well-rotted manure! Rhubarb is a gutsy feeder and performs best when grown in soils rich in organic matter. Rhubarb leaves contain toxic levels of oxalic acid and should never be eaten or fed to livestock, but can be safely added to the compost pile.

Rhubarb Spray for Aphid Control

Make a spray to get rid of aphids by boiling three pounds of rhubarb leaves in three quarts of water. Strain this and add one ounce of soap flakes, dissolved in one quart of water. Before spraying, do a test patch.

Rhubarb is either green- or red-stalked; the latter are sweeter but less productive. However, the green-stalked varieties are better suited to forcing, so it may be a good idea to grow some of each type. There are a surprising number of varieties: 'Victoria' and 'Sutton's' are well known green-stalked varieties, while 'Valentine', 'Canada Red' and 'Cherry Red' are good red-stalked types.

Rhubarb responds well to forcing, producing an earlier harvest of tender, pink blanched stalks. At the turn of the 20th century, gardeners used specially designed terra cotta forcing pots for rhubarb, but these are not commonly available today. In mid-February I simply cover dormant rhubarb with the biggest terra cotta pot I own, and delight in peaking underneath to see the long, pale rhubarb stalks leap out of the ground.

Rhubarb can be harvested for a period of eight to ten weeks during spring. Harvest the stalks when they are between one and two feet long, and before they become tough.

TIP: Pull stalks off the crown with a twisting motion, rather than cutting them off. By mid-summer, stop harvesting, as not only does rhubarb get sour from a build-up of oxalic acid, but it's best to leave some foliage on the plant to feed the roots.

To keep the crowns producing, divide them every three years. It's best to divide rhubarb in the fall, and replant it with plenty of manure or compost to help it re-establish by spring. Divide the crowns so that you have pieces with at least two or three good buds on them. Replant these three feet apart, with the crowns buried three inches deep.

TIP: Not harvesting any fruit the first year from newly divided rhubarb means more fruit the next year. Remove seed heads when they appear, to direct energy back to the roots and leaves.

Good news for weight watchers! Rhubarb is one of the lowest calorie foods, providing only ten calories per four ounces. The sweetener is the problem, so try sweet cicely or stevia as a sugar substitute. Rhubarb is a good source of vitamin A and vitamin C, and also contains potassium, calcium and thiamin (B1).

Rhubarb – one of the earliest plants to stir in the winter.

Foolproof One Crust Rhubarb Pie

It doesn't matter how rough this pie appears when it goes into the oven, it always looks fantastic when it comes out!

Preheat oven to 400°F (200°C)

Crust:
12 ounces of shortcrust pastry (see recipe page 106)
1 egg yolk, beaten
3 Tbsp. semolina

Filling:
1 pound rhubarb cut into one-inch pieces
1/3 cup granulated sugar
1-2 pieces preserved ginger in syrup, drained and finely chopped (or substitute candied ginger)

Topping:
1/4 cup coarsely chopped hazelnuts
2 Tbsp. turbinado sugar

Roll out pastry into a 14-inch circle. Transfer onto a baking sheet. Brush a little egg yolk over the pastry. Scatter semolina over the centre, leaving a wide rim all around.

Mix rhubarb pieces, sugar and ginger in a large bowl. Pile onto the middle of the pastry circle. Fold the pastry rim roughly over the filling so that it meets in the middle and almost covers it. Some of the fruit will remain visible in the middle.

Glaze the pastry with the remaining egg yolk and scatter the hazelnuts and turbinado sugar over the top. Bake 30-35 minutes or until the pastry is golden brown. Serve warm.

TIP: Freeze rhubarb you don't use fresh. It keeps well frozen for up to a year, and there's nothing better than serving up a bowl of piping hot rhubarb crisp in the middle of winter.

Squeaky Beans

Properly cooked, fava beans are tender and sweet with 'melt-in-the-mouth' appeal. Freeze those you don't eat fresh, and throw the still frozen beans into a pot of boiling water for exactly ten minutes, after which they taste as good as fresh. My husband, Guy, loves it when they appear on his dinner plate, so I grow four different varieties – *Green Windsor, Mr. Bartons* (larger seeded favas), *Crimson Flowered* (1778), and *Walter Krivda's* (smaller sized bell beans).

Vicia faba is the botanical name for this legume, in the pea family Fabaceae. The genus *Vicia* indicates that favas are vetches, nitrogen-fixers, which means favas can also be grown as cover crops to improve soil nitrogen. They have a deep taproot that helps to break up compacted soils. I like the fact that I can grow a delicious crop of beans in winter and improve my soil at the same time. When grown as a cover crop, the plants are turned under in late spring before they set seed, allowing two to three weeks for them to break down before planting. Half a pound of small seeded favas, or bell beans, will add nitrogen to 250 square feet of garden.

By sowing the seeds in February, or even early March, you'll be harvesting these *squeaky* beans in July or August. Being a cold-hardy crop, they

can also be planted in late October or early November for earlier harvests in May or June, but be prepared to overseed in spring, as some seeds may rot in the cold, wet soil of winter.

Pods are produced in pairs on four foot tall stalks; each seed can produce up to three stalks with several pairs of pods on each. *TIP:* Wrap twine around your patch of beans later in the season to prevent the plants falling over under considerable weight.

Broad beans are harvested for fresh eating when the seeds swell in the green pods, but they can also be harvested for dried beans when the pods turn black. Dried beans need to be soaked overnight and cooked for about 75 minutes. You can also eat young leaves in winter salads and the new shoots as a steamed vegetable.

Black aphids can be a problem in late spring, as they colonize on the succulent tips of the plants. Watch out for aphids and snap the tips off the stalks to prevent a build-up of aphids. These pests do not affect the quality or production of the beans in the pods, but are an eyesore. However, these pesky aphids are a food source for beneficial ladybugs, which they attract in large populations to the garden.

Favas have no cholesterol and little oil, but are high in carbohydrates and protein, averaging about 30% protein, which is high for beans. If you haven't yet tried these buttery beans, why not give them a try? After all, they are buttery without the cholesterol!

Taking a Soil Test

How do you know if your soil needs amending or if a particular plant will thrive in it? How can you best find the solution to problems with plants in your garden? There's only one surefire way, and that's by having your soil tested. Once you become familiar with your soil conditions, it's much easier to answer these questions.

Knowing what specific nutrients are either lacking, or are in excess in your soil can solve problems and improve plant growth drastically.

If you have moved to a new garden, or have established new beds, a soil test will take the guesswork out of gardening. Ideally you should have your soil tested every three years. Your local garden centre can put you in contact with a laboratory that conducts soil tests.

Different tests provide you with varying amounts of information. The most basic test gives you the soil pH and macronutrient analysis (NPK), but by paying more you can get a detailed analysis of your soil. You can find out the levels of nitrogen, phosphate, potash, iron, zinc, sulfur, copper, manganese, magnesium, sodium, calcium, organic matter, soluble salts, lime, and the cation exchange capacity (CEC), which indicates the nutrient holding capacity of the soil. This analysis will be accompanied by appropriate fertilizer recommendations, based on the results of the test.

How to take a soil sample for testing
You'll need several random samples from the area you want to test. In total the laboratory will need about 250 to 500 ml of soil.

With a shovel, dig a hole from the soil surface to the root zone. Remove a thick one-inch slice from the smooth side of the open hole, including the surface crust of the soil. Remove the slice from the blade of the shovel, and place a two-inch wedge of it into a clean container (plastic is best). Repeat this procedure at random across the area you want to have analyzed.

Mix the representative slices thoroughly, removing all foreign matter such as roots, stalks, rocks, etc. Make sure some of the surface crusts are mixed into the final sample, as they contain soluble fertilizer salts that can affect plants.

Place your sample in a zip-lock bag, and identify it for the laboratory records.

The Soil Food Web

Let's take a journey underground for a moment to explore what goes on beneath the surface of the soil. It's like discovering an unexplored planet, teeming with life forms that affect everything going on in the garden.

An amazingly diverse web of life exists in the soil, without which plants would not exist, and therefore, nor would we. Soil-dwelling organisms range from one-celled bacteria, algae, fungi and protozoa, to more complex nematodes and micro-arthropods (microscopic bugs), to creatures we are more familiar with, such as earthworms, insects and small vertebrates.

The role of these combined organisms is to decompose organic matter, fix nitrogen from the air, store nutrients and make nutrients available to plants, enhance soil tilth, and manage or destroy pests and pollutants. They are critical in creating, regulating and maintaining healthy soils and plant growth.

Soil organisms follow seasonal and daily patterns, being subject to temperature and moisture fluctuations. The greatest activity occurs in spring when temperature and moisture are optimal. When your garden bursts alive in spring, it's the soil web of life below ground becoming active again that has triggered this growth spurt.

In view of this it only makes sense to get to know what goes on below the soil, so here's a brief introduction to the different levels of the soil web of life.

The primary level consists of plants – lichens, moss and algae – which are photosynthesizers fuelled by the sun's energy to fix carbon dioxide.

The next level consists of decomposers – bacteria and fungi – which convert complex materials into nutrients, and make them available to plants and other soil organisms.

The next level comprises the shredders – predators and grazers – represented by earthworms, nematodes and macro-arthropods (bugs such as cutworms, millipedes, weevils, beetles, etc.). Their activities enhance soil structure and control root-feeding pests and disease.

The highest level is represented by mice, birds and above-ground animals and insects – predators that control and keep a balance of the populations of the lower level predators.

These organisms are found wherever there is organic matter to feed on, but mainly in the top few inches of soil. They are most concentrated around roots, in plant litter, on humus, and on the surface of soil aggregates. Tillage, insecticides, fungicides and herbicides have an enormous impact on non-target species in the soil food web. Disruption of the intricate relationship and balance between the pathogens and beneficial organisms opens the door to problems with pests and diseases.

Organic gardening practices respect the fragile interdependency of the soil food web. Feeding the soil with organic matter, avoiding synthetic chemical pesticides and fertilizers, minimizing tillage, mulching and using green manures all help to sustain and protect this wonderful world of life below the soil.

I hope you enjoyed your brief journey underground, and that it helps to reinforce the reason why it is so vitally important to garden organically.

Getting Your Vegetables Off to a Fast Start

In a climate of uncertainty, we can never be sure what the weather is going to throw at us in spring. Despite this, as soon as spring is in the air, we want to get our gardens off to a fast start. We want to get the earliest crops from our vegetable gardens, so here are a few tips to get around the 'dodgy-weather doldrums'.

- Seed lettuces in an unheated greenhouse or cold garage by a window, any time from mid-February onwards. When seedlings reach two inches in height, grow them on outdoors, off the ground to avoid slugs and bugs. When established, transplant them, evenly spaced, into the garden.

- Peas can be grown under protection in used gutters, and an establishing row of peas can be transplanted outdoors once plants have reached four to six inches high and are well-rooted. (See *Little Pea Secrets,* third week of January.)

- As soon as the ground warms up, direct seed arugula, beets, kale, spinach, coriander, corn salad, orach and a summer mesclun mix. After lightly raking the seeds under, spring rains take care of the rest, until early thinnings provide tender spring greens.

TIP: Plant your rows in a north/south direction, which exposes both sides of each row to maximum sunlight and results in increased yields. Beware not to overshadow crops needing sunlight with taller plants. However, plants that prefer cooler growing conditions, such as lettuces and spinach, will benefit from being overshadowed. If you need protection from wind or ocean salt sprays, consider planting a row of Jerusalem artichokes, which make an admirable windbreak.

- In late February, sow onion and leek seeds directly into punnets, and germinate them inside an unheated greenhouse or a coldframe. When seedlings reach one inch in height, the punnets can be grown on outdoors, until they reach a skinny pencil size in thickness. The seedlings can then be transplanted into the garden to get a head start for fall.

- Squash and artichoke seedlings resent disturbance, so seed them in individual pots so the roots are not disturbed transplanting outdoors.

TIP: When planning the layout of your food garden, practise the principles of crop rotation to relieve the stress on the soil from nutrient depletion.

Vegetables fall into three categories: heavy feeders, heavy givers and light feeders. Heavy feeders (corn, tomatoes, squash, lettuce and cabbage) take large amounts of nutrients from the soil. Plant the areas where these crops were grown last year with heavy givers, nitrogen-fixing plants or legumes, such as peas, beans and fava beans, or light feeders, which include all the root crops.

- Heat-loving beans rot in cold, wet soil. Get a head start by growing them in a greenhouse, on top of the fridge or on a windowsill in bright light. Wait until the soil has well and truly warmed up before transplanting outdoors.

- Other heat lovers, like dill, perilla and amaranth, prefer being grown from direct seedings, but wait until the soil has warmed up (late May, early June) or they will not germinate.

TIP: Your food garden should be in a site that receives 11 hours of sunlight or more daily. Seven hours allows plants to grow adequately, but four hours may only work for cool season crops. If your garden receives less than 11 hours of sunlight, you will have to experiment to get the best results from a diversity of food plants.

- Grow tomatoes on in gallon pots, and wait until they have flowers before planting them out. Feed weekly, alternating one week with liquid seaweed and the next with fish fertilizer.

Fourth Week of February

The Primary Seeding

The primary seeding at *The Garden Path Nursery* always happens at the end of February, and involves some extensive preparation first. We empty the greenhouse of all overwintering plants, which go into a coldframe or under plastic to get hardened off. Then we thoroughly clean the inside of the greenhouse – glass panes, all surfaces and benches and the floor, taking special care to get into corners and on top of ledges.

Our intention is to get rid of any algae, botrytis, overwintering pests, spores and egg masses. A clean start is imperative for healthy seedlings. You'll hear me repeating this mantra throughout the season, "If you want to prevent disease and pests you must remove them!"

We sow all our seeds except for those of heat-loving plants, which require higher temperatures for germination, e.g. beans, corn, squash, red malabar spinach, basil, zinnias and cleome.

TIPS: Sow eggplants and peppers, which need 70-75°F (21-24°C) for germination, on bottom heat using thermostatically controlled heater cables. This way they'll germinate in a week or two, instead of taking a month to six weeks. Peppers and eggplants give better yields from an early start.

Organize your seeds by filing them alphabetically in a shoebox behind recipe cards marked A-Z. You can also create sections for cool-weather seeds for earlier sowing, seeds that require light for germination, seeds that need heat for germination, and winter vegetables for sowing later in the year.

> *Flowers That Need Light for Germination*
> African violet, arum, begonia, calceolaria, campion, coleus, columbine, coreopsis, foxglove, hesperis, heuchera, impatiens, lobelia, nicotiana, penstemon, petunia, portulaca, primula, sanvitalia, snapdragon, stocks, venidium

Ten Tips For Happy Seedlings

1. Fresh seed is best

Using fresh, high quality seeds that have not deteriorated through age or poor storage conditions gives the best start for seedlings. Stored seeds constantly exchange gases through the seed coat to regulate moisture, which consumes nutrients stored in the endosperm. Over time, the deterioration of nutrient levels affects the viability of the seed, which in turn affects germination rate and performance. Seed vitality is least affected if seeds are stored in a cool, dark, dry place, but all seeds have a shelf life. Seeds of Alliums (e.g. onions and leeks) and Umbels (e.g. carrots, parsnips, parsley, sweet cicely and dill) remain viable for one year only, whereas pea and bean seeds are good for three to five years. Check the seed catalogue or seed packet for usual seed life, and make sure you use seeds within this time.

2. Timing

Seeds germinate when conditions are conducive to survival. They germinate best when close to their optimum temperature range, which for most vegetables is around 65-80°F (18-27°C). Peas, favas, lettuce and spinach will germinate at cooler temperatures around 40°F (5°C), while snap beans, corn, melons and peppers refuse to germinate at temperatures much outside their optimum range of 75-80°F (24-27°C).

Starting your seeds at the right time avoids stressing seedlings, or losing them later to unfavourable conditions in the garden. Sow your seeds so they will be ready for transplanting when the conditions for their growth outdoors are favourable.

3. Light or dark for germination?

Some seeds will not germinate without the stimulation of light, while others need to be in darkness. Usually larger seeds require darkness, and one way of providing it is to cover them with newspaper until the seedlings emerge. Another is to make sure you cover them to three times the depth of the seed size.

4. Overcrowding

When seedlings are overcrowded they are either impossible to separate or they grow poorly. Sound familiar? For years I overseeded nicotiana because the seed is miniscule. It was only when I mixed the seed with dry sand, and then sowed the sand, that I managed to stop doing this. *TIP:* Try this for direct seeding tiny seeds in the garden. Remember that each tiny seed will grow into a large plant that needs room to thrive.

5. Growing medium

Choose a sterilized, lightweight seeding mix that will provide a moisture-retentive, disease-free, well-drained medium best suited to delicate seedlings. Never use garden soil to start seeds. It compacts when it dries out, making it impossible for fragile root hairs to penetrate, and it also harbours potential disease problems.

The Garden Path Seeding Mix

1 part peat
1 part vermiculite
1 part perlite
1 cup dolomite lime for each 12 litres of mixture to counteract the acidity of the peat

6. Moisture, temperature and light

Make sure you have adequate levels of three critical factors to ensure seedlings thrive once they have germinated: moisture, light and temperature. Underwatering or overwatering causes stress. Yellow or spindly seedlings are often the result of too little light. Too much warmth, together with too much moisture, leads to a fungal problem called *damping off.*

By paying close attention to light levels, watering and temperature control, your seedlings will grow into healthy, sturdy plants.

7. Things that bug seedlings

The most common pests that attack seedlings are fungus gnats, sowbugs, slugs, whiteflies and aphids. Good hygiene and cleanliness make a huge difference in controlling these pests. Scrub and clean your growing area thoroughly at the start of each new season.

The appearance of pests around seedlings often indicates that the tiny plants are stressed. Maybe they are rootbound and need transplanting? Possibly they need to be fed? Perhaps they are being overfertilized or underwatered? Try to find out what the problem is and correct it. Making minor adjustments to cultural conditions helps protect plants from further attack.

TIP: Yellow sticky traps catch insects around plants. Use these as indicators of a potential insect problem.

8. Food

Food stored in the seed's endosperm is sufficient to nourish the plant through its period of dormancy and germination, into its initial period of growth. Beyond this, nutrients must be provided by the medium the seed is grown in. If the medium has been sterilized, there will be no nutrients in it, so here's where you come in with a regular fertilization program.

I feed my 'green babies' with a weekly feed of organic liquid fish fertilizer and liquid seaweed. If you cannot find a combination product, use fish fertilizer one week and seaweed the next. Alternate these feedings until you transplant the well-rooted seedlings into nutrient-rich garden soil.

9. Hardening off

Seedlings do not appreciate being placed outdoors in cool spring conditions when they have become acclimatized to a protected environment. Gradually harden off young plants outdoors by putting them out in the day and bringing them in at night for at least ten days. This way they can adjust to cooler temperatures more gradually.

10. Transplanting

Once they have developed their second set of true leaves, the roots of seedlings are established enough to be transplanted into their own pots or into the garden. Use only clean pots to prevent disease problems. (See page 35 for the Garden Path Potting Mix recipe.)

Give new transplants a helping hand by feeding them either liquid fish fertilizer or liquid seaweed once a week for the first three or four weeks of their new lives in the garden. This not only helps them get established faster, but also helps them recover from transplant shock. Until young plants have developed secondary feeder roots to access nutrients from the soil, this supplemental feeding is of great benefit to them.

TIP: Interplant rows of fast-growing plants, such as lettuce, radish, spinach and mustards with slower-growing crops, such as cabbage, garlic, onions and peas to help get the maximum yield from a small food garden.

Companion plants that grow well together are lettuces interplanted with radishes and carrots, corn grown with squash and beans, and tomatoes planted with onions, parsley or basil.

Make a simple inexpensive cloche using PVC pipe and 6 ml plastic. Placing a cloche over beds helps harden plants off and gets seedlings off to a fast start.

Tricky Seeds

Plants produce seeds to ensure the continuation of the species, so their seeds are well-equipped to cope with harsh conditions. Most seeds are produced toward the end of the year, so many have hard seed coats to prevent the uptake of water during unfavourable winter conditions. Hard seed coats are common in the pea and bean family, which is why abrasion with sandpaper or chipping of sweetpeas, using a sharp knife or metal file, a process called *scarification,* ensures quick and even germination.

Some seeds have biochemical recording mechanisms to prevent germination until a certain number of hours of cold temperature has passed. This enables the seed to remain dormant until the warmer days of spring. Some plant seeds, such as those of peony, davidia, cardiocrinum and lilies, have multiple dormancies, and will take more than a year to germinate. These seeds should be covered with coarse grit 6 mm (1/4 inch) thick to avoid mosses and liverworts growing on the surface of the growing medium. Seeds with such biochemical recording mechanisms will not germinate in spring without having first been exposed to a period of chilling, a process called *stratification,* to break dormancy.

Some plants do not produce viable seed reliably. *Acer palmatum* Japanese maple, is unreliable, and beech only sets viable seed once every seven years. Some plants, such as hellebores, anthriscus, primula, meconopsis and pulsatilla, only germinate when the seed is sown fresh, soon after collection. Some seeds, such as lettuce, cyclamen and primula become dormant at temperatures above 25°C (77°F), so need cooler conditions for germination.

If you are experiencing difficulties getting seeds to grow, or are unsure of specific germination requirements, sow the seed in fall and overwinter it in a coldframe. Bringing the seed tray into a warmer environment in spring (15-25°C) (59-77°F) will encourage germination.

The majority of seeds are not particular in their requirements for germination, but understanding the needs of trickier seeds is obviously vital in getting them to grow.

March

I wandered lonely as a cloud
That floats on high o'er vales and hills,
When all at once I saw a crowd,
A host of golden daffodils;
Beside the lake, beneath the trees,
Fluttering and dancing in the breeze.

Continuous as the stars that shine
And twinkle on the milky way,
They stretched in never-ending line,
Along the margin of a bay;
Ten thousand saw I at a glance,
Tossing their heads in sprightly dance.

The waves beside them danced, but they
Outdid the sparkling waves in glee,
A poet could not but be gay,
In such a jocund company;
I gazed and gazed but little thought
What wealth the show to me had brought.

For oft, when on my couch I lie
In vacant or in pensive mood,
They flash upon that inward eye
Which is the bliss of solitude;
And then my heart with pleasure fills,
And dances with the daffodils.

William Wordsworth (1804)

First Week of March
- Four Secrets of Successful Soil Building
- Composting Is Not Rocket Science!

Second Week of March
- Quiet Please – Weeds Growing!
- Divide…
- …And Multiply!
- The Golf Green Lawn
- Spring Tonic Nettle Soup

Third Week of March
- Get to Know Your Clematis
- Last Chance to Prune

Fourth Week of March
- Best Care For Seedlings
- Top Tips For Terrific Tomatoes
- Propagating Herbs

First Week of March

The Fours Secrets of Successful Soil Building

For years I have been experimenting with feeding my soil so I can grow the healthiest plants. Now the plants in my garden are so lush and healthy I feel I have hit the nail on the head, so I want to let you in on my discoveries. They are so simple, and use only materials from natural sources. Best of all, they're all free!

Before I share my 'secrets' with you, I'd like you to consider this little bit of basic logic. If soil provides nutrients essential for plant growth, then soil quality will determine the health of the plants. As they grow, plants constantly remove nutrients from the soil. If these nutrients are not replenished, then plant health is jeopardized. Insects and disease are attracted to unhealthy plants, so all the gardener's problems begin when soil becomes depleted of essential plant nutrients. This is why the basic tenet of organic gardening is "feed the soil, and the soil will take care of the plants."

Soil organic matter is created by decaying plants and the dying leaves, twigs and flowers that pile up loosely on the soil surface. Millions of soil-dwelling insects and organisms assist in the process of breakdown and decomposition, and their carcasses will eventually also enrich the soil. This continual process of decay is an essential part of nature's cycle, and it is from this that fertile soil is created.

Contrary to popular belief, chemical fertilizers with synthetic origins do not restore soil health and fertility; in fact, they actually destroy physical and biological properties of soil. They can even combine with minerals already present, making them unavailable to plants. High concentrations of nitrogen, phosphorus and potassium from chemical fertilizers glut and overload plants. Plants outwardly look lush, but fast growth produces weak and watery tissues that attract pests and disease.

Replicating nature, by replenishing soil nutrients and protecting the fragile soil web of life, results in healthy plants that do not attract problems with pests and diseases. All it takes is a bit of time in the dormant seasons – November, December, January and February – feeding the soil. These are the months when it's cold out and you will relish some outdoor activity and exercise. (See *The Soil Food Web,* third week of February.)

Number One: Add compost to your garden. Compost is the gardeners' version of humus, but it is produced much more quickly. The quality of compost as an organic soil additive depends on the residues from which it is made, as well as the extent to which decomposition has occurred. *TIP:* For best results, vary the layers of material when building the compost pile as much as possible, and provide air, moisture and heat for the fastest and most thorough breakdown.

Number Two: Add leaves and leaf mulch to the garden. Shredded leaves break down very easily, and create a soil tilth that is wonderful to work with and teems with earthworms. *TIP:* In the fall, run a lawnmower over a pile of leaves on a driveway. This reduces bulky leaves to one tenth of their volume, and results in a manageable pile of shredded leaves. Spread these over your beds in six-inch layers as a soil-building mulch.

Tree roots penetrate widely through topsoil and deep into subsoil, taking up valuable nutrients, that are then stored in the leaves. When leaves break down, they return these nutrients to the soil. Take full advantage of fall by stockpiling leaves. I heap mine in a corner of the driveway and just forget about them. By spring the pile has started to break down into a coarse leaf mulch, which we use in potting mixes and as a garden mulch. After one full year, the pile will have broken down into a beautiful, rich black leaf mulch, the texture of superb garden soil. This is perfect for mulching and enriching the garden. (See *Lots of Lovely Leaves*, second week of October.)

Number Three: Add seaweed to your garden. After winter storms, head down to the beach and scoop the top off piles of leafy kelp that has been washed up. Seaweed contains all the micronutrients and trace elements essential for the healthiest plant growth. It can either be added directly to the garden as a mulch or layered into compost. Many gardeners worry about salt build-up, but in over twenty years of adding seaweed to my garden, I have never encountered any problems. The proportionately small volume that is spread on the garden, and the fact that winter rains wash and dilute any salt residues, puts this issue into perspective.

Number Four: Add animal or green manure for a boost of nitrogen to the soil. Local farms are always eager for gardeners to take away their stockpiles of manure. I have cultivated a friendship with a neighbour who owns three horses. She only treats them homeopathically and with acupuncture, so I know there are no drug residues in their manure. This manure has no weed seeds either, as she uses untreated woodchips in the horse paddocks. Be cautious about manure mixed with hay, as it can spread grass and weed seeds over the garden.

Organic gardeners are concerned about the use of growth hormones and antibiotics in conventional livestock farming, as well as genetically modified grains used in livestock feeds. Try to find a source of animal manure – horse, cow, chicken, sheep, llama or rabbit – that has not been subjected to these inputs. If manure is not aged (if it's either still steaming or retains a strong odour), it's important to age it before you spread it on the garden. Do not harvest food from a garden that has been manured until 120 days have passed, allowing time for the manure to be broken down and potential pathogens to be neutralized by myriad soil microorganisms.

If you prefer, you can add nitrogen to soil using plant matter rather than animal residues. Grow a winter green manure crop of fall rye, winter pea, fava beans, winter barley or winter wheat, and plough it under in early spring. In spring/summer you can grow a warmer climate green manure crop using vetches, clovers, buckwheat, alfalfa or phacelia. (See *Green Manures*, first week of November.)

Try this to screen compost easily. Place a screen on a log balanced across a wheelbarrow. 'Rock and rolling' it back and forth with a friend quickly fills the wheelbarrow with screened compost.

Trench compost by digging kitchen waste in a deep trench to break down in the garden.

Composting Is Not Rocket Science!

What's all the mystery about composting? It's only about decay! Nature composts continually: things fall on the ground, naturally decay and eventually become absorbed into the soil. This process builds vibrant soil, feeds the complex host of soil-dwelling organisms, and provides nutrients for healthy plant growth. To me, the mystery is why gardeners rake up and remove debris that falls on the garden, when they could be turning it into 'black gold'.

Composting is the key to returning large quantities of nutrient-rich organic matter to the soil. Best of all, it's recycling free materials and putting things we no longer want to good use. The ingredients of successful composting are good aeration, moisture and materials added in layers no more than six inches thick at a time. Heat builds up as the pile breaks down. *TIP:* This happens more quickly when the compost heap is located in a place that gets sunlight.

The more varied the materials you add to your pile, the better the quality and nutrient content of the finished product. (See *The Greens and the Browns,* fourth week of November.) Avoid weeds that have gone to seed, diseased matter and invasive plants such as couch grass, ivy, goutweed and morning glory. Layer with many different things: green for nitrogen, brown for carbon. Grass clippings produce nitrogen, shredded leaves or spoiled hay add carbon; comfrey, nettles and seaweed provide trace elements; while manure, weeds and herbaceous prunings contribute nitrogen.

Avoid problems with rats by using a rat-proof plastic cone composter for kitchen wastes. When the cone is full, bury the contents in a deep trench in the garden and cover it with soil. The compost breaks down to enrich the soil for plants growing on top of the trench.

Building a Composting System

- *The most basic method:* Build a pile not exceeding four feet tall by four feet wide. Turn it once, moistening, not soaking, as you turn. Cover the pile to trap in heat, resulting from the process of decay, and to stop winter rains from washing out nutrients. If you use plastic or old carpets, take care that they do not break down over time and contaminate the compost. In six months you should have compost ready to spread on your garden.

- *Create a structure to contain compost:* Use fencing wire, four feet tall, to create a circular cage. Fill it with layers of garden waste and forget about it. With this system, air flow and moisture penetrate the pile, but there is little insulation, so breakdown takes longer.

- *The one, two or three bin system:* Use free wooden pallets from lumberyards, nail them together, and tie the front side on with twine for easy access for turning. Build as many bins as you want by adding more pallets. When you have filled up one bin, turn it once while moistening the layers with a hose. *TIP:* Put a wooden cover on top to insulate from rain and trap in heat, and as a reminder not to add more to this pile.

- *The Windrow Method:* If you garden on acreage, create a windrow, a straight row as long as you want, but no more than four feet tall. Start with twiggy stalks on the bottom for aeration, layer with no more than six inches of as many different materials as possible. With acreages, this shouldn't be a problem. If the materials are dry, moisten the pile. At the end of the season, use leaves as a final layer for insulation. Optional: Cover the pile for faster breakdown. If you use plastic, choose a heavyweight grade to make sure it doesn't break down and contaminate the compost.

For large quantities of compost in the shortest time possible, build a windrow and insulate it with hay bales along both sides and at the ends, using stakes to hold the bales in place. Cover the top with black plastic. If you site it in full sun, you should have useable compost in spring from a windrow built in November.

Three-bin composting system: one bin for building the pile; one bin for turning compost into and leaving it to break down; one for holding well-rotted, ready-to-use compost.

Second Week of March

Quiet Please, Weeds Growing

The onset of warm weather stimulates plant growth, which also means weeds! Now's the time to turn your attention to what's coming up in the garden. An ounce of prevention is worth a pound of cure. It's much easier to hoe up young weeds now, while the earth is moist, than later when it's dry and compacted. Make sure you hoe up spring weeds before they set seed and multiply your weeding task. Mulching smothers weeds and mowing chops off their heads, which keeps them at bay.

Annual weeds, such as chickweed, are easy to hoe. The piles can be left to dry out. Either turn them back into the soil or add them to the compost pile. Unless you can achieve hot temperatures, it's best not to compost weeds that have gone to seed. Don't compound a problem by spreading it.

Perennial weeds are easier to spot before being hidden by lush spring growth. Some, such as dandelions and plantain, have deep tap roots and must be dug out removing the entire root, as any segment left produces a new plant.

Go round the garden now, digging out dandelions, buttercups or plantain wherever you spy them. I love the *schlucking* sound of deep roots as I pull weeds out from the soil. Pernicious weeds, such as morning glory, couchgrass or ground elder, have underground roots that spread rampantly. Removing young plants as soon as they appear saves hours trying to eradicate infestations later.

Once you have weeded, keep weeds in check by mulching beds with leaf mulch, compost, aged manure, or a mix of all three! This not only smothers dormant weed seeds, but also improves soil tilth, and locks moisture into the soil, which makes future weeding easier.

TIPS: Many gardeners take a tolerant view of lawn weeds such as daisies and speedwell. If you don't, established weeds can be tackled one at a time by pouring salt on them, taking care not to salt the grass at the same time.

For emerging weeds growing out of cracks in driveways, etc., spray with vinegar. It's the latest method of organic weed control for removing young weeds.

Divide…

Take the opportunity, while going around checking for emerging weeds, to take stock of your perennials. Anything need dividing? Most perennials need dividing every three years when they get woody in the centre or overcrowded in the bed. Divide fall flowering perennials now, but leave the summer and spring flowering ones until after flowering, or you'll lose the show.

TIP: Use an axe to cut through solid rootballs. One good swing and you'll have it in half. Then sections are easy to pry apart. Take another

---

The Garden Path Potting Mix

In a wheelbarrow mix together until well blended:

2 buckets* of screened compost or sieved garden loam (biologically active soil medium)
1 bucket of composted leaf mulch or peat (moisture retention)
3/4 bucket perlite or coarse washed sand (aeration)
12 cups granulated organic fertilizer (Contents: non-gmo seedmeals, dolomite lime, rock phosphate, sul-po-mag, greensand, zeolite and kelp meal)

*1 bucket = 20 litres

good swing if they are not – just remember your ten toes when swinging that axe!

Asters and Michaelmas daisies benefit from being divided every year. Clumps of phlox need lifting and dividing every third year. Solidago, sedum, rudbeckia and helenium respond well to being divided if the clumps have spread too much in the border, or if they are not flowering as well as they should. Now's also the best time to lift and divide ornamental grasses. Healthy pieces can be separated and used to start new clumps.

... and Multiply!

The secret to getting cuttings to root successfully is to use bottom heat. We built a propagation box, six feet by four feet, from recycled wood. We simply tacked a 25 foot-long heater cable with a thermostat to the bottom, which was covered with a two-inch layer of sand. This is the only regular source of heat provided to plants in our Zone 8 greenhouse over the winter.

You can take softwood and hardwood cuttings all year round, but the main times are summer and fall. Cuttings, in pots of rooting mix, sit on top of the warm sand all winter. When new roots poke through the drainage holes or new growth emerges from the tips, the cuttings have struck. Then the rooted cuttings go into their own four-inch pots to provide them with

The Garden Path Rooting Mix
Measure equal parts of sterilized ingredients by volume* and mix well:
Coarse washed sand
Peat
Perlite
Optional: Add granular rock phosphate to stimulate rooting (1/6th of total volume)

*A 4-litre ice cream bucket works well.

nutrients and a good medium for continued growth and root development.

We put nine cuttings in a six-inch square pot filled with rooting mix, using a chopstick or dibber to make holes to place them in. The square pots fit compactly onto the six by four propagation table, so that each table can have as many as 500 hundred cuttings rooting over the winter months.

You'll be amazed how easily some plants take root, e.g. rosemary, hebes, shrubby lavatera, buddleia, penstemon, erysimum and cistus. Some take much longer for roots to develop e.g. camellia, cotinus and corokia. When it comes to rooting roses, trial and error pays off. Some root easily, e.g. 'Dublin Bay', 'Perle d'Or', 'Queen Elizabeth'. Some are harder to root, and others are darn right near impossible! Experiment with lots of cuttings – it's fun and rewarding.

Cuttings on the propagation table.

The Golf Green Lawn

Gardeners work hard to achieve their ideal lawn – the 'golf green' lawn, maintained as a high maintenance monoculture, in which no diversity of plant species other than grasses is tolerated. Even though monocultures do not thrive in nature, this is what is demanded from the perfect lawn. Considering that in Victoria, the 'City of Gardens' where I live, 88% of pesticides used are herbicides, it is clear how costly to the gardener and the environment such lawns can be.

Creeping speedwell, clover, moss, buttercups, daisies, plantains and dandelions have no place in a 'golf green' lawn. Fortunately, as an organic gardener, instead of being instantly impelled to eradicate them, I have come to appreciate some of the above mentioned plants in my lawn.

Aerate the lawn after a wet winter to prevent soil compaction. This provides a freer draining medium for new grass roots to grow. (I leave the core plugs to break down and feed the lawn.) Aerating machines are inexpensive to rent.

If there is a build-up of thatch (dead plant matter) over the root zone, you'll need to dethatch first. This involves the rental of another dandy machine, which I think of as a mechanical comb.

This doesn't mean to say that the lawn is always full of weeds, but that I enjoy a lush expanse of green not comprised of one hundred per cent grass plants. Heck, if it's that difficult to accept natural plant diversity in a lawn, I just call it a meadow!

After aerating is the best time to topdress with lawn sand, a mix of fifty per cent topsoil and fifty per cent sand. Alternatively, if you have a stockpile of compost, spread this over the lawn. Spread the topdressing one to two inches thick, and rake it level to fill in the holes from aeration. *TIP:* Regular topdressing with compost helps decompose thatch and may eliminate the need for dethatching altogether.

I appreciate the influence of a green lawn on the landscape. I actually have two expanses of lawn, which I manage differently. The 'upper lawn', in the semi-shade garden, is maintained as a formal lawn with regular cutting, edging and close attention to weed control. It's a miracle the 'lower lawn' survives at all! It grows in baking hot sun on two inches of topsoil over fifteen feet of clay fill. I leave it to go brown every summer and it miraculously struggles back in fall. This is the lawn I refer to as a meadow!

Organic lawn maintenance includes regular aeration, dethatching if necessary, proper watering, seasonal fertilizing and, most importantly, mulch mowing with sharp blades set at the correct height. These practices go a long way toward creating a healthy green lawn that keeps moss and weeds at bay.

Keeping soil neutral, around pH 6.5, is important here on the wet west coast, where heavy winter rains tend to acidify soils. I apply dolomite lime to the lawn every year to neutralize acidity and add the macro-nutrients calcium and magnesium.

TIPS:

- Do not remove grass clippings as they feed soil microbes, which play a vital role in feeding the lawn.

- To avoid compaction, do not walk on or cut the lawn after watering or a heavy rain.

- Always cut grass higher than two inches.

The best time to apply a natural source fertilizer to the lawn is when the weather warms up, and the soil becomes biologically active. Warm, moist soil activates myriad soil microorganisms, which slowly break down the fertilizer to release nutrients to hungry grass plants. To protect soil health, avoid synthetic lawn fertilizers with high NPK ratios (nitrogen, phosphorus, potassium). These disrupt the intricate web of life in the soil and cause weak cellular growth, which is more prone to disease.

Natural source slow-release fertilizers are best. In spring, use a blend with high nitrogen for leafy grass growth (NPK 10-3-3), and in fall a high potassium blend for hardiness and strong root development (NPK 3-3-8).

TIP: Applying a mycorrhizal product at this time will boost microbial activity in the soil, which means grass will grow more vigorously and experience less water and heat stress later in the season. This can be applied as a foliar feed from a hose end or backpack sprayer. Mycorrhizae work by creating networks of fungal filaments in the soil around plant roots, which enhances the ability of the plant to absorb water and nutrients from the soil.

When my 'meadow' starts to look raggedy it's time for a lawn renovation. To overseed, I need a grass seed blend that will withstand full sun and high traffic, so I choose a low maintenance seed mix, comprising primarily fescues: hard fescue, creeping fescue, and chewing fescue, with 10% perennial rye grass. The hard fescues have two hundred and fifty times the root density of other grasses, which means they stand up well to adverse conditions such as drought. It's important to choose a lawn seed mix suited to your soil, light and traffic conditions.

After seeding, I topdress with a layer of screened compost – pure heaven for the lawn – and then I roll. Rolling over the area establishes good contact between the seed and the soil. You can rent a lawn roller where you rent an aerator or dethatcher.

Hopefully it rains just after the lawn is seeded, and every day thereafter, because the most important thing to get a new lawn established is to keep it *constantly* moist, and never allow it to dry out.

> *TIP:* To keep birds away from a newly seeded lawn take a cedar stake about eighteen inches long and hammer a nail in one end, leaving it to stick out. Make a small hole in an aluminum pie plate. Tie the plate to the nail with twine, allowing it to bang around. Hammer the stake into the newly seeded lawn. Repeat this all over the lawn; the flashing of foil and banging of plates frightens birds away.

A Spring Tonic

When the nettles appear down by the creek it's time for a spring tonic. Nettles are full of life-enriching minerals, vitamins and chlorophyll, which add pep to your step. Plants love a boost of nettle tea as well (see *Special-teas,* second week in April). If you want to stop nettles going to seed, just cut them back regularly and add them to the compost pile. Of course a good pair of gloves is recommended for this job.

Spring Tonic Nettle Soup — Preparation time 30 minutes

1 chopped onion (or 4 chopped leeks)
1 Tbsp. butter with a drizzle of olive oil
2 bay leaves
4 medium potatoes, chopped
4 cups tender nettle tops, rinsed
4 cups water
Salt and pepper to taste

1 cup milk and 1 cup light cream
   (or 2 cups soymilk)
1 bulb roasted garlic (optional)
Garnishing options:
Parsley, finely chopped
Yoghurt
Croutons

Sauté onions (or leeks) with bay leaves in butter and oil until softened. Add potatoes and cover with water. Season with salt and pepper. Bring to a boil, reduce heat and cook until potatoes are soft. Add nettles and allow to cook for about ten minutes until wilted and soft. If adding roasted garlic, squeeze out the softened cloves into the soup now.

Remove the bay leaves. Purée everything in a blender until smooth. Return to heat and slowly add dairy or soymilk, stirring while soup gently reheats. Do not allow to boil, or soup will curdle. Serve garnished with a dollop of yoghurt topped with a sprinkle of chopped parsley. Croutons also taste great in this nutritious soup.

Third Week of March

Get to Know Your Clematis

Once established, *Clematis armandii* is an evergreen vine so vigorous that you can almost watch it growing. It can grow as much as fourteen feet in one season, so be careful where you plant it. Fortunately, it responds well to hard pruning and can be cut right down to the ground. It's best to control it, though, by selective yearly pruning, which is best done after flowering in May. In spring, the main feature of *Clematis armandii* is a profusion of showy, fragrant blossoms, which beautify any structure these vines sprawl over. Gardeners relish this plant because it's easy to grow, with attractive glossy-green leaves year round. I value it most because it's one of the few evergreen vines that thrive in shade.

The Curse of Clematis

Clematis wilt, also known as clematis die-back, is the most serious problem affecting clematis. The youngest leaves suddenly droop, and then the upper parts of the vine wither and die. Lesions may appear on the stems near ground level and dark patches may appear on leaves. This can happen in just a few days.

To remedy clematis wilt, cut affected plants back to just below soil level. New shoots will arise that are not affected by the disease, and your plants will recover. If the problem reoccurs, dig out and remove the affected plant. Then remove the soil to a depth of one foot around the site, and replace with fresh soil before replanting.

TIPS: When planting clematis, sink it six inches deeper in the soil than the soil mark on the stem. This encourages the formation of shoots from the lower part of the stem, which are less prone to infection. This is one of the very few instances where deep planting is actually beneficial.

Keep the roots of clematis cool by mulching over them or planting low-growing shading plants over the root zone.

How to Prune Your Clematis

There are three different groups of clematis, classified by their flowering time.

Group 1: Varieties that flower in early spring on wood produced in the previous year, e.g. *C. montana* and *C. cirrhosa.* Prune after flowering when they outgrow their allotted space. If necessary, cut them down completely, but don't do this more than once every three years.

Group 2: Early summer, large-flowered cultivars, e.g. *C.* 'Nelly Moser', that bloom twice, once on the previous season's growth and again on new shoots produced in summer. Staggered pruning helps prolong the display from established Group 2 clematis. Keep a framework of old wood on which the first flush of flowers will form. Cut other stems, including any that are weak or damaged, back to a pair of healthy buds nearer the base. You can hard prune every three to four years. You will lose the first flowering, but the second will be much stronger.

'Nelly Moser', a large flowered clematis that blooms twice a year.

Group 3: Varieties that flower in late summer on growth made in the current season, e.g. *C. jackmanii, C. viticella* and *C. texensis.* Once established, they should be hard pruned every year when the buds show signs of new growth. Remove any stems killed by frost. Cut back to a strong pair of buds six to twelve inches above the ground. New vines will develop from ground level.

Last Chance to Prune

Here's a reminder of other plants that need attention now, if they have not already been pruned.

* *Roses:* Cut out dead, diseased or damaged wood and all spindly shoots from hybrid tea and floribunda roses. With rambling and climbing roses, prune back to only the strongest canes from which vigorous shoots arise. Tie these to supports to encourage lateral growth from which the blooms arise.

* *Hydrangeas:* Selectively prune mophead and lacecap hydrangeas, taking off the old flower heads by cutting just above a strong pair of buds. Remove any spindly canes. On old congested bushes, take out the oldest canes at ground level. New ones will grow in their place.

* *Mahonia:* Mahonias can easily get out of control, so each year, after flowering, prune away one or two flowering shoots. Old leggy shoots can be cut down to the ground, which encourages new shoots to grow from the base. Alternatively, shoots can be shortened to a variety of lengths to give mahonias shape and structure. Don't worry if you are left with leafless stems; new shoots will soon sprout from them.

* *Heathers:* Trim winter-flowering heathers with hedge shears to remove old flower heads and enhance the shape of the plants. Be careful to remove only the blooms, and avoid cutting into old wood which will not grow back.

* *Bamboo:* Bamboo needs pruning once a year. The proportion of canes that need to be removed will vary from a third to almost two-thirds, depending on whether the clump in question has been pruned regularly. In this case, remove about a third of the canes. Aim for an open and airy effect. There should be clear daylight between the bare lower stems and the leafy upper parts. *TIP:* Start by removing the thinnest canes around the perimeter of the clump; things will gradually become clearer as you do this. Don't just remove canes from the edge of the clump; the centre must be tackled too, as this is where overcrowding is most likely to lead to loss of vigour.

> ### Bamboo Mite Spray
> (For large stands of bamboo)
> 500 ml dish soap (phosphate free)
> 250 ml vegetable oil (used)
> 20 litre sprayer filled with water
>
> *When to spray:*
> Twice, with the sprays one week apart. Apply out of direct sun to prevent burning the foliage. Spray in summer when the mites become active, after thinning older growth and removing damaged and crooked canes (around the time new growth comes in). This is a good annual practice, as mites like crowded foliage for shelter.

* *Grasses:* Ornamental grasses should be trimmed back annually in spring. Leave the flowerheads of many species for winter display, but tidy them up as winter takes its toll. Cut deciduous grasses, such as miscanthus, to about four inches (10 cm) from the ground. Hedging shears work well for this satisfying task. For pampas grass, rake out dead material from the base to let light and air into the centre. If the species is less hardy, leave the pruning until later in spring to give extra frost protection.

TIP: Before you start, get a good pair of leather gloves. Many grasses have razor-sharp leaves. Paper cuts – Ouch!

Fourth Week of March

Best Care for Seedlings

If you started plants from seed earlier in the year, you should have lots of seedlings to take care of now. The first set of seed leaves are called cotyledons; at this stage the roots are not developed enough, so do not disturb the seedling. It is not until seedlings develop their first set of true leaves that they can be moved into their own pots, a process called *pricking out*.

When pricking out, handle delicate seedlings carefully – by their leaves ideally – rather than their fragile stems. It's easy to snap a stem when handling. Use a dibber or a chopstick to make a hole in the premoistened medium, and place the seedling into it. Carefully cover over the roots and water in. The seedling is now in *transplant shock*, and needs to be kept out of direct sun for a few days until it recovers. In sun it will wilt immediately, and may never recover.

Keep seedlings evenly moist, and don't let them dry out. Watering in the morning is best so seedlings don't sit cool and wet all night. This could trigger a fungal problem called *damping off*, which is caused by soil-borne fungi, usually rhizoctonia, occasionally pythium and less often botrytis or phytophthora.

Seedlings put on a lot of new growth at this stage, so after three or four waterings, start to fertilize weekly with liquid fish fertilizer or liquid seaweed. Once their roots have established, periodically check that your plants have not become rootbound. Then either pot each plant on into a larger pot, or harden it off to prepare it for transplanting outdoors.

Problems?

- *If seeds have not sprouted,* they may not be viable. Check the date on the seed package. Do a viability test by sowing ten seeds on a dampened piece of paper towel. Fold it over. Keep it damp. Check a week or so later to see how many seeds have sprouted. Three out of ten indicates only 30% germination. In this case I would recommend buying a fresh packet of seeds. A germination rate of no less than 65% indicates acceptable viability.

- *If there is no germination,* the seed may require longer to germinate. Sometimes seeds take from four to six weeks to sprout. Parsley requires 21 days for germination. Check a germination guide before you give up on your pots of seeds.

- *If seeds are taking a long time to germinate,* the temperature may be too cold for germination. For heat lovers like peppers, basil and tomatoes, which require temperatures around 75-85°F (25-30°C) for germination, put seed trays on top of bottom heat, or just wait longer until the weather warms up.

- *When seedlings are yellow,* it's an indicator that they are starving due to lack of nutrients in the growing medium. Apply a weekly feed of liquid fish fertilizer or liquid seaweed.

- *If seedlings are spindly and leggy,* there's not enough light for them. Increase the light by moving the pots closer to a bright window or using grow lights. Rotating seedlings daily helps them straighten up, or you can try planting spindly seedlings deeper.

- *If seedlings are growing very slowly,* it may be due to overcrowding, or the growing medium may have insufficient nutrients to supply all the seedlings. Try to prevent overcrowding by sowing seeds less thickly. If possible, transplant seedlings into individual pots to relieve this stress, and then apply a foliar feed of liquid fish fertilizer or liquid seaweed.

- *If seedlings collapse at soil level,* it is damping off, caused by a soil-borne fungus. Damping off is aggravated by overseeding in warm, moist conditions.

- *If seedlings are being eaten,* you've got a critter in the area. Check for slugs or sowbugs that love munching on tasty new seedlings. Check between and under the pots and trays, and find the culprit before it dines on all your plants!

Top Tips for Terrific Tomatoes

Finding the best variety for your region and garden microclimate requires some experimenting. A tomato that astounds one gardener may disappoint another, because growth, flavour and yield are dependent on weather, soil and the garden microclimate. It makes a world of difference whether you grow tomatoes in gardens subject to cooling summer ocean breezes or in protected inland gardens.

Grow cherry tomatoes for early ripening.

Extend your season of harvest by growing a diversity of tomatoes, ranging in size and days 'til ripening. Choose a range of early to late season cultivars, and select those that perform best in your garden, and those you find most flavourful.

By growing open-pollinated rather than hybrid tomatoes, you can save the seeds of those that perform well in your garden, and those with the best flavour and the highest yields. Heritage varieties have not been hybridized between two parent strains, so you can save seeds from 'tried

and true' heritage favourites such as Brandywine, Amish Paste or Stupice.

"Which is the best tomato to grow?" I get asked this question hundreds of times by customers. There's no 'best' tomato in such a world of diversity, so I suggest making a decision based on what tomatoes do best. Tomatoes are grown for a variety of uses: salads, snacking, slicing, soups, canning, sauces and paste. Choose a variety that meets your needs. A uniformly round tomato such as Moneymaker is perfect for salads. A beefsteak variety such as Costoluto Fiorentino is a juicy slicer, whereas a jumbo cherry like Gardener's Delight makes a great fresh eating and snacking tomato.

Seventy-five per cent of all tomato cultivars are *indeterminate. Indeterminate,* or vining, tomatoes continue to grow and produce throughout the season, so give a longer season of harvest. Indeterminates need the support of sturdy stakes or trellises. *Determinate* tomatoes are compact bushy plants, which make better choices for container growing, but have a shorter period of harvest. That's because growth is stopped by the development of terminal flower buds; this means they only set fruit once and then stop producing. They may still need the support of a stake or a tomato cage. If you are growing mostly determinate varieties, I recommend growing some indeterminates too. Then you can pick tomatoes all season long.

Tomato seeds need 75-85°F (25-30°C) for germination; seedlings need daytime temperatures of 60°F (15°C) and nighttime temperatures of 45-50°F (8-10°C). Six-week-old seedlings are ready to be hardened off to go outside.

TIP: Make sure the ground has warmed up before transplanting outdoors. Black landscape fabric over beds warms the soil by day and holds in warmth at night. You can also use cloches or bell jars to cover newly transplanted plants.

A neutral soil pH of 6 to 6.5 is ideal. Prepare the planting hole with compost and a handful of slow release organic fertilizer that contains lime, with a balanced NPK around 6-8-6. Calcium prevents blossom end rot. Tomatoes love fish heads planted underneath them, if you can get your hands on some.

TIP: New roots develop on all parts of the stem planted underground. These will provide the tomato with more nutrients. Strip all the leaves off the stem except for the top truss of three or four leaves when transplanting. Either dig a deep hole or lay the tomato plant diagonally in a shallow trench, but bury most of the stem except for the upper truss of leaves to encourage the formation of these roots.

Provide supports for tomato plants when first transplanting, with cages for determinate varieties or sturdy five-foot tall cedar stakes for indeterminate vining varieties. Proper staking and tying as the tomato grows exposes leaves to sunlight and results in increased fruit production.

Fertilizing plants weekly with liquid seaweed, with a high phosphorus content, boosts fruit production. Don't overwater; a deep soaking once a week is better than several light waterings. Fruit splitting and blossom end rot are caused by erratic watering.

Suckers are sprouts that grow between the main stem and the leaf axils. Removing suckers directs the plant's energy from vine production to fruit production. Remove suckers from indeterminate, vining plants diligently, and train them to one or two main stems. Beware of suckering on determinate, bushy plants, which cuts back on tomato production.

Tomato blight is the most serious disease of tomatoes, especially after long periods of wet weather in August and September. Blight can wipe out a whole crop in a matter of days if left unchecked. It is caused by the fungus

When transplanting into the garden, pound a sturdy stake into the hole, and tie the tomato plant to it.

Phytophthora infestans, and first appears as brown blotches on the leaves and then blackened stems on the plants. To control blight, remove all infected plant debris from the garden and do not compost it. Once blight shows up in your garden, practise crop rotation diligently in future years to prevent reoccurrence.

Leaf curl early in summer is caused by viral diseases spread to plants by aphids, and by sap on fingers and tools. Practise good hygiene and aphid control. Yellowing between veins of older leaves, which then turn brown, is due to magnesium deficiency. Digging one teaspoon of Epsom salts (magnesium sulphate) into the planting hole at the time of transplanting will help to prevent this problem.

Yellow pear tomatoes

Propagating Herbs

Experience the elemental pleasure of growing herbs, and preparing culinary delights and herbal concoctions from your garden. Herbs are among the easiest plants to grow and, once established, require little attention. They thrive in any garden soil, as long as it is well drained, but will do best in full sun.

Annual herbs, such as basil, borage, dill and chervil, and biennial herbs, such as parsley, are easily grown from seed. Grow them under controlled conditions in a starter mix, or direct seed them into warm garden soil. Seeds of herbs such as basil and dill, which need more heat to grow, germinate best when they have a source of heat.

In the garden, members of the Umbelliferae family (angelica, dill, parsley, sweet cicely, lovage and fennel) self-seed readily – sometimes to the point where volunteers can be a nuisance. When growing these herbs under controlled conditions, it's a different matter. The secret of success is to use fresh seed, as after one year seed viability drops dramatically, along with germination.

Medicinal herbs are denoted by the Latin name *officinalis*, e.g. *Melissa officinalis* lemon balm, *Calendula officinalis* pot marigold, *Valeriana officinalis* valerian and *Taraxacum officinalis* dandelion.

Alliums, such as chives and garlic chives, also need to be grown from fresh seed. Allium seeds are viable for one, maybe two years, but after one year the germination rate drops. Growing alliums from seed is slow, so it's much quicker and easier to propagate them vegetatively by division. Simply dig up 'mother' clumps and tease them apart into well-rooted sections.
TIP: Cutting tops back by one-third helps plants establish new roots.

Perennial herbs, such as lemon balm, oregano and sweet marjoram, are also slow growing from seed, taking up to a year before plants reach a harvestable size. The fastest way to propagate them is by division from established 'mother' plants, when well-rooted sections are easy to separate and pot on.

Cuttings are the best way to propagate woody perennial herbs such as rosemary, bay, winter savory, thyme and sage. Softwood cuttings taken in summer root easily in the warmth and light of long summer days. (See *Softwood Cuttings*, third week of July).

Artemesia dracunculus sativa, French tarragon, and *Aloysia triphylla* lemon verbena, represent the pièce de résistance of culinary herbs. Divisions of established clumps of French tarragon can be taken in spring. Cuttings of lemon verbena are taken in late summer and should be overwintered with a heat source.

Once cuttings have rooted, as indicated by new top growth or roots emerging from the bottom of the pot, move them on into four-inch pots, in a growing medium with free drainage. To stimulate growth, begin a weekly feeding program using liquid fish fertilizer.

TIP: The best way to keep lemon verbena growing well is to prune it back heavily after taking cuttings, removing any spindly branches. Plants will sprout back vigorously. Lemon verbena is not reliably winter hardy, so I grow it in a container and provide winter protection under cover.

Mints – From Fruity to Fragrant
There are many different varieties of Mentha, some which are more winter-hardy than others. Mints range from fruity, e.g. pineapple, ginger, and apple mint, to fragrant, e.g. lavender, chocolate, basil and eau de cologne mint, to savory, e.g. spearmint and peppermint. Beware if you plant mints in the garden; they are notoriously invasive, so they may be best grown in a planter. Place pots of mint outside the kitchen door, accessible for snipping.
TIP: Throw a sprig of mint into the pot when cooking new potatoes.

Drying Herbs
Harvest herbs on a sunny day, after the dew has dried from the leaves and before the flowers have opened. This is when the flavour is at its peak. Pick young, fresh shoots about six inches (15 cm) long. Gather together and tie into small bunches. To capture the essential oils, put them in a paper bag and hang it in a warm, dark place with good air circulation. After a few days, the dried herbs should be ready to store in airtight jars in a dark place, which prevents deterioration from light. *TIP:* Herbs lose flavour over time, so replenish them annually.

April

Noise, by Pooh

Oh, the butterflies are flying,
Now the winter days are dying,
And the primroses are trying
To be seen.
And the turtle-doves are cooing,
And the woods are up and doing,
For the violets are a blue-ing
In the green.

Oh, the honey-bees are gumming
On their little wings, and humming,
That the summer, which is coming
Will be fun.
And the cows are almost cooing,
And the turtle-doves are mooing,
Which is why a Pooh is poohing
In the sun.

For the spring is really springing,
You can see a skylark singing,
And the blue-bells which are ringing
Can be heard.
And the cuckoo isn't cooing,
But he's cucking and he's ooing,
And a Pooh is simply poohing
Like a bird.

A.A. Milne (1928)

First Week of April

Watering

It's a challenge to stay on top of watering when the weather warms up, so getting into a regular watering schedule is important. On sunny days the temperature in the greenhouse can get as high as 90°F (32°C), so seedlings can dry out quickly.

Watering puts you in touch with your plants. While watering, make observations and take mental notes. Which plants need more light? Which need a good soak? Which need feeding? Which need repotting? Observation is the key to healthy plants.

Watering in the morning works best so that seedlings do not sit cool and wet at night, which could trigger the fungal problem called damping off. We often 'spot water' from a 45 gallon black plastic barrel that we keep, filled, in the corner of the greenhouse. The water in the barrel stores the sun's heat by day and releases it at night, acting as a passive solar water heater. Warm water is less stressful to tender seedlings. For city dwellers on chlorinated tap water, another benefit is that chlorine evaporates from stored water.

Rules for Outdoor Watering

- When it's cool at night, water in the morning. Young plants don't enjoy being cold at night. Cold wet soils lead to fungal problems.
- If a plant is seriously wilted, water it regardless of the time of day.
- One inch depth of water at a time is said to be sufficient. *TIP:* To measure this, check how long your system takes to fill a tin can to a depth of one inch. That is the length of time you should use your system for each watering.
- One good weekly watering is better than brief daily waterings. Roots seek water. Water penetration encourages roots to grow more deeply. Surface roots are vulnerable to desiccation.
- Put drought-resistant plants in areas that are difficult to water. *TIP:* Group plants with similar watering requirements together.

Did You Know?

- An existing border with mulch can go seven days between waterings.
- Sandy soils need more watering than clay soils.
- Water runs off slopes and berms very quickly, without soaking in.
- Terracing helps prevent water run-off.
- Lawns are major consumers of water. *TIP:* Why not plant an eco-meadow of yarrow, speedwell, clover and English daisy where a lawn struggles to thrive? It needs very little water and no fertilization, and looks beautiful in bloom. Best yet, it only has to be mowed every four weeks!
- Mulching on steep slopes, windy sites and between exposed plants reduces evaporation, protects plants and smothers weeds.

Dry Gardens

Marnie McNeill's garden overlooks the ocean and is built on rock covered with six inches of topsoil. It has been landscaped with every drought-tolerant plant imaginable, and is a perfect example of a *xeriscape*, or dry garden. Not only do her plants sail through winter, but many bloom early in the season, a result of free drainage and heat stored and reflected by the rock.

Marnie has an incredible collection of euphorbias. Two clumps of 'gasp-producing' *Euphorbia wulfenii* 'John Tomlinson' and *Euphorbia myrsinites* donkeytail spurge, create a spectacular bloom. They happily thrive along with cultivars of lavender, cistus, hebe, verbascum, helianthemum, romneya, echium, phormium, phlomis and eryngium – all great examples of drought-tolerant plants.

Also magnificent are the sulphurous, cone-shaped blooms of a four-year-old *Aeonium arboretum atropurpureum* (the AAA plant). Aeoniums can live up to ten years, but after blooming each single rosette dies, and is replaced by a new cluster of rosettes.

Aeonium arboretum atropurpureum 'Swartzkopf' is a three-foot tall branched 'tree' bearing succulent rosettes of purple-black leaves about nine inches across. The pigmentation of the leaves depends on sunlight. As the summer draws on, they darken to burgundy, then almost black, hence the variety's name. They're so easy to propagate that one plant will produce enough offsets to last forever. A juvenile rosette, with a short stem attached, snapped off and stuck into a sandy potting medium, will quickly root to grow a new plant.

TIP: When overwintering succulents, keep them dry or they will rot. It's not the cold that gets them – it's a wet freeze that does them in.

Marnie McNeill's spectacular Euphorbia wulfenii *'John Tomlinson'*

Dry Garden Plants

Lupinus arboreus, the yellow tree lupin, is a shrub that will thrive on dry, eroded banks overlooking the ocean. In my rich garden soil I have to prune it back regularly, as it grows so vigorously. In late spring, masses of pale yellow lupins cover this bushy shrub to create one of my favourite floral shows. *Lupinus arboreus* is a short-lived perennial shrub, living up to three or four years. However, it's so easy to grow from seed and so fast growing, it's easily replaced.

Cistus, rock rose, is another fast-growing, evergreen shrub with beauty and drought tolerance. The sight of *Cistus purpureus* in full bloom can take your breath away; buds open into large, deep pink, rose-like blooms with dark purple centres. Give cistus a heavy pruning, about a third off, after blooming, to stop it getting straggly and improve the floral show next year.

TIP: Grey leaves and glaucous foliage indicates that a plant is drought-tolerant, e.g. romneya, senecio, stachys, dorycnium, santolina.

Lavatera arborea, tree mallow, is so easy to grow that it will grow out of cracks in sidewalks. Lavateras root very easily, so take cuttings when pruning them after flowering in August. They look so much better when pruned back hard; otherwise, they become leggy and are prone to winter breakage. *TIP:* Lavateras resent being planted in wet soils. To overwinter them successfully, plant them in a free-draining site.

Buddleias, butterfly bushes, also grow out of cracks in sidewalks. I've seen them thriving along railway tracks in Europe, where they have self-seeded. So adaptive and successful is this shrub that it's been placed on the 'regulated plants list' in some areas. I've never experienced buddleia as a problem, and value the fragrant panicles of summer flowers, which attract butterflies. Deadheading after blooming is a simple way to keep them from self-seeding.

Lavandula stoechas, Spanish lavender, loves heat. It's exceptionally drought-tolerant with finely divided, silver-grey foliage and spikes of dark purple flowers. Spanish lavender has a long period of bloom from April to July, and as it fades, *Lavandula angustifolia,* English lavender, takes over. Growing both species means you can stay in purple paradise much longer!

Stachys lanata 'Primrose Heron' is very different from the woolly lamb's ears that is commonly grown. The foliage is primrose-yellow, rather than silvery grey, and provides a perfect contrast to darker foliage plants.

Second Week of April

What To Do in the Flower Garden

- Tall or weak-stemmed plants, such as delphiniums, achillea, alstromeria, anthemis, and heavy-headed flowers such as peonies need supports set in place to avoid future floppiness. *TIPS:* Harvest twiggy tree prunings in late winter. These can be plunged firmly into the soil, so that rapidly growing plants can grow through them in the next few weeks. An upside-down tomato cage with the three ends bent into the centre at the top works great for peonies.

- Continue deadheading fading daffodils and tulips. Allow the foliage to die down to feed next year's bulbs.

- Pour boiling water on emerging weeds on driveways or in gravel, or spray vinegar on them from a misting bottle.

- Pinch out the growing tips of fuchsias, pelargoniums, snapdragons, tagetes and sweetpeas to get bushy plants and more flowers.

- After flowering, lift and split polyanthus into smaller pieces to create more plants for next year.

- Check for aphids on the new tender shoots of roses. A jet stream of water from a hose will dislodge them, or try an insecticidal soap spray to prevent an infestation. Aphids are wingless insects, so can be easily controlled by disrupting an established colony.

- Watch for and control black spot and powdery mildew on rose foliage. Both are easy to control in the early stages, but can quickly get out of hand, especially if you leave rose leaves around the plant. Powdery mildew can be controlled with a foliar spray of compost tea (see *Special-teas* at the end of this week). *TIP:* Lack of air circulation is often the problem. Keeping the bottom 12 inches (30 cm) of your rose bushes clear of foliage greatly improves air circulation.

To Control Black Spot
1 tsp. baking soda
1 litre water
1 tsp. soap flakes
Dissolve baking soda in 1 litre of warm water. Add soap flakes to help solution cling to leaves. Remove infected leaves. Spray top and bottom of remaining leaf surfaces to control spread of the disease.

Powdery Mildew?
Powdery mildew is a fungal disease that affects squash, peas, roses, phlox, verbena, dahlias, and many other garden plants. It is caused by the following conditions:

- stress on plants from extended periods of dry weather
- inadequate watering, resulting in dry soil
- too much shade, congested growth or poor air circulation

Try this recipe developed at Cornell University to control powdery mildew:
1 tsp. baking soda
1 quart water
1 tsp. light vegetable oil
A few drops insecticidal soap (to emulsify oil)
Shake mixture before and during spraying.

Or try this simple milk recipe:
1 part milk
9 parts water
Spray on with sprayer. (Wash out sprayer afterwards.)

TIP: Before proceeding, test spray by applying to small area of plant and waiting 48 hours to check treated area. Make sure infected plants are well watered before spraying, and apply in the evening after the sun is off the plants.

- Check for rust on hollyhocks, which appears as orange pustules on the leaves and stems. Spores will spread to other parts of the plant, so remove infected leaves as soon as you see them, but do not compost.

- Lawn repairs using turf or seed should be completed soon, before the weather warms up and the soil dries out. (See *The Golf Green Lawn*, second week of March.)

- Trim box, hyssop and germander hedges and topiaries now for fresh, new foliage by mid-summer. *TIP:* Always use sharp hedge shears. Trim hedges freehand if you've got a good eye for following contours. If not, put a string marker along the desired height to help you cut straight.

- Apply a high-nitrogen, organic fertilizer around the drip zone of hedges to encourage growth. *TIP:* Keep the rooting area of a hedge weed-free in its first three seasons.

- Magnolias are sensitive to magnesium deficiency and dry conditions. If your magnolia is not performing well, water the roots with Epsom salts diluted in water (20g per litre) twice during the growing season.

- Feed all ericaceous (acid-loving) plants with an appropriate fertilizer. This includes plants such as azaleas, rhododendrons, pieris, hydrangeas, heathers, camellias and skimmias.

- Carefully inspect the rhizomes of stored cannas, making sure there is no sign of rot. Divide if necessary and pot up using lightweight, screened organic compost. Transplant once new shoots appear and the weather has warmed up.

- Plant gladioli in free-draining soil in a warm, sunny site, about 10 cm (4 inches) deep. For best effect, plant the corms in groups of five or seven, spacing them about 15 cm (6 inches) apart. Plant at intervals until the end of May to achieve a succession of flowers. *TIP:* If your soil is heavy, rest corms on a layer of grit.

- When sprouts appear on tubers of begonias, they are ready for planting. Make a mix of equal parts peat, sand and sieved compost (or garden loam) and cover the tubers well, as begonias develop their root system all around the tuber.

Dazzling Dahlias (Part One)

Divide large clumps of tubers into sections to prevent overcrowding. Overcrowded dahlias do not flower well.

- Pot on your favourites under cover to get them off to an early start.

- Plant the remaining tubers in a trench in the garden, and cover with earth until they sprout. *TIP:* Sprinkle environmentally safe slug bait around them to protect tasty new shoots from slugs.

- When they have sprouted and put on four inches of top growth, dig up and transplant them to where they will grow. (I usually do this around the end of May.)

- Plant dahlias in rich, fertile soil amended with aged manure or good quality compost.

- Pound a stake into the ground while transplanting to prevent future damage to tubers.

To Keep Earwigs Under Control

To keep earwigs under control, cover stakes with an upturned terra cotta pot stuffed with newspaper. Shake earwigs out daily into a bucket of soapy water.

When dahlias have reached half their potential growth, make a soap solution in a bucket using 75% dish detergent and 25% water. Cover your hands with this soapy solution and run them up and down the dahlia stalks to coat them. This makes it difficult for earwigs to crawl up the slippery stalks and also deters aphids, which are wingless creatures.

See fourth week of October for *Dazzling Dahlias (Part Two)*.

Special-teas

Compost Tea

Can you believe there's something even better than compost for your garden? Compost tea! Compost tea is made from an extract of compost containing microorganisms, nutrients and organic matter. At the end of a well-oxygenated 'brew' cycle, using a special pump, aerated compost tea contains millions of microorganisms. The tea can be used as a foliar spray to suppress disease, or a soil drench to stimulate high populations of beneficial soil microorganisms.

Liquid extracts of compost tea should be used fresh, ideally no more than twelve hours after brewing. They can be diluted as much as 1:10 parts water for a soil drench to reach into root systems. A more concentrated dilution of 1:3 or 1:5 is used as a foliar spray.

The benefits of this non-toxic tea are many:
- It makes the benefits of compost go farther.
- It helps to suppress foliar diseases.
- It increases the amount of nutrients available to plants, boosting plant growth.
- It speeds up the breakdown of toxins.
- It has been shown to increase the yields, nutritional quality and flavour of vegetables.
- It enhances soil biofertility.
- It reduces transplant shock.
- It controls black spot and powdery mildew.

The soil food web consists of myriad microorganisms – bacteria and fungi (decomposers), and protozoa and beneficial nematodes (predators). Amongst them are good and bad organisms, some of which aid plant growth and some of which cause disease. Good bacteria work against detrimental ones in four ways. They consume the bad guys, they produce antibiotics to inhibit them, they compete for nutrients and they compete for space.

Anaerobic conditions enhance bad bacterial decomposers, so introducing a highly aerobic compost tea can eliminate a large percentage of disease-causing bacteria. Increasing the proportion of good bacteria, by watering compost tea into the soil or spraying it onto plant leaves, takes care of potential or existing pests and diseases.

Plants know what's good for them. They exude sugars, carbohydrates and proteins into the soil as energy-rich food, which feeds the good bacteria and fungi. When we kill off beneficial organisms by using pesticides and chemical fertilizers, we disrupt the delicate inter-relationship between plants and the soil food web. One of the best things you can do for your garden is to spray your plants or soil with compost tea to restore populations of beneficial organisms.

Comfrey liquid teas are made in the demonstration area at Ryton Gardens, the headquarters of the Henry Doubleday Research Association (HDRA) in the UK. On the far left is a comfrey column, ideal for smaller quantities. (Two comfrey plants will produce half a litre of concentrate.) Larger quantities of concentrate for comfrey tea are made in the plastic barrels.

Comfrey Tea

Comfrey is one of the easiest plants to grow. The leaves contain nitrogen, phosphorus and potassium, which are readily released to plants when comfrey leaves break down. *Symphytum x uplandicum,* Russian comfrey, is the best for producing garden fertilizer. The 'Bocking 14' cultivar has been shown to be most productive, because you can cut it down three to four times a year. Another good reason to grow it over other strains is that it produces little viable seed.

Comfrey leaves are nutrient rich, containing 75% water, 74% nitrogen, 24% phosphorus and 1.19% potassium.

Ready-to-Use Comfrey Tea

Method:
Pack 1 kg (2.2 lbs) of comfrey leaves into a container with a lid.
Add 15 litres (3.3 gallons) of water.

Cover to keep the smell in and the flies out! Leave to brew for 4 to 6 weeks. Strain. Use undiluted.

TIP: Top up with leaves during the season or make new batches after each cut. Put the residue that collects in the bottom of the container into the compost heap. Hold your nose!

Comfrey Concentrate

Method:
Drill a 1/4 inch hole in the bottom of a 20 litre (5 gallon) container with a lid. Place a piece of wire mesh over the hole to prevent blockage.

Stand the container on bricks, so that a collection bottle will fit under the hole. Pack in enough comfrey leaves to fill the container. (Do not add water.)

The leaves will decompose into a black liquid, which can be stored in a stoppered bottle. If kept in a cool, dark place, it will store for up to a year. Always dilute the concentrate before use. If it is black and strong, dilute it 20:1 (20 parts water to one part concentrate), if it is brown and thin, dilute 10:1.

Uses

- A general feed for outdoor planters. Feed once weekly.
- A good compost heap activator. Water onto the pile.
- A feed for fruit bushes. Water in before fruiting.

TIP: Do not use regularly on acid-loving plants.

Nettle Tea

Nettles are full of life-enriching minerals, vitamins and chlorophyll. Follow the above directions for comfrey concentrate, using nutrient-rich nettles instead. Pack 11 lbs of nettles into a container and fill with 1 gallon of water. Cover and leave for 2 weeks, stirring occasionally. Strain. Dilute 10:1 before using as a plant fertilizer, ground soak or foliar feed.

Third Week of April

What To Do in the Vegetable Garden

- If you have stripped the lawn to make room for new beds, beware of wireworms, which will eat new seedlings. *TIP:* Monitor populations of wireworms by planting potatoes as a bait. After three weeks, pull up the potatoes to check the number of wireworms. Beneficial nematodes are the least toxic biological control. Purchase nematodes at your local garden centre. *TIP:* Check the "sell by" date, as this is a living product with a limited shelf life.

Biological nematodes destroy cutworms, whitegrubs, leatherjackets and weevils. They carry bacteria in their intestines that are deadly to host larvae. Within 24 hours the bacteria kill the host, and feed on the remains. Nematodes are safe to all non-target organisms, such as earthworms.

- Direct seed radishes, and cool weather greens, such as spinach, lettuce, arugula and mesclun mix (baby salad greens).

- Dig under green manure crops. Make sure fall rye is well dug – it's a brute to dig out once it has become deep rooted!

- Plant Jerusalem artichoke tubers away from the main garden. They are so invasive that, once established, they can take over your entire garden.

- Mulch your garlic patch with 50% compost: 50% aged manure for bigger garlic bulbs.

- Plant potatoes if the soil has started to warm up. Plant tubers about 4 inches (10 cm) deep, in a shallow furrow. They will need to be earthed up once the shoots are 10 inches (25 cm) tall. Rows should be two feet apart.

- Sow beets now. Sow thickly in shallow furrows 12 inches (30 cm) apart. *TIP:* For the best beets, add uncontaminated wood ashes when seeding (7-8% potassium).

- Check if vining peas are growing up their supports. Tie them on with twine if they are sprawling along the ground.

In the Fruit and Berry Patch

- Check your cane fruits for adequate support. Supports and wires need to be well secured at the start of the season to support the canes' new growth.

- Raspberries, loganberries and blackberries should have had all the old canes removed from the base by now. These are easiest to detect by getting on your knees and viewing them at ground level. Old canes that need removing are brown and woody rather than green and supple. Strengthen canes by tip pruning them to remove any spindly growth.

  TIP: Remove weeds from under fruit bushes and trees to suppress competition for nutrients, then mulch with compost.

Self-Seeding Vegetables

Once you introduce vegetables that are self-seeding to your garden, you'll never have to plant them again. I'm always amazed how many plants come back automatically every year. Experienced gardeners know that volunteers are always the healthiest and most robust plants in the garden.

Valerianella locusta, *Corn salad, or mache, can be direct seeded in early spring and again in late August. Easier yet, leave some to self-seed to come back automatically!*

Arugula, rocket salad, is a prolific self-seeder. I relish the nutty, slightly peppery flavour of young arugula seedlings. As it matures it develops a pungent mustard kick. Arugula has ornamental black and white flowers, rather than the typical yellow flowers of the mustard family. In cooler spring and winter months, arugula maintains its milder flavour longer, which is when I put it in toasted sandwiches, salads, and lightly sauté the greens.

Corn salad, or mache, is a reliable, self-seeding, cool season vegetable that has become very popular. Its mild, slightly crunchy rosettes of greens taste wonderful in salads or layered in sandwiches anytime from October until it warms up in May, when corn salad sets seed.

Purple orach, mountain spinach, is an ornamental edible, providing a colourful accent in vegetable or flower gardens. It is best grown in part sun, where it does not bolt to seed so quickly. *TIP:* Pinch out the tips to make it bushier, to produce more leaves for harvesting.

Purple orach sets so many seeds it even outgrows me!

Perpetual spinach is a cross between chard and beet greens, but has a finer-textured leaf and smoother flavour than true spinach. I prefer perpetual spinach lightly steamed – it's a sweet and juicy green that doesn't coat the tongue with oxalic acid like spinach. It grows in the garden all year round, and tastes even sweeter after a few hard frosts. It's so tender I tear leaves into salads, and often use it as a base for vegetarian lasagnas.

New Zealand spinach is sometimes described as an acquired taste, but I prefer it to spinach. It will self-seed, and can take over your garden if you let it, but it's easy to pull out plants you don't want.

Swiss chard 'Fordhook Giant' is a variety I have grown successfully for years. It thrives in our cool coastal climate and overwinters without any problems. Use the large leaves as a replacement for cabbage in roll-up recipes, and also for succulent steamed greens. The juicy white stalks are perfect steamed or stirfried, and hard to distinguish from celery in recipes. I grow 'Bright Lights' Swiss chard in summer for an extra splash of colour, and because I find it does not overwinter as well as 'Fordhook Giant'.

'Russian Red' kale or 'Dwarf Green Curled' kale are both good varieties to grow in summer because the leaves are tender enough for salads. The coarser Scotch kales, such as 'Winterbor' or the Tuscan Blue kale 'Lacinato' are best for winter eating.

Fourth Week of April

Shedding Light on Shade

A question we often get asked at *The Garden Path* is "what can I grow in the shade?" The answer depends on the type of shade, and the accompanying soil conditions.

Partial shade, or half shade, means half a day of direct sun and half of shade, caused by the sun moving around blocking structures or trees. It is usually morning or afternoon shade, with full sun the rest of the day. The soil is often moist, which suits plants such as ajuga, viola, asarum (wild ginger), pulmonaria, cyclamens and ferns.

Filtered shade, also referred to as light shade, occurs under sparse foliage and open branches, allowing a shifting pattern of sunlight throughout the day. Plants that thrive in filtered shade are astilbe, hostas, dicentra, tuberous begonias, impatiens and epimedium.

Dense shade, or deep shade, means all-day shade created by heavy foliage, evergreen trees or tall buildings. Dense shade is often accompanied by dry soil from tree roots or buildings that block rainfall. Plants that can prosper in dense shade include lamium, euphorbia 'Robbiae', lunaria, galium (sweet woodruff) and doronicum (leopard's bane).

I have gone one step further into the shade by choosing plants with dark foliage for my border without full sun. Deep-hued plants are intriguing, but it's the dazzle of their bright, often white, flowers in the shade that are most captivating. A few of my favourite black foliage plants are *Anthriscus sylvestris* 'Ravenswing', *persicaria* 'Red Dragon', *Artemesia lactiflora* 'Guizhou', *Eupatorium* chocolate snakeroot, and *Cimicifuga racemosa* black snakeroot. Intersperse these black beauties with hostas, whose provocative fleshy leaves provide a striking contrast. The glaucous, ribbed leaves of *Hosta sieboldianii elegans,* the bold-green and white leaves of *Hosta* 'Francee', and the lime-green

Perfect Plants for Impossible Places

For dry shade
(including dry, shady pockets under trees)
Doronicum leopard's bane, *Euphorbia amygdaloides var. robbiae, Galium odoratum* sweet woodruff, *Geranium phaeum, Geranium macrorrhizum, Lamium maculatum* spotted deadnettle, *Convallaria majalis* lily-of-the-valley, *Lunaria annua* honesty, *Luzula nivea* snowy woodrush, *Luzula sylvatica* greater woodrush, *Tiarella cordifolia* foamflower

A winning combination: false Solomon's seal with variegated hosta.

For moist shade
Ajuga spp. bugleweed, *Alchemilla mollis* lady's mantle, akebia vine, *Anemone japonica* Japanese anemone, *Aruncus sylvester* goat's beard, *Athyrium niponicum var. pictum* Japanese painted fern, astilbes, begonias (fibrous and tuberous), *Bergenia* spp., *Brunnera macrophylla, Caltha palustris* marsh marigold, *Carex morrowii, Clematis armandii*, corydalis, *Cyclamen* spp., *Darmera peltata, Dicentra* bleeding heart, *Digitalis x mertonensis* strawberry foxglove, *Epimedium* bishop's hat, ferns, *Filipendula* meadowsweet, *Garrya eliptica* silk tassel bush, *Hakonechloa macra* 'Aureola', *Fuchsia magellanica, Helleborus* spp., *Heuchera* spp., *Hosta* spp., *Meconopsis* spp., *Mertensia* Virginia bluebells, omphaloides, pachysandra, *Polygonatum hybrida multiflorum* false Solomon's seal, *Primula* spp., *Pulmonaria* spp. lungwort, *Ribes sanguineum*, tree peonies, *Vinca minor* periwinkle, *Viola odorata* sweet violet

and yellow *Hosta* 'Gold Tiara' unfurl in perfect unison with the dark shoots and foliage. Everyone loves a stroll down my shade border in early spring. There's so much to oohh and aahh about!

Slick Slug Control

If you've got shade, especially moist shade, then look out for slithering, slimy-bodied molluscs! Spring is when slugs get moving, as the rain and luscious new growth tempt them out from their hiding places. Let the battle begin! Gardeners have many weapons in their arsenal against slugs, from innovative traps to barriers and slug pellets. Here are some ways to keep these pesky molluscs under control, but they are not all tasty!

- Beer traps provide a perfect lure for slugs to get sozzled. They're easy to use, but they need regular emptying. *TIP:* If you don't want to share your favourite brew with slugs, make your own: 1 cup water to 1 tsp. sugar to 1/4 tsp. yeast. It's the yeast that attracts slugs, so why waste good beer?

- Use a non-toxic slug bait made from ferrous sulphate pellets, which don't harm birds, pets or wildlife. When slugs eat this they crawl away and will eventually dehydrate.

- Copper barriers create electrical currents that repel slugs but do not kill them.

- Barriers of anything with sharp edges (e.g. hair, crushed egg shells, sharp grit) keep slugs at bay, but have to be renewed as they break down.

- Lay wooden planks around the garden. Slugs will take refuge beneath them. Regular checking and removal help keep populations under control.

- Spray blenderized slug spray (ugh!) into nooks and crannies where slugs hide, or onto slugs' favourite plants. You'd stay away too if your relatives were being blenderized! (Can I borrow your blender?)

- Learn to recognize and eradicate slug eggs: they look like clusters of translucent tapioca.

- Encourage natural predators into the garden by providing a variety of habitats such as hedges and ponds. Birds, beetles, ground beetles, garter snakes, frogs, toads and ducks all eat slugs.

- Eliminate slug hiding and breeding places by keeping your garden free of piles of weeds, plant containers and garbage.

- Use sharp mulches of shredded bark, crushed rock, woodchips or rock screenings to keep slugs away. Ring plants you want to protect with these sharp-edged mulches.

Slugs Love:
Delphiniums, lupins, tender seedlings, marigolds, orchid flowers, impatiens, pansies, primroses, daffodils, hostas, tulip shoots, iris, dahlias

Slugs Do Not Like:
Scented, leathery and furry leaves, begonias, snapdragons, cistus (rock roses), mulleins, aubretia, basil, alliums, alyssum, fennel, wormwood, chicory, ferns, camellias, rosemary, lavender

Diane's List of Deerproof Plants

Diane Pierce shares these suggestions for plants that deer never eat in her garden:
- Aromatic herbs, e.g. nepeta, sage, rosemary, helichrysum, lavender
- Boxwood
- Ceanothus (only flowers, not leaves)
- Epimediums
- Euphorbias
- Ferns
- Ornamental grasses
- Hellebores
- Phormiums

May

Gather ye rosebuds while ye may,
Old time is still a-flying:
And this same flower that smiles today,
Tomorrow will be dying.

Robert Herrick (1591-1674)

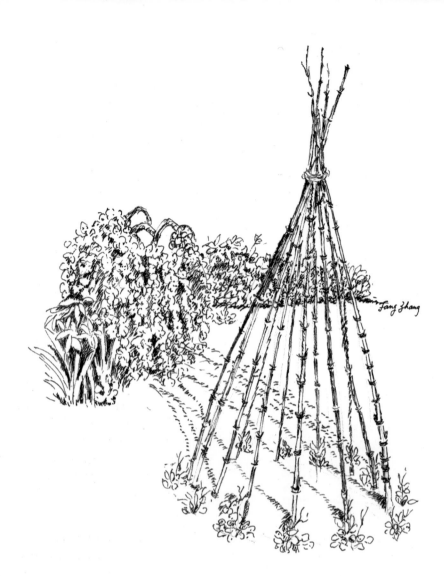

First Week of May

It's All About the Microbes!

Microbial soil life plays a vital role in plant health because it's these microorganisms that break down organic matter to create humus compounds, which serve as sites for nutrient adhesion. Plant roots 'shop' for these nutrients by exchanging their positively charged hydrogen ions with the positively charged nutrient ions adhering to humus. It's simply by balancing their inner chemistry that plants choose which nutrients they need. All quite amazing, but what's more amazing is the fact that we are only now recognizing the importance of protecting the microbial life in the soil.

Although plants can't distinguish between nutrients from natural or synthetic sources, it's synthetic compounds, applied as fertilizers, that damage and destroy microbial soil life. In today's world soils continue to be depleted by higher and higher inputs of petrochemical-based fertilizers. Every time crops are removed without restoring organic matter, soil nutrients are depleted, which results in reduced fertility, decreased plant health and soil erosion. Slow-release, natural source fertilizers do not destroy soil life, and break down gradually, providing plants with the correct proportions of nutrients when needed.

When a soil is regenerated by inputs of organic matter, by using crop rotations, green manures, mulch and compost, nutrients that have been removed by plants are restored. Beneficial soil microbes are also kept fed, so they can continue their job of slowly breaking down and releasing essential elements to plants. So it is understandable that the basis of healthy plant growth is really all about the microbes.

Crop Rotation

Many gardeners are confused about crop rotation, an important practice in food gardens that prevents the build-up of soil pests and diseases. If brassicas, prone to club root, are grown in the same bed every year, eventually a spore-borne fungal disease will establish and infect all future brassicas grown there.

Homemade Fertilizer

Blended organic fertilizers are useful when soil fertility is in question, when starting a new garden or trying to revitalize a garden. Natural source fertilizers are slow release and continue to work as they slowly break down. Over time, once soil fertility is re-established, the need for these supplements will decline.

Steve Solomon's Formula (NPK 1:1.5:1)
Measure by volume:
4 parts seedmeal (canola, alfalfa or soy) or fishmeal
1 part dolomite lime
1 part rock phosphate or 1/2 part bonemeal
1 part kelp meal

Blend well, but mix again before application. Work in lightly under young transplants, or sidedress along existing plants. Apply around the drip line of plants and work in gently so as not to damage the roots. Granulated fertilizer takes three to four weeks to break down before roots can access it.

Seedmeals = nitrogen source (N) for healthy leafy greens
Rock phosphate = phosphorus (P) for fruits and flowers
Kelp meal = potassium (potash) (K) for roots and overall good health
Lime counteracts soil acidity and adds calcium and magnesium

If *Phytophthera infestans,* tomato blight, has occurred, spores remain in the soil to infect future crops of the Solanaceae family: tomatoes, peppers, eggplants or potatoes.

Avoid carrot fly by not sowing carrots on ground that has recently been used for carrots, parsnips or any of their Umbelliferae relations, as maggots or pupae may still be in the soil, waiting to feed on a new crop.

Rotating crops around the garden breaks the cycle of attracting and accumulating pests and diseases. There are eight main families of vegetables, so plant members of each family in a different place each year. The chart below clarifies how you can plant using simple crop rotations.

What To Do in the Vegetable Garden

- Direct seed root crops of parsnips, celeriac, carrots, beets and radishes.

- Plant out onions, leeks and Brussels sprouts as transplants, or sets, in May.

- Do not sow beetroot in freshly manured or fertilized ground. Sow in one inch (2.5 cm) deep lines with rows twelve inches (30 cm) apart. Sow thickly, as beet seeds have a higher failure rate than most. *TIP:* For better beets, add wood ashes to the prepared plot.

- Carrots are best grown in deep, light soil. If you suffer from heavy soil, make holes approximately 18 inches (45 cm) deep by three inches (7.5 cm) wide with a crowbar and fill with light, sandy soil. Sprinkle a few seeds on top of each hole and cover with a thin layer of soil. Thin out later.

- Fertilize young transplants with liquid fish fertilizer to help them get established.

- Foliar feed transplants with liquid seaweed to help them recover from transplant shock.

- Keep your beds free of weeds.

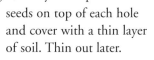

Dividing the garden in quadrants makes crop rotations easier to keep track of.

Suggested Crop Rotation

Suggested Rotation	Family	Some of the Crops in Family
Brassicas	Cruciferae	arugula, broccoli, Brussels sprouts, cauliflower, kale, radish, rutabagas
Squash	Curbitaceae	cucumber, squash
Greens	Chenopodiaceae Compositae	chard, spinach endive, lettuce
Legumes	Leguminosae	beans, peas
Alliums	Liliaceae	leeks, onions, shallots
Roots	Umbelliferae	carrots, celeriac, celery, parsnips
Solanoids	Solanaceae	eggplants, peppers, potatoes, tomatoes

- Heat lovers such as corn, basil, squash and beans can be started off under protection now. Plant them out only once the soil has warmed up. *TIPS*: Squash resents root disturbance. Sow seeds individually into pots to avoid disturbing the roots when young seedlings are transplanted into the garden. Zukes, cukes, pumpkins and butternut, spaghetti, buttercup, acorn, delicata and patty pan squash can all be seeded in early May.

- Beans need warmth to germinate and are sensitive to cold, wet soils. Erratic weather means unreliable germination and the possibility of rotting bean seeds. Start beans under controlled conditions and plant them out when they are six inches tall and well-rooted. This way you can be sure of a good start and a reliable harvest.

- Watering the food garden regularly is important, as new transplants and newly germinated seedlings are very susceptible to dehydration. Check your garden daily, and be sure to water well during hot spells.

- Asparagus is harvested from established crowns from early May onwards. Harvest for up to six weeks, then leave the spears to grow feathery foliage, which feeds the roots for next year's crop.

- Look out for black aphids clustering around the tips of broad beans (favas). They are easily removed by cutting off the tops where the colonies have established. This will help prevent an unsightly infestation, and will not affect the production of beans below. If necessary, tie twine around your bean patch to stop the plants from falling over.

- Draw extra soil up around young shoots of early potatoes. This gives the underground tubers extra protection from light so that they don't turn green.

- Kitchen garden soil can be replenished by planting green manure crops that are dug back into the soil to replace nutrients. Fast maturing, warm weather green manures include clover, alfalfa, buckwheat and phacelia. (See *Gardening with Green Manures*, first week of November.)

A Nifty Trick For Carrots

- Fill a four-inch pot with a sterile seeding mix (to make your own, see page 27).

- Sprinkle 12 to 15 carrot seeds evenly across the top. Cover lightly.

- As the seedlings establish, feed them weekly with liquid fish fertilizer.

- When the foliage has reached four inches high, remove the entire rooted plug, and plant it in the garden without disturbing the roots. The scent of carrot foliage attracts the carrot rust fly. Not thinning the carrots avoids attracting these pests.

- Plant plugs in blocks six inches apart in all directions. Your carrots will now outgrow the weeds.

- Harvest the entire bunch of baby carrots or leave the carrots to grow on and harvest them singly at a larger size.

TIP: Mulch the carrot patch with coffee grounds. The strong aroma of drying coffee confuses the female carrot rust fly and stops her from laying her eggs on the carrots.

Harvest an entire bunch of baby carrots using the Nifty Carrot Trick.

Winning Tomato Tips

Tomatoes come in every colour – red, pink, orange, black, purple, yellow, and even striped. They come in all sizes from tiny currants to bite-sized cherries to whopping beefsteaks, in every shape from round to pear to oval, and in all flavours from sweet to tart, to smoky to fruity. They can be grown for any purpose – fresh eating from the vine, tossing into salads, drying, roasting, juicing, or using in sauces and soups. Get adventurous with tomatoes and open up to a new world of culinary delight.

Tomatoes will produce earlier if you keep the establishing plants in pots until the first flowers open. Otherwise, when you plant them out, they put all their energy into growing new roots, delaying the formation of the first flower truss.

When planting out, strip all the leaves off the stem except for the top truss. Bury the entire plant into a deep hole, where roots will form on all parts of the buried stem to feed the plant for fruit production. Keep vining tomatoes to one or two main stems by pinching out the suckers, which grow between the main stem and the leaf axils, as the plant grows.

Tomato cages only suffice for bushy determinate varieties. Vining tomatoes need staking. Use a five-foot tall, two-inch wide cedar stake for semi-determinate and vining tomatoes. There's nothing worse than finding your loaded tomato plants flopped over! *TIP*: Pantyhose makes the best ties for tomato plants, as it does not cut into the soft stems. Cut pantyhose into stretchy strips, and use these for tying plants to stakes in the garden.

Recommended Taste Sensations

- Try eating asparagus raw. It tastes like crunchy, tender peas. Delicious with a dip!
- When you pinch out pea plants to make them bushier, eat the pea shoots. Use them in salads, or stirfry with them.
- Roast Jerusalem artichoke tubers for 20-25 minutes with a drizzle of olive oil. Nutty and delicious. Also good raw with veggie dips.
- Raw celeriac, celery root, peeled and sliced, tastes wonderful, especially with a dip.
- Decorate green salads with calendula petals, violas or violets, borage flowers, primrose petals, or brassica and mustard flowers.
- Use fresh leaves of sweet marjoram, chives, or Greek oregano in salads, soups and stews.
- Steam flowering shoots of kales, collards and cabbages for a tender and delicious side vegetable. (Best just before the flowers open.)
- For an early hit of garlic, use garlic scapes steamed as a side vegetable, sautéed, stir fried, chopped raw in salads, or blended into salad dressings.

Second Week of May

In the Fruit and Berry Patch

- To ensure a good harvest, fruit must be thinned now. If thinning is not done, the harvest may be poor, with small, low-quality fruit. In addition, fruiting may become biennial, with heavy crops one year and little or no fruit the next. Thin by hand, removing any disfigured or damaged fruit. Select well-positioned fruits to develop fully. Apples and pears should be thinned to two fruits per cluster, six inches (15 cm) apart; plums should be selected to leave a single fruit every three inches (7.5 cm).

- If you have fruit trees, now is the time to hang up pheromone traps to trap the codling moth. This helps prevent damage from apple maggots. Traps are a safe alternative to spraying your trees with insecticides.

- Band apple and pear trees in spring with one or two six-inch removable wraps, such as burlap sacking, and tie tightly around the tree with twine. Coat them with a sticky paste, such as Tanglefoot™. These sticky bands trap the larvae of the codling moth when they crawl down the tree to pupate in the soil.

Codling moth *Cydia pomonella* is a common problem for apples and pears throughout North America. The wingless female moth climbs the tree to lay her eggs on fruit, leaves or twigs. Larvae burrow into the fruit core, usually from the blossom end. The fruit interior becomes dark and rotted, and young fruit may drop. Larvae leave the fruit in fall to pupate under the tree bark or in ground litter.

- In the berry patch, make sure canes are supported before fruit production. Tie canes to supports with wire or jute twine. This not only makes harvesting easier, but also exposes fruit to the sun to help it ripen.

- Do not clear-cut your rhubarb patch. Leave some stalks to feed the roots for better fruit production next year.

- Check gooseberry bushes for sawfly caterpillars, which need to be picked off before they defoliate the bushes.

- Check gooseberries and other fruiting plants for signs of mildew. *TIP:* A solution of one part milk and nine parts water makes a natural and effective fungicide spray.

- Remove weeds from under fruit bushes and trees, and mulch with compost to suppress further weeds, which compete for nutrients.

- Bumper crops of luscious strawberries are ripening now. Before they touch the ground, the fruits need a mulch of straw to keep them clean, and control weeds. Fluff up the straw, allowing air to circulate and water to drain away, and tuck it right under the berries.

A mulch of straw keeps strawberries clean and controls weeds.

Strawberry Shortcakes

Makes 12 shortcakes
Preheat oven to 350°F (175°C)

2 cups strawberries, hulled and halved
1 fresh squeezed lemon
1/4 cup granulated sugar
1/3 cup dark brown sugar
4 cups unbleached flour,
  plus extra for work surface
4 tsp. baking powder
1 1/2 tsp. salt
12 Tbsp. (1 1/2 sticks) unsalted butter,
  chilled and cut into small pieces
1 3/4 cups half and half cream
2 Tbsp. heavy cream (set aside)
1 egg yolk

Chop strawberries. Place in a bowl with lemon juice and 1/4 cup granulated sugar. Let stand about 1 hour, until berries are very juicy.

Mix 1/3 cup dark brown sugar with flour, baking powder and salt. Using a fork or pastry blender, cut butter into the mixture until it resembles coarse meal. Add 1 3/4 cups half and half cream and mix with a fork until dough just comes together.

Transfer to a lightly floured board or countertop and pat into a 1-inch thick square. Using a 2 1/2-inch round cookie cutter, cut into 12 rounds. Transfer onto a lightly greased baking sheet.

Cover and refrigerate for 20 minutes or overnight (optional).

Remove rounds from refrigerator. Whisk together remaining 2 Tbsp. cream with egg yolk. Brush tops with egg wash. Bake until golden brown for 20 minutes. Cool slightly on wire racks for 15 minutes.

Make Your Own Devonshire Cream:
1/2 sour cream : 1/2 whipping cream
Mix in an open glass jar and leave overnight in the fridge. That's it!

To Assemble:
Slice shortcakes open and place bottom halves on serving plate. Add a dollop of cream, the strawberries and their juice, and top off with matching shortcake halves.

Why not interplant fruit with herbs? These Shuswap strawberries with pretty white blossoms make a perfect partner to the variegated lemon balm's bright yellow and green foliage. The red strawberries that follow will also look good against this colourful backdrop.

Keeping Cut Flowers from Your Garden Fresh

- Soon after cutting, put stems into water. Use tepid rather than cold water.

- Remove lower leaves, so that none are below the water in the arranging vase.

- If the flowers flop, freshen the water in the vase and recut the end of the stems. If severely wilted, try re-trimming and plunging stems into boiling water for thirty seconds.

Homemade Floral Preservative
Mix:
3 cups water
1 Tbsp. sugar
1 tsp. vinegar
1 crushed aspirin

Third Week of May

In the Flower Garden

- When petals on tulips drop, deadhead them by cutting back each flower stem to the first leaf. Then dig the bulbs up for drying, which improves your chance of getting them to perform well again. This would ruin most bulbs, but tulips are tough. Knock the soil from the bulbs, and place them one layer deep on newspaper in boxes. The bulbs gradually reabsorb nutrients from the withering leaves, to promote next year's growth and flowering. No sunlight is required for this, but provide adequate ventilation. Once the leaves are entirely dry, store the bulbs in their boxes until planted again in fall.

  TIP: If the bulbs are in planters, bring them under a deck or into a garage. Don't water the planters to allow the bulbs to dry out. Later clean, label and store the bulbs as above. Replant in the fall.

- Add something spectacular to your garden by planting a variety of sunflowers. Dwarf varieties such as 'Teddy Bear' or 'Music Box' are ideal for planting in pots.

- Consider starting tender annual climbers such as *Ipomoea* annual morning glory, *Thunbergia alata* black-eyed Susan vine, *Cobaea scandens* cup-and-saucer vine or *Tropaeolum canariensis* canary creeper, which can be planted out in June when the soil has thoroughly warmed up. These plants add vertical interest to the garden. Plant either in the ground or in containers, where these vigorous climbers can cover a trellis or pergola in one season.

  TIP: Plant one of the above climbers at the base of plants that have stopped flowering, such as clematis, or with plants that do not flower, such as grape vines. Or try planting a climber to scramble horizontally over a rock wall.

- Fill in spaces where spring flowering plants have finished with summer flowering plants such as dahlias. Don't forget to tie the dahlias to strong stakes. *TIP:* Protect dahlia flowers from earwigs by applying a two-inch wide band of petroleum jelly or barrier glue round each stem, about six inches above the ground. Try sprinkling organic coffee grounds around dahlias to deter slugs and snails. Apparently caffeine, harmless to soil and plants, drives slugs and snails away. Check your local coffee shop for free grounds.

- Cut back euphorbias when their show is over so fresh new foliage will emerge. *TIPS:* Beware when handling euphorbia plants, as the cut stems leak a milky sap that irritates the skin and causes a bad rash. If sap drips onto skin, wash it off immediately before exposure to the sun.

- Inspect the growing tips of all herbaceous plants for signs of aphid infestation. Brush the aphids off carefully or zap them with a strong jet of water. If necessary, give them a good squirt of an organic soap solution.

- Pull up or cut back plants such as forget-me-nots, cerinthe, wallflowers and *Centaurea montana* (perennial cornflower). These plants produce prolific numbers of seeds that can be a nuisance if they are allowed to seed all over the garden. Leave a few plants to set seed where you want to encourage them; otherwise, remove them altogether. This is how plants such as *Centranthus ruber* get right out of control.

Cerinthe major purpurescens

- Collect and sow the seed of hellebores as soon as it is ripe. It should germinate during the spring, after a period of cold winter weather. Trim any leaves that are lying against the soil, leaving the upright leaves intact. This helps to prevent the plant from succumbing to *Coniothyrium hellebori,* a disease that blackens foliage.

- Keep deadheading spent flowers and roses. This job pays dividends, as it not only spruces up the appearance of the garden, but makes plants flower longer since they don't spend energy producing seed.

- Adjust your mower blades to a higher, summer cut height. Cutting too short will stress the lawn and turn it brown. Grass grows quickest when the weather is warm and moist, so taking off small amounts by mowing more often keeps lawns looking their best.

- Build the compost heap throughout the season. Remember to add no more than six-inch layers of grass clippings at a time. Layer clippings with other materials to avoid a smelly, anaerobic pile.

Pressed Flowers

Pick your flowers just before full bloom and collect some buds as well as full flowers. Bug-eaten flawed flowers look even worse pressed, so seek perfection! Gather your specimens on a dry day, after the dew is off the garden, and press flowers soon after gathering.

The Simple Telephone Book Method

Separate smaller delicate flowers from the larger specimens. Place your collection between sheets of tissue paper (or facial tissue). Press flowers in profile and face on, and don't forget some buds.

Place the sheets between the pages of a telephone book that lives in a warm place. (A long, slow dry is best.) Your pressed flowers will be safe between the 'Yellow Pages' for a long time, but use bookmarks so you remember where they are!

I have used pressed flowers to make beautiful bookmarks, candles, coasters, bath salts and greeting cards – the possibilities are endless! My favourite thing is to open up a book with pressed flowers in it to discover a forgotten delight.

How to Make a Flower Press

Take two matching squares of wood. Paint or decorate the outer sides with a floral motif. Layer 6 to 8 sheets of corrugated cardboard, cut to size, between the wood squares.

Drill a 1/4" hole through the wood and the cardboard at each of the four corners. Place four long bolts through each of the holes. You will need a compatible wing nut to tighten each bolt.

A Tissue Paper Sandwich

Arrange your flowers between sheets of tissue paper, and sandwich the tissue paper between the layers of cardboard. After building the sandwich, clamp the press by tightening the bolts. Beware too much downward pressure!

Recommended flowers and foliage to press:

Alyssum, coral bells, cosmos, forget-me-nots, Johnny Jump-Ups, Queen Anne's lace, fern tips, herbs, aegopodium, clematis and other vining plants, dusty miller, euphorbia, small grasses

Feature of the Month

Going Potty

I happily plant in anything that will contain a growing medium, from olive oil cans to old boots, even if it means I have to punch drainage holes in it first. Container gardening is perfect when you live in a townhouse with a small patio garden, or an apartment with a balcony. Maybe you want to add interest to your front door or some colour outside your window? So what do other plant addicts do when they run out of space? They go potty and start planting containers!

You can grow anything in containers: bulbs, winter and summer annuals, perennials, grasses, climbing plants, herbs and veggies. Bamboos provide impressive screens for privacy, and containerizing them keeps them from taking over the garden. Experimenting is half the fun.

Try growing lettuces, radishes, green onions, zucchinis, tomatoes or scarlet runner beans in planters. Herbs, being Mediterranean plants that thrive in hot, dry conditions, are perfect for planters in full sun. In summer, pick fresh sprigs of mint, parsley, chives, oregano or basil from a pot outside your door.

In cedar boxes on a sundeck plant climbing roses, clematis or honeysuckle with bulbs for spring colour and lavender for summer fragrance. Massing colourful planters together is all the rage in gardening circles. When a planter has passed its best, simply replace it with another, just coming into its best show. This way you always have a fabulous display.

The most important thing to keep your planters looking good and maintain plant health is to topdress them every year with screened compost, mixed with a balanced organic fertilizer, NPK 6-8-6. Rework planters when they get rootbound or overcrowded. Dig out mature plants and find them a new home in the garden. Refill planters with fresh, screened compost mixed with organic fertilizer, and redesign them using exciting new combinations of plants.

When you come across a new plant you are not sure about, consider growing it in a planter. You can get to know it up close and personal before choosing an appropriate site in the garden. Young shrubs and trees look spectacular grown in terra cotta pots and ceramic planters, grouped together for mass effect. *Acer palmatum* 'Sango Kaku', *Corokia cotoneaster*, *Cotinus coggygria* smoke bush, *Nandina domestica* heavenly bamboo, *Fremontodendron* 'California Glory', *Pieris japonica* 'Variegata', *Gingko biloba* maidenhair tree saplings, are just a few suggestions.

THE Don'ts of Container Gardening

Don't use 100% garden soil, as it sets to concrete when it dries out in a container. Add amendments to create a lightweight, free-draining growing medium, and a slow-release fertilizer to feed plants all season long.

Don't site sun lovers in the shade, or shade lovers in the sun.

Don't plant your containers so that all the interest happens at the same time. Plan for sustained interest throughout the season. Consider varying heights, colours and textures, as well as bloom time.

Don't think you always have to combine plants. A single specimen with attractive foliage or beautiful flowers can be just as striking as a mass of different plants.

Don't forget to grow edible plants in containers. Patio tomatoes, salad greens, parsley, mints and climbing beans make perfect container specimens.

Don't leave pots that may need extra protection out all winter. Bring them in if necessary. Winter wet with a deep freeze is a killer combination for container plants.

Making Wire Hanging Baskets

1. Stand the wire basket in an empty pot to stabilize it.

2. Fit a small saucer in the bottom of the basket to hold a small reservoir of water, which is extremely useful in the height of summer when you go away.

3. Line the basket with a layer of sphagnum moss, or choose a synthetic liner made from coir (coconut fibre) or dyed sheep's wool, which are reusable and more sustainable.

   TIP: Be innovative, and use bamboo leaves, fern fronds or even phormium swords as an environmentally friendly alternative to sphagnum moss.

4. Cover the base with lightweight potting compost pressed down firmly to exclude air pockets.

5. Plant your basket in layers, starting at the lowest layer with trailing plants, use the middle layer for hanging plants, building up to the top layer for tall, upright plants.

   Lay bedding plants on the compost through the wire mesh from the outside. Press down to secure roots in place. When this layer is fully planted, cover well with compost to make the next layer. Continue to fill the basket with plants followed by layers of compost to within two inches of the rim.

6. Plant the uppermost layer with taller plants such as geraniums or marigolds. (Do not overcrowd the basket, as annual plants have a naturally spreading habit).

7. Check that the supporting chains, ring and bracket are strong enough to cope with the considerable weight of a full, watered basket.

Good Choices For Baskets In Full Sun:
Bacopa, felicia, geraniums, helichrysum, lobelia, lotus vine, marigolds, nemesia, petunias, scaveola, tagetes, trailing schizanthus, verbena

Good Choices For Baskets In Shade:
Alyssum, fibrous begonias, fuchsias, ivy geraniums, hedera, impatiens, trailing ivy, lobelia, tuberous begonias

8. To ensure displays last throughout the summer, remember to feed, water and deadhead the basket regularly. Give plants a regular watering with a potash-rich fertilizer such as liquid seaweed every week.

9. Don't hesitate to cut back growth that trails too far. A good pruning helps plants grow bushier, and often results in a second flowering.

10. Once planted up, it's a good idea to harden off the basket for ten days or so, leaving it outdoors during the day but protecting it from the cold at night.

Choose an alternative to spaghnum moss to line hanging baskets. Try burlap sacking, green-dyed sheep's wool matting, or a coir (coconut fibre) lining.

Fourth Week of May

True English Cowslips

The first time I spotted *Primula veris* flowering in my garden, I was instantly transported back to England on a wave of nostalgic ecstasy. Cowslips have always been central to English country life. Shakespeare mentioned them 400 years ago in his plays and today, even though their natural habitat is diminishing, the common cowslip is considered by many to be the quintessential British wildflower.

Primula veris - *the English cowslip*

This adorable spring plant, rarely seen in Canadian gardens, is well suited to temperate growing conditions. *Primula veris* is easily grown from seed, and also seeds itself readily. *TIP:* Seeds germinate best if sown fresh, as soon after collection in June/July as possible.

Like all primroses, established clumps can be divided to create spectacular colonies. Primulas grow best in moist soils in lightly shaded settings, as they are woodland plants.

The true English cowslip has a light but persistent scent, a perfume that softens the air. Bring a posy of flowers into the house and their delicate perfume will surprise you. I adore the cheerful stalks of the lemon-yellow flowers nodding in my garden. Grow *Primula veris* to add a touch of the 'Olde Country' to your garden.

Lovely Lilacs

As much as we love them, lilacs have weaknesses as garden plants, which are overlooked in our appreciation for their showy, fragrant early-spring blooms. Lilacs often keep you waiting several years before they begin to flower, and in some seasons fail to flower at all. They hang on to their spent flowerheads for months, which turn brown and look messy. If you want to be sure of getting flowers next year, you are forced to balance precariously on a ladder, reaching out to snip them off.

However, although lilacs lack interest when flowerless, they are good for providing a screen or a backdrop in the garden. As screen plants they do well, constantly growing suckers from the ground up, which makes them spread to become very bushy.

Here are some useful lilac tips:

- Lilacs are happiest in soil that contains lime.
- Lilacs grow and flower better if given an annual dressing of compost.
- They should be positioned in full sun, and grown in well-drained soil.
- Be sure to trim off spent flower heads as soon as they finish blooming, to give them the best chance of flowering the following year.

Azaleas and Rhododendrons

Other plants that flower best when their spent flower heads are removed are azaleas and rhododendrons. This is a good time to purchase them, while they are in bloom. This way you can be sure of getting the colour you want and avoid mishaps with mislabeling.

Rhododendron macrophyllum *'Unique'*

Here are some useful growing tips:

- Plant azaleas and rhododendrons where they will get wind protection.

- Often characterized as shade-loving, be aware that dense shade is not suitable. Partial shade of early morning sun followed by dappled shade in the afternoon is ideal.

- They must have an acid soil, most thriving at pH 5.0 to 5.5.

- Most azaleas and rhododendrons are shallow-rooted, so it's important to ensure that the soil does not dry out. Applying a mulch, such as leaves, sawdust or pine needles, conserves moisture around the roots. A dry summer and fall adversely affects the display the following spring.

- As the roots grow close to the surface, it's important not to disturb the area within the drip line around the root ball when cultivating.

- Use fertilizer formulated for acid-loving plants and make sure you water it in well.

- Leaves turning yellow indicates an iron deficiency. This can be cured by using a chelated iron fertilizer. A sprinkling of iron sulfate in fall hardens growth for the winter and helps prevent iron chlorosis.

The Prettiest of Peonies

Peonies, like roses, have to ability to captivate gardeners by invoking nostalgic memories and cherished associations with the past. Peonies are adored for their beauty, colour and fragrance, and because they establish into grand clumps, which even thrive on neglect. Be prepared to wait three to five years for them to achieve full perfection. After the showy spectacle of blooms in late spring or early summer, peonies continue to provide handsome foliage for the remainder of the season. Their attractive foliage covers up for early-flowering bulbs as they die back, and continues to create a luscious foil for summer and fall-blooming perennials.

Peonies thrive in rich, slightly-acid, but well-drained soil. The most common mistake gardeners make is to plant the tubers too deep, which means they will not bloom. Plant or divide peonies in the fall, keeping in mind that shallow planting encourages flower production. Initially the tubers benefit from a mulch of evergreen boughs or straw where the ground freezes, but once established need no winter protection.

You can choose from a range of exquisite double-flowered varieties, which are the most popular. These require a flower ring (I use an upturned tomato cage) to support the considerable weight of their blousy blooms. I have been smitten by the more delicate anemone-like flowers of the species peony, which flourishes in filtered sun at the entrance to the shade garden. Peonies are easy to grow, but in wet, cool seasons, botrytis can be a problem. Remove affected leaves at the first sign of sinister black blotches.

Feeding Roses

Ensure the best show from your roses by applying rose fertilizer now before blooming. Roses are heavy feeders and flower better if well fed. Here's a simple, inexpensive home recipe that works really well.

Organic Rose Food Recipe

Before blooming:
Mix well:
1 cup alfalfa pellets
1/4 cup rock phosphate
2 Tbsp. magnesium sulphate
Scatter mix around the drip line under your rose bushes and work in gently.

After blooming:
1 cup alfalfa pellets
2 Tbsp. magnesium sulphate
Mix with 2 gallons of water. Steep for 24 hrs. Water this mixture around the root zone of each rose bush.

TIP: Stop feeding your roses by the end of August, as new growth can be injured in winter. When roses start to leaf out in spring, foliar spray with liquid seaweed or compost tea to improve disease resistance. Cleanliness is very important in rose gardens. Fallen leaves can harbour disease and insect pests over the winter, so rake fallen leaves away from the base of roses to prevent problems.

June

If Jove would give the leafy bowers
A queen for all their world of flowers,
The rose would be the choice of Jove,
And blush the queen of every grove.
Sweetest child of weeping morning,
Gem, the breast of earth adorning,
Eye the flow'rets, glow of lawns,
Bud of beauty, nursed by dawns:
Soft the soul of love it breathes,
Cypria's brow with magic wreathes;
And to Zephyr's wild caresses,
Diffuses all its verdant tresses,
'Til glowing with the wanton's play,
It blushes a diviner ray.

Sappho of Lesbos (c. 600 BC)

First Week of June

Rambling Roses

It's not often that gardeners need to replace a climbing rose because they live a lot longer than other roses. Therefore, it's important to choose the right plant and the right site from the start, and not to muddle climbing roses with ramblers.

People often confuse climbing and rambling roses, but their parentage differs so they have quite distinct modes of growth. Ramblers renew themselves every year from ground level, putting out new canes many feet long. They should be pruned annually after flowering, allowing new canes to eventually replace old ones. This prevents vigorous growth from becoming a bewildering tangle.

'Royal Sunset' – an exquisite climbing rose, that blooms all season long.

Climbers are better behaved, flowering on wood from an enduring framework. As a result of being more restrained, climbers are the better choice for planting over arches and pergolas, so you won't get attacked as you walk by. Ramblers are the best choice for growing on fences or for scrambling over trees or hedges.

When planting a rose, dig a large hole and enrich the soil with plenty of aged manure, especially if you're planting against a building, where there is likely to be an accumulation of rubble. Add a slow-release organic fertilizer to the planting hole, choosing one with a high phosphorus (P) content to promote better blooms.

TIP: Roses love banana peels! Compost banana skins around your roses. Bury three cut-up banana peels around each bush. The peels provide 3.25% phosphorus and 41.76% potash, which really get roses blooming.

Encourage climbing and rambling roses to flower more profusely by tying the main growth down horizontally, to increase the number of flowering laterals that develop. Prune by shortening these laterals to about six inches in late winter.

TIP: Choose varieties that are perpetual flowering, which will give you a show through summer and fall, instead of just one magnificent June flush. 'New Dawn' is a climber that has fragrant, semi-double blooms of soft-pink and flowers freely from June to October.

Recommended climbers
Royal Sunset, Mme. Alfred Carriere, Aloha, Iceberg

Recommended ramblers
Amaglia, Veilchenblau, Kiftsgate, Lady Bank's Rose *(R. banksia lutea)*, American Pillar, Paul's Himalayan Musk

TIP: To keep deer off roses (which they love): Beat eggs with water (one egg to one litre water) and spray this mixture onto foliage every five days. The egg white acts as a sticking agent. A bonus is that the sulphur in the eggs acts as fungicide and keeps powdery mildew and blackspot off roses.

My Interview with David Grierson

If you're a night person like me, you'd find conducting a radio interview on tomatoes at 8 a.m. in the morning challenging too! From a sudden surge of early morning inspiration I jotted down some thoughts on paper, and instantly created the four S's as a framework for the interview. The next thing I knew I was chatting to David Grierson about tomatoes on *The Early Edition,* live on CBC radio.

"So," asked David. "What are your tips on growing the best tomatoes?"

"Let's start with the first of four S's," I replied. "Seaweed. If you want to get bumper crops of tomatoes, it's important to feed your plants throughout the growing season. Seaweed is high in potash and trace minerals, which boost fruit and flower production. If you plan ahead, you can gather seaweed from the beach in winter, and mulch beds where you'll be growing tomatoes with it. If you don't get round to doing this, use granular seaweed in the planting hole or feed tomato plants with liquid kelp. Both products are readily available from your local garden centre."

"What's the second S stand for then?" said David, his interest obviously piqued.

"Suckers," I replied. "The aim is to maximize fruit production versus foliage. If you are growing vining tomatoes you need to pinch out the suckers as they develop. A sucker is the new growth that develops in the leaf axis between the main stem and the leaves. If you keep your plant pruned to one or two main stems, you focus the energy on fruit production, and get way higher yields of tomatoes."

"The third S stands for staking," I continued. "There's nothing worse than finding your tomato plant, loaded with fruit, keeled over. Tomato cages are OK for shorter bush tomatoes, but not for vining varieties. For them you need a good strong stake, preferably a two-inch cedar stake, pounded a foot deep into the ground. Tie your plants onto their stakes as they grow, which maximizes their exposure to sunlight for ripening, and also makes harvesting easier."

"What do you tie the tomatoes onto the stake with?" asked David. I could tell that he was now making mental notes, as he was planning on growing tomatoes too.

"Well, this could pose a problem for the gentlemen in the audience, but I use pantyhose," I replied. "I save them and cut them into strips, and they make the perfect stretchy ties for tomatoes and other soft-stemmed plants."

This must have been a stretch for David, who wanted to know what he could use instead of pantyhose. "Green jute twine is perfect," I responded. "Just avoid wire ties, which cut into the soft stems of the tomatoes as they grow."

Thus we came to the fourth S – Strip!

"I know it's hard to believe that this doesn't damage the plants, but towards the end of the season of fruit production, which is the end of August here on the west coast, you should strip all the leaves off your tomato plants and cut the tip off the main leader. This diverts the plant's energy into ripening the existing fruit, rather than producing more fruit, which will come to nothing so late in the season. It also exposes all the green tomatoes to the sun to ripen. Defoliating your plant completely at this stage doesn't affect it, and means you don't end up with bushels of green tomatoes."

"I know what the fifth S is," quipped David to end the interview. "S for sweet, and I'll be out this afternoon to buy my tomatoes!"

Noah Spriggs, the sweetest little tomato of all!

Sweet Strawberries

"Doubtless God could have made a better berry, but doubtless God never did."
  Dr. William Butler, 17th century writer

Nothing invokes the pleasure of summer more than a bowl full of sweet, sun-ripened strawberries. If you are growing June-bearing varieties such as 'Royal Sovereign' or 'Totem', then bountiful harvests of juicy berries will be yours. If you're growing day-neutral, everbearing varieties such as 'Tristar', you'll be picking luscious, ripe-red berries until the end of August. *TIP:* If it's jam you're after, choose June-bearing varieties for larger yields at the same time. If you want to enjoy occasional berries throughout the summer, plant ever-bearing varieties. Better yet – grow both!

The only downside to growing strawberries is that they only bear well for two to three years, so you need to plan for year three or four. Here's how:

- Renew your strawberry patch every year by replanting strawberry runners, or 'offsets'. Leave runners attached to the parent plant (as long as it is disease-free), and pegged down in the garden or into pots sunk into the soil. Once rooted, offsets can be cut off and replanted elsewhere. *TIP:* Do this no later than the end of August, or they may not produce a good crop next season.

- Replant rooted offsets in well-drained, slightly acidic soil in full sun, spaced 12 inches (30 cm) apart in rows 30 inches (75 cm) apart. Cover the roots but not the crowns when transplanting. Water well to help new plants establish.

TIPS: Once fruit production has stopped, cut the foliage down to the ground to keep your strawberry patch disease-free. Hedge trimmers work fine for this. The first time I did this my heart was in my mouth, but when I saw the vigorous regrowth of healthy new leaves, I felt reassured that this was a good idea.

- After fruiting, clear straw and other debris from around the plants to get rid of any diseased or pest-damaged material. If there's any sign of disease in your strawberry patch, start a new one elsewhere, preferably not where potatoes, tomatoes, eggplant or peppers (Solanaceae family) have been growing, which may encourage verticillium wilt.

The Beneficial Ladybug

One of the best natural predators for aphids is the little red and black spotted beetle in the garden, *Hippodamia convergens,* the native ladybug. Ladybugs eat aphids in both their adult and larval stage; adults consume up to 5,000 aphids during their lifetime. As well as keeping a check on aphids, they also eat other wide-bodied, slow-moving plant pests. Adults depend on a diet of pollen and nectar for maturation, but a supply of aphids or other prey is needed for egg production.

In winter, ladybugs hibernate under loose bark, in rock crevices, and in nooks and crannies. They wake up in March or April, mate, and lay their eggs in clusters of three to twenty on lower leaf surfaces. After two to five days the eggs hatch into larvae. It's important to recognize the larval stage of the ladybug so it is not mistaken for a pest. Larvae look like six-legged crocodiles, dark brown in colour with bright orange spots on the back of their lumpy bodies.

A mature larva can eat as many as 50 aphids a day, and between 200-500 aphids in a three-week lifespan. After 21 days the larvae pupate, attaching themselves to the undersides of leaves by their tails. After two to five days the adults emerge and continue to feed. Ladybugs produce up to six generations a year, which accounts for a lot of aphids.

As long as there is prey and a source of water, there's no reason for a ladybug to 'fly away home' and it will stick around in the garden. Broad spectrum insecticides can be fatal to these beneficial beetles, but encouraging healthy populations of ladybugs and other beneficial insects in the garden should make it unnecessary to use such products. No wonder we consider the ladybug to be lucky!

Second Week of June

Solutions to Pesky Plant Problems

Aphids

Description: Tiny (2-3 mm long) pear-shaped insects, often green, but also grey or black. They affect many plants, and are often found crowded in colonies on them.

Damage: Aphids suck plant sap, causing curled and distorted leaves and buds. Aphids secrete sticky honeydew onto leaves that become black and sooty as mould grows on the honeydew. The honeydew can be washed off with water.

Prevention:
- Check new shoot tips on shrubs, perennials, annuals and fruit bushes throughout the season, and squash aphids on sight between your thumb and finger.
- Attract predatory insects such as ladybugs and lacewings.

Control:
- Wash off with a strong jet of water.
- Release aphid midges or ladybugs.
- Spray with soapy water or insecticidal soap.

Caterpillars

Description: Caterpillars have elongated, segmented bodies with many short legs. Some are hairy while others are smooth. Different species include leaf rollers, cabbage loppers, tent caterpillars and cutworms.

Damage: Caterpillars chew large ragged holes in leaves. The presence of silk webbings indicates a caterpillar attack. Damage to plants is unsightly, but there's usually little long-term damage as they often grow new leaves.

Prevention:
- Cultivate the garden to remove weeds that may harbour caterpillars.
- Turn soil over several weeks prior to planting, to allow birds to feed on exposed cutworms.
- For tent caterpillars, remove egg masses from branches while the tree is dormant and before the larvae hatch.
- Attract birds to your garden by putting up birdhouses, birdfeeders and birdbaths.

Birds are incredibly valuable in the fight against pests. Robins adore caterpillars and grubs, especially cutworms, starlings help to control wireworm and gypsy moth populations, tits and finches devour bud-frequenting insects, woodpeckers search out cranefly larvae, and thrushes adore snails.

Control:
- Hand pick caterpillars, or prune out infested branches and drown caterpillars in soapy water.
- Spray dormant oil to kill overwintering eggs on trees.
- In the case of a severe infestation, spray with Bacillus thuriengensis (Bt), which will kill larvae when they eat the leaves of a sprayed tree.

Earwigs

Description: Dark brown and elongated with prominent rear pinchers.

Damage: Seldom more than a nuisance, but in high numbers, they can damage tender plants.

Prevention:
- Eliminate daytime hiding places such as woodpiles, empty flowerpots and other debris near the garden or house.

Control:
- Make traps from slightly dampened, tightly rolled newspaper, or stuff newspaper inside pots. Place near the plants being eaten or in other infested areas. Check traps daily, and shake trapped earwigs into soapy water to drown them.

Root Maggots

Description: Whitish larvae (6 mm long) that tunnel in the roots of host plants.

Damage: Maggots kill the host plant directly or indirectly by allowing diseases to infect the plant. Root maggots include cabbage maggots, which attack the cabbage family, including turnip and radish; carrot rust fly, which attacks carrots, celery, parsnips and related plants; and the onion maggot, which attacks onions, shallots, garlic and leeks.

Prevention:
- Rotate crops (see *Crop Rotation,* first week in May).
- Remove crop debris immediately after harvest and destroy infected roots.
- Use floating row covers (such as Remay) to cover seedlings and transplants. Covers can be left in place until harvest.

Control:
- Apply parasitic nematodes to soil around affected plants when the soil temperature is between 55-68°F (12-20°C).

Spider Mites
Description: Spider mites are minute, have eight legs, and resemble fine specks of dust. They are red, pale green, or yellowish.
Damage: Damage appears as yellow speckled areas on leaves, and in severe infestations, leaves turn yellow with brown brittle edges. Damage is the most severe in hot, dry conditions.

Prevention:
- Mist plants daily to suppress reproduction.
- Inspect plants for mites before purchasing them to avoid problems.

Controls:
- Spray infected plants with water regularly to hose off mites.
- Spray with insecticidal soap.

Whitefly
Description: Tiny insects with powdery white wings. They colonize in large numbers on the undersides of leaves.
Damage: Whiteflies feed on plant juices and excrete sticky honeydew. Infested leaves become pale or discoloured, may wilt and fall off.
Prevention:
- Inspect all seedlings and plants before purchase, to ensure they are free from whiteflies.

Control:
- Place sticky traps near the tops of plants to capture adults.
- Apply insecticidal soaps to control adults.

Simple Home Remedies

Simple Soap Solution
2 Tbsp. soap flakes
1 litre warm water
Dissolve soap flakes in water and apply directly to infested areas every 5-7 days. Note: Too much soap can cause burning on plants.
Pests affected: Aphids, spider mites, and whiteflies.

Garlic Oil Spray
10-15 cloves of minced garlic
2 tsp. mineral oil
600 ml water
1 tsp. liquid dish soap
Soak garlic in mineral oil for 24 hours. Strain garlic out and add 600 ml water and 1 tsp. liquid dish soap. Mix thoroughly. Spray plants with this solution.
Pests affected: Aphids, spider mites, and whiteflies.

Fungicide for Mildew and Black Spot
1 tsp. baking soda
1 litre water
1 tsp. soap flakes
Dissolve baking soda in 1 litre of warm water.

Add soap flakes to help solution cling to leaves. Remove infected leaves from plant, then spray top and bottom of remaining leaf surfaces to control spread of the disease.

Sticky Traps
1-2 Tbsp. Vaseline or Tanglefoot™
4"x 8" plastic cards or cardboard
Waterproof yellow paint
Apply paint onto both sides of the card and let it dry. Once the paint is dry, apply Vaseline or Tanglefoot™ liberally over both sides of card. Place the card just above the plant canopy.
Pests controlled: Flying pests, such as fungus gnats and whiteflies.

Sowbug Traps
1 small plastic container with lid
2 Tbsp. cornmeal
Cut a small hole at the base of the container, large enough and close enough to the bottom to allow sowbugs to climb in. Place cornmeal in container. Place container into area infested with sowbugs. After feeding on the cornmeal, the bugs will drink and then explode! (Replace cornmeal frequently.)

Plants That Keep Bugs at Bay

Over the years I've discovered a way to keep pest problems to a minimum – by growing plants that either repel them or attract their predators to the garden. Such plants assist nature in keeping a balance of the pesky bugs in your garden. By leaving it up to nature to control pest problems, you'll save countless hours of toil and worry.

Strongly scented marigolds planted throughout the garden either confuse pests or mask plants from them. The heady aroma of 'Taj Mahal' hedging marigolds gives a long season of protection as they bloom until first frosts.

'Taj Mahal' hedging marigolds – two-foot tall bushy plants covered in strong-scented flowers that repel pests.

We all love basil for its culinary uses, but Italian sweet basil repels aphids, mosquitoes and mites, and enhances the growth of many plants nearby. So it's not just a great companion to tomatoes, but to many other plants too.

Cabbage pests and aphids dislike the strong smell of members of the *Mentha* family. Set pots of mints around the garden so they can do their work, but not become invasive.

Tanecetum vulgare, tansy, is also very invasive, but worth growing for its refreshing lime-green, ferny foliage in spring and showy 'gold button' flowers in fall. Tansy repels cucumber beetles, Japanese beetles, ants and squash bugs, so they

will leave your plants alone. The one downside is that it attracts cabbage worms, so keep it away from cabbages. Plant thyme with cabbages instead, as it controls flea beetles and cabbage white butterflies.

Nasturtiums often act as trap plants for aphids, and can be viewed as saviours of other susceptible plants. This is another way of looking at plants infested with aphids – to appreciate them for drawing annoying pests away from plants you want to protect.

Members of the Compositae family, such as sunflowers, zinnias and asters, have a long season of bloom so attract beneficial insects for a long period of time.

Plants that lure 'good guys' to your garden
Fern-leaf yarrow (lacewings, ladybugs), angelica (lacewings), candytuft (hoverflies), cosmos (parasitic wasps), evening primrose (ground beetles), nemophila (syrphid flies), solidago (parasitic wasps and predaceous beetles)

Some plants act as mini-insectaries for beneficials. Allowing woolly grey aphids, specific to the lupin, to colonize on *Lupinus arboreus,* the tree lupin, attracts large numbers of parasitic wasps and predators. Having this strong presence of beneficials in the garden takes care of aphids trying to establish on nearby plants before problems arise.

Dragonfly on lemon verbena

Centaurea cyanus, cornflower or bachelor button, is a blue wildflower with extrafloral nectaries, which means the plants release nectar even when the flowers are not blooming. Research in Germany has found that bachelor button nectar has a sugar content of 75%, highly attractive to ladybugs, lacewings and beneficial wasps. Sow cornflower seeds directly in the garden in fall or early spring; plants usually reseed energetically.

Lobularia maritima, sweet alyssum, makes a highly fragrant, beneficial-attracting, weed-smothering ground cover. Numerous studies have confirmed that sweet alyssum is highly attractive to aphid-eating flower flies.

Anthemis tinctoria, golden marguerite, produces bright yellow daisies that are highly attractive to five key kinds of beneficials: ladybugs, lacewings, flower flies, tachinid flies and mini-wasps. Golden marguerite thrives in poor soils, growing two to three feet high and wide.

Anthemis tinctoria

Phacelia tanecetifolia, 'Bee Friend', has the loveliest purple-blue flowers that are irresistible to hoverflies. The ferny foliage can also be dug under as a green manure crop.

Amaranth is a magnet for ladybirds, shield bugs (which gorge on mites), parasitic wasps and even slug-hungry ground beetles.

Beneficial insects only stay in a garden when there are plants to provide food and shelter for them. They need food to sustain them from spring until fall. Herbs that are members of the Umbelliferae family, such as fennel, dill, anise,

coriander and parsley, have flower clusters that are easy for beneficials to feed from. Caraway, catnip, hyssop, lemon balm, lovage, rosemary and thyme are herbs that also attract beneficial insects.

Borago officinalis, borage, has bright blue clusters of edible, cucumber-flavoured flowers. Studies in Switzerland have shown borage to be exceptionally attractive to good bugs, with an average of over 100 beneficials found in just one square yard of borage. In addition, common green lacewings have a very strong preference for laying their eggs on borage. Once you grow borage and allow a few to self-seed, you will always have it in your garden.

Agastache foeniculum, anise hyssop, has fuzzy violet flower spikes on plants with licorice-scented leaves. The nectar-rich flowers are very attractive to both butterflies and pest-eating beneficial insects.

Foeniculum vulgare, fennel, flowers are extremely attractive to nectar-feeding beneficial insects such as parasitic wasps, lacewings and hoverflies. Fennel is also a host plant for the caterpillars of the anise swallowtail butterfly.

Salix spp., pussy willows, are especially valuable because they produce pollen early in spring when many beneficials are emerging.

All clump-forming ornamental grasses provide excellent summer shelter and overwintering sites for ground beetles, ladybugs and other beneficials. Studies in England found more than 1,500 predators per square yard in grass-covered "beetle banks" planted in arable fields.

The Heart of the Artichoke

Give globe artichokes a lot of space, because they grow rapidly to three to five feet tall, and can eventually reach a width of six feet across. They grow so fast that you can harvest artichokes in September from a March seeding.

These stately, silver-green plants produce flower buds resembling elongated, green pine cones. These cones are layered with edible bracts, but it is the very heart of the cone that is sought after. *TIP:* If left to mature, the large flower buds open to reveal purple thistle-flowers, which can be dried and used most effectively in floral arrangements.

Don't confuse globe artichokes, *Cynara scolymus,* with its relative, cardoon, *Cynara cardunculus.* You would choke if you tried to eat a cardoon flower. It's the midrib of the leaf that is enjoyed from this exotic plant.

'Green Globe' is an open-pollinated artichoke variety, well suited to cultivation on the west coast, as the days 'til maturity are only 180. The best harvest follows in the second and third year, but then artichokes get crowded

and need to be divided. Replenish in early spring by carefully digging down to remove young offsets and set them out or pot them up. The leaves always go into serious wilt, but don't panic – they eventually recover.

Globe artichokes are heavy feeders that need rich, friable garden soil with plenty of compost. Mulching with seaweed, or adding a handful of granular seaweed for extra potassium really boosts flower production, and hence the number of delicious artichokes you'll get to enjoy eating.

Artichokes prefer full sun, requiring a minimum of ten hours of sunlight a day. They are frost-sensitive perennials, which do not overwinter in areas with deep ground freezes. I cut mine back to six inches above the ground in November, and cover them thickly with mulch to keep the roots from freezing.

TIP: Artichoke seedlings do not transplant well, as they have a very sensitive tap root. Sow seeds individually in their own pots, so they can be transplanted into the garden with a minimum of root disturbance.

A Slow Food Experience

Harvest the artichoke flowers just before they start to open, leaving three inches of stalk attached. Stand them in a saucepan of boiling water with a sprig of bay leaves and a lemon cut in half. Boil, covered, for 25 minutes. Drain and eat as soon as you can. While cooking, prepare the dipping sauce.

The Dipping Sauce
Sauté 6 French shallots, finely chopped with
2 Tbsp. white wine
2 Tbsp. white wine vinegar
Slowly stir in 1/4 cup butter 'til melted and sauce thickens
Add 2 Tbsp. lemon juice
Salt and pepper to taste

Remove each bract individually from the flower bud, and swoosh it gently across the sauce. Delicately scrape the seasoned fleshy base off the bract with your teeth. As you get closer to the heart, each bract will have more flesh to enjoy. The fleshiest part of the flower bud is the heart. Before eating it, make sure you remove the thistly hairs or they will choke you. The sweetest delicacy awaits, as you finally savour the succulent heart – a moment worth waiting for!

Third Week of June

Why Save Seeds?

There are many benefits to saving your own seeds. One is that you are collecting seeds from plants that have adapted to the specific growing conditions in your garden. Another is that you can choose the healthiest plants to collect seeds from, and select for the traits you want, such as high yields, large fruit, early ripening, great fragrance or wonderful flavour.

By saving your own seeds, you know you are starting with the freshest seeds with the highest germination rate – the best start a plant can hope for. You can grow plants that may not be commercially available, such as hollyhocks that have been growing in your grandmother's garden for fifty years, or beans, passed along by a wizened gardener in the community.

Instead of paying a lot for a little pinch of seeds, you can have containers full of them for free! Plenty to share with family and friends. Best of all, you can barter your precious seeds at a community seed show, such as Seedy Saturday, and exchange them for specialty seeds collected by other gardeners.

Most importantly, by saving seeds you are empowering yourself to look out for your future security. In these times of climate change, threats of war, and rapid population increase, who knows what's going to happen to the global food supply? It's reassuring to know that you can collect the seeds you'll need to grow your own food.

Saving Seeds Successfully

As a seed saver, you participate in the selection process to encourage those qualities in a plant you most value. Choose flowers for beauty, colour or fragrance. For vegetables, traits such as early ripening, disease resistance, high yields, size and good flavour are all important. Of course it always makes sense to select seeds from the healthiest and best performing plants in the garden. These seeds will grow plants that display the greatest vigour.

Here are a few basics you need to know about saving seeds:

Choose open-pollinated rather than hybrid seeds to guarantee that you get the same plant year after year. Hybrids result from crossing two parent plants. If you save seeds of hybrids, the plants will not come true in the next generation. The resulting plant may revert back to characteristics from one or the other of the parent plants, or display an undesirable mix of both. Species of plants that have not been hybridized will reproduce to the original plant. Open-pollinated vegetables will grow into the same vegetable as the parent plant, as long as cross-pollination with a different variety of the same species has not occurred.

Determine whether plants are self-pollinating or cross-pollinating. Plants such as tomatoes, beans, peppers, lettuce and peas are self-pollinating. They have 'perfect flowers', which means their flowers hold both male and female parts, so they can be pollinated without the assistance of bees, insects or the wind to carry the pollen. This allows the gardener to grow different varieties in close proximity to one another.

Use isolation distances to be sure accidental crossing does not occur. Different tomato varieties should be separated by a distance of 6 feet (30 feet if they are potato-leaf varieties), different varieties of lettuce should be 10 feet apart, bush beans need to be separated by 10 feet, and pole beans by 30 feet. These are all self-pollinating vegetables.

Male squash blossom. The smaller flower is on a long stalk.

Female squash blossom. A larger flower with a small swelling at the base on a short stem.

Many plants, such as squashes, have 'imperfect flowers', which means each plant has separate male and female flowers. In this case the gardener must take further isolation distances into account when planting. Squash needs to be isolated by 1/4 mile to prevent insects spreading pollen from the male flowers of one variety to the female flowers of another variety. If you've ever had an unidentified squash volunteer in your garden, it was the result of cross-pollination between different varieties of squash grown there the previous year.

Biennial crops, such as beets, carrots and cabbages, produce their edible crop in the first year and set seed the following season. These crops need isolation distances of 1/4 mile to prevent cross-pollination. Carrots will cross with wild carrot, Queen Anne's Lace, if they are grown within 1/4 mile of each other. Brassicas, e.g. broccoli, Brussels sprouts, cauliflower, collards, kale and kohlrabi must be separated by 1/4 mile to prevent cross-pollination. Get to know your isolation distances for saving vegetable seeds, or you will be harvesting a future crop of mutant veggies!

Collect seeds before they disperse naturally. The timing for seed collection is critical; observation is the key to success. Wait until the seed is ready and ripe enough for collection, but don't wait until the seeds have scattered all over the garden or the birds have swooped in and eaten them.

Label seeds. If you've ever found an envelope of seeds and wondered what they were or how old they were, you will know how important labeling is. For everything you collect, identify the species and variety, record any special features, and record data such as the place and date the seeds were collected.

Dry seeds thoroughly. I'll never forget my friend's dismay at discovering her container of precious hollyhock seeds had gone mouldy. Drying seeds thoroughly is critical before storing them in sealed containers or envelopes. The larger the seeds, the longer they need to dry properly. I spread mine out on ceramic plates and let them dry in a warm area away from direct sunlight. I allow two weeks or more for drying.

Before storing, clean seeds. Remove the chaff and other debris by sieving seeds through screens of different-sized mesh. Winnow seeds in a light breeze to remove any tiny particles or dust. I use a hairdryer on a low, cold setting to do this.

Tomatoes are cleaned by a wet process, where they undergo a fermentation process for a few days, which also eliminates seed-borne pathogens. Melons, squashes, cucumbers and tomatillos are also cleaned using water, allowing dead seeds to float to the surface and good seeds to sink to the bottom of the container.

Store seeds in a cool dark area, away from fluctuations in light and moisture. The ideal temperature for storage is 55°F (13°C). Paper envelopes or airtight containers, such as yoghurt tubs, work fine for seed storage. Keeping seeds in an airtight, waterproof container in the fridge prolongs seed life, longer if you freeze them.

This may sound like a lot to remember, but you will discover that saving seeds is relatively straightforward. The satisfaction of taking out containers of your own seeds in spring to begin a new cycle of growth, will more than compensate for your efforts the previous year.

How To Save Tomato Seeds

If you are growing more than one tomato variety, choose the best performing ones, those displaying desirable traits such as high yields, early ripening, disease resistance or excellent flavour.

Cut the tomatoes in half. Squeeze the seeds and pulp into a container, and put a plastic label in with them for identification purposes. (Notice the protective, gelatinous layer around each seed, which prevents it from germinating.)

Leave the seeds to ferment for four days, during which time a white 'scum' will form on top. This dissolves the gelatinous seed layer, preparing the seeds for future germination, and destroys any seed-borne pathogens. (I put a saucer over the container, because fruit flies love this process!)

After four, but no more than five days, rinse the seeds in a large bowl by filling the bowl with water. Good viable seeds sink to the bottom, and 'dud' seeds float to the top. Gently pour the water and floating 'scum' off, repeating the rinsing as many times as you need, until all that's left in the bottom of the bowl are cleaned seeds.

Pour these into a sieve and give them a final rinse; tap off any excess moisture. Spread the seeds onto a plate to dry. Keep the label on the plate, so you don't muddle up which varieties are being collected. (I avoid drying seeds on paper towel, as seeds stick to it and have to be picked off, although some people tell me they sow the seeds stuck on the paper towel!)

Place the plates of seeds in a sunny window for a day or two to dry them. Crumble the seeds with your fingers to separate any that are stuck together. Leave them spread out on plates for another week or two in a warm place to thoroughly dry. Store the seeds in labelled, airtight tubs. Tomato seeds stored properly will germinate for at least five years.

You'll be amazed how many seeds you can save from a handful of tomatoes. There's no better start for tomatoes than your own fresh seed, collected from the healthiest plants. (I find tomatoes grown from my own seeds improve as years go by. They have become ideally acclimatized to my garden's unique growing conditions.)

Go on, give it a go – squishing and squeezing is good for the soul!

Choose tomatoes for desirable traits. Cut the tomato in half.

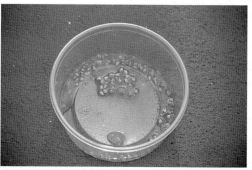

Squeeze the seeds into a container. Add a plastic ID label.

Leave to ferment for 4-5 days. Then wash the 'scum' off, and rinse the seeds thoroughly through a fine sieve.

Tap off excess water, and place seeds (with label) on a plate to dry for two weeks.

Fourth Week of June

What To Do in Your Garden Now

- Remove spent blooms of repeat flowering roses to encourage a later flush of flowers. Deadheading used to involve cutting back the shoots to three to five leaves, but it has been shown that the more foliage the plant retains the better it performs. So deadhead hybrid tea and floribunda roses by snapping off spent flowers at the natural break point on the stem, usually one to two inches (2.5 cm to 5 cm) below the flower. This promotes repeat flowering earlier.

- Keep on deadheading. Plants set seed after flowering to attract pollinating insects and then have no need to keep flowering. Deadheading encourages an ongoing show of flowers. *TIP:* Picking sweet peas regularly prevents them from going to seed and encourages continued flowering.

- Deadhead rhododendrons and lilacs before they set seed. This improves the floral show for next year by channeling the plant's energy into growth instead of setting seed.

Papaver orientale, *perennial poppy*

- Shear back plants that have finished blooming, e.g. oriental poppies, hardy geraniums, pulmonaria, omphaloides, alchemilla, centaurea montana, euphorbias. Cut them just above ground level. They will go into a period of semi-dormancy followed by a flush of new foliage to fill in the gap.

- Plant rudbeckia, dwarf sunflowers, cleome, nicotiana, scented geraniums, dahlias, chrysanthemums, helenium or asters to provide follow-up interest to plants that have finished blooming.

- Shear back rockery perennials such as aubrieta now. This prevents the plants from becoming overgrown or woody, and encourages new growth for next year.

- Spring flowering shrubs such as deutzia, weigela, lilacs, philadelphus and forsythia should be pruned after blooming. Cut out older stems, leaving younger more vigorous ones to grow. Other spring flowering shrubs, such as *Viburnum tinus,* berberis, chaenomeles, choisya and flowering currants should be pruned now after flowering. Remove one stem in three from *Kerria japonica.* Rhododendrons can be lightly pruned after flowering if necessary. If deciduous magnolias need pruning, do this now when in full leaf, as pruning when dormant can lead to dieback problems, and pruning in late winter can result in bleeding. Prune overcrowded stems of *Clematis montana* once flowering is over.

Philadelphus, *mock orange, is a highly fragrant shrub that should be pruned after flowering.*

- If planting with granular organic fertilizers, work these well into the planting hole before planting. Natural source fertilizers (contents: seedmeals, gypsum, greensand, sul-po-mag, rock phosphate, zeolite, kelp meal) break down slowly and feed your plants with trace elements they need as they grow. It takes three to four weeks for granular fertilizers to break down and become available to plants, so help transplants initially with a liquid feed of either fish fertilizer for leafy greens or liquid kelp for fruiting and flowering plants.

- Variegated plants tend to revert to more vigorous green non-variegated foliage, which should be removed as soon as it is detected.

- Store lifted spring bulbs after allowing them to dry. Clean off any dried soil and place them in labelled brown paper bags or boxes until replanting in fall.

- Mow in a different direction each time you mow the lawn; otherwise, grass will begin to lean one way and your mower won't cut as well. Now that the weather is heating up, the soil will dry out quickly and the lawn will start browning. Raise the mower blades so you don't scalp the lawn, and mow less often, as longer grass copes better with drought conditions.

- When you dig a hole for transplanting, if it's dry at the bottom, fill it up with water and let it soak in before planting.

- Seed of biennials, such as foxgloves, campanula, wallflowers and forget-me-nots can be collected now and sown. The seed of primula is best sown when green, so harvest and sow seeds of *Primula veris*, *Primula bulleyana* and *Primula japonica* as soon as it can be collected.

- Attract hummingbirds to your garden with red and orange flowers such as *Crocosmia masonorum* 'Lucifer', *Zauschenaria californica* California fuchsia, *Phygelius capensis* Cape fuchsia and *Lychnis chalcedonica* Maltese cross.

- After bearded irises have flowered, dig up any large clumps and split them. Select the most vigorous rhizomes with one or two fans attached. Replant them in full sun with the tops of the rhizomes just showing. If you replant them too deep they will not flower the following year. *TIP*: Cut leaves back by half, to prevent irises from being uprooted while the shallow roots are re-establishing.

- Remove suckers off grafted shrubs as soon as you see them. Cut them off as close as possible to the stems or roots from which they grow. Inspect grafted roses regularly for suckers developing from the base of the bush. Remove them by scraping back the soil to expose the sucker and rootstock. Pull the sucker away from the rootstock, as this also removes any dormant buds. Refill the hole with soil and firm down.

- Wisteria stems quickly get long and whippy after flowering. Prune them back, leaving about five buds on each lateral stem. Wisteria is traditionally pruned twice a year, once in summer and again in winter, to promote a good spur system with plenty of flowering buds. The long, whippy laterals that have developed since flowering should be pruned back to 12 inches on the current season's shoots. At the same time, select laterals to extend the framework and tie them in.

  TIP: Wisterias need a sunny, sheltered position to flower well, and must be watered regularly during dry spells to help the buds form. If plants have been reluctant to flower, feeding them with a granular seaweed through spring and summer should encourage them.

- Dianthus are not long lived and tend to become unattractive after three years. Replace them by taking cuttings from now until August. They prefer alkali conditions, so root the cuttings in loam rather than peat. Keep cuttings in the shade, uncovered. Pinch tips to make them bushy. By fall they should be large enough to plant out.

- Resist the temptation to give regal pelargoniums too much root room, as they like to be cramped in their pots. Feed them every week to get them to go on flowering. These plants have one determined enemy: whitefly. They need constant observation to see that these pests do not become a problem, especially under the leaves.

Winter varieties of squash when properly stored will keep throughout the winter.

In the Vegetable Garden

- Try growing squash or pumpkins on the compost heap. They love a nutrient-rich medium and will go bananas. The compost should be well rotted before you sow the squash seeds or plant transplants.

- To promote better fruiting, feed plants such as tomatoes, eggplants and peppers with granular seaweed, high in potash. It can be worked into the soil as a side dressing around established plants or incorporated into planting holes.

- Feed pots of tomatoes, peppers and eggplants weekly with liquid seaweed. As plants establish and their roots fill the pots, it is harder for them to absorb nutrients from the medium in the containers. A weekly liquid feed of manure tea, compost tea or liquid seaweed will compensate for this, and more fruit will result.

- Provide asparagus beds with organic fertilizer when the last crop has been harvested. Allow the remaining spears to continue growing into ferny canes, to replenish strength in the roots.

- Run out of space? Vertical gardening is the answer! Tie strings of garden twine up and down a horizontal support frame and attach beans, vining tomatoes, red malabar climbing spinach or cucumbers to this framework.

- Continue direct sowing beans, squash, carrots, corn, sunflowers and beets.

- Remove winter vegetables that are going to seed, such as chards, purple sprouting broccoli and kales. (Leave one or two of the best plants to set seed for a winter crop.)

- Squash roots hate disturbance. It's best to make a mound, plant four seeds on it, and then thin to the best two seedlings. If using transplants, gently tap the seedling from its pot and plant it on the mound with minimum disturbance to its roots. The same applies to artichoke and cardoon seedlings.

- Weed control is important as competition for moisture and nutrients increases. Hoe between rows during dry weather. Better yet, lay down a thick layer of straw or hay mulch to suppress weeds.

Floating row covers, such as Remay, protect crops from pest problems.

- Never sow carrots on ground that has recently grown carrots, parsnips or any Umbelliferae relations. Maggots or pupae of the carrot rust fly may still be in the soil, waiting for a new crop. *TIPS*: Create a physical barrier against the carrot rust fly by covering carrot seeds with horticultural fleece (Remay) or fine mesh netting. Alternatively, confuse the fly by disguising the carrot smell with a stronger one. I have had great success mulching my carrot patch with organic coffee grounds. Marigolds and onions also work well.

- Keep checking hardneck (rocambole) garlic for seedheads (scapes). Cut the stalks down as far as the leaves, or the seedheads will compromise the size of the garlic bulbs. *TIP:* Enjoy the scapes as a mild garlic green in salads, stirfries or as a side vegetable.

- Harvest small early potatoes by gently foraging around the roots of the plant without actually digging it up. Potatoes need earthing up to ensure good harvests, and to prevent tubers from turning green and becoming inedible.

Try growing some of the many fascinating varieties of heritage potatoes.

- Impoverished patches of garden soil can be replenished by planting green manures, crops that when dug back into the soil will replace nutrients. Quick-maturing green manures include mustard, fenugreek and buckwheat. Or try phacelia, a pretty crop with ferny foliage and bright blue flowers, much loved by bees. Dig these crops under before they set seed.

In the Fruit and Berry Patch

- Tie in new canes of trailing vines such as blackberries and loganberries as they grow.

- Pull out raspberry suckers appearing beyond the supported rows.

- Gooseberries are potash hungry. Layer around the base of the plants with comfrey leaves or wood ash, and cover with a layer of mulch such as compost, grass clippings or leaves. This helps to retain the right amount of moisture, keep weeds down, and keep mildew at bay.

- Straw down strawberries to keep fruit clean from soil splash. Peg down strawberry runners if new plants are needed. This will encourage rooting along the stem.

Raspberries will benefit from a topdressing of grass clippings, unless the grass has been treated with a herbicide.

Native Plants: The Right Plant in the Right Place

Putting the right plant in the right place is key to successful gardening. Plants that are best adapted to an area are the native (or indigenous) plants that grow there. Indigenous plants are adapted perfectly to their native habitat, which makes them drought-tolerant, pest and disease-resistant choices.

> A North American native plant: One that existed in the region before European settlement. Not all wild plants are native. We can thank European settlers for introducing Queen Anne's lace, dandelion, broom, ivy, and Himalayan blackberry, which are all invasive and sometimes habitat-destroying plants.

It's strange to think that we do not value the native plants that grow around us so successfully. That's apparent because they are usually all removed, along with the topsoil, during property development. Urban gardeners, therefore, don't become familiar enough with the plants that were originally growing in their gardens and as a result do not consider them worthy plant choices.

Attitudes toward native plants are changing as we come to appreciate their value, beauty, diversity and appropriateness. If you see the flush of pink from a bank of *Arctostaphylos uva-ursi,* kinnickinnick, in spring, you know what a great groundcover it makes. With glossy, evergreen leaves, it happily spreads to a dense carpet in sun or shade. The best part is that kinnickinnick's flowers also attract butterflies and bees in spring, and the red berries in fall and winter are an excellent food source for wildlife.

Have you ever noticed the heady fragrance of the creamy-white flowers of *Oemleria cerasiformis,* Indian plum, which heralds spring? Did you know that Indian plum also produces clusters of plum-coloured berries in summer, which are surprisingly sweet to eat?

For a shrub that thrives in shade, try *Vaccinium ovatum,* evergreen huckleberry, which also has attractive evergreen foliage and pink flowers followed by edible berries. If it's fall colour you are after, plant *Viburnum opulus,* highbush cranberry, which has stunning red leaves in fall, along with orange-red fruit.

The greatest benefit of integrating native plants into a home landscape is that they are of great value to wildlife. They provide habitat and forage, such as berries, seeds and nuts for mammals and birds, and flowers that feed beneficial insects.

Native plants attract hummingbirds to the garden year round. From March to April, hummingbirds are lured by the bright red flowers of *Ribes sanguineum* red flowering currant; from April to July by the fragrance of *Lonicera involucrata* twinberry and *Rubus spectabilis* salmonberry and the cerise-red colour of *Dicentra formosa* Pacific bleeding heart. From July to October the pink flowers and red pods of *Epilobium angustifolium* fireweed, keeps them humming.

Anna's hummingbirds *(Calypte anna)* overwinter on southern Vancouver Island. They lay two broods a year, starting in February. They have been sighted in many places in British Columbia, but nest mainly in Victoria, a few in Nanaimo and Greater Vancouver. It is estimated that there are 500 breeding Anna's hummingbirds around Greater Victoria.

Selecting the right native plant for your garden is important if you want it to thrive. Right plant – right place means not planting a moisture-loving plant in a dry spot, or one that needs well-drained soil in a wet spot. Initially, just like any other introduction to your garden, you'll need to water native plants to get them established. Once established, though, they will be low maintenance and will not require watering. As they thrive in native soils, native plants do not need feeding, but will benefit from a yearly application of leaf mulch and compost.

There's a native plant for every garden. It's just a question of looking at them with new eyes and appreciating them for the perfectly adapted plants that they are.

Erythronium californicum *Fawn Lily. Plant in groups under trees, in rock crevices or beside water features for dainty spring blooms.*

July

Dust If You Must

Dust if you must, but wouldn't it be better
To paint a picture or write a letter,
Bake a cake or plant a seed,
Ponder the difference between want and need?

Dust if you must, but there's not much time
With rivers to swim and mountains to climb,
Music to hear and books to read,
Friends to cherish and life to lead.

Dust if you must, but the world's out there
With the sun in your eyes, the wind in your hair,
A flutter of snow, a shower of rain,
This day will not come round again.

Dust if you must, but bear in mind
Old age will come and it's not kind.
And when you go, and go you must,
You yourself will make more dust!

Anonymous

Fang Zhang

First Week of July

Cut-and-Come-Again Vegetables

Mesclun may sound like a hallucinogenic drug, but the word merely means a mix of baby salad greens. I often say that the experience of eating such a tantalizing blend of fresh-cut greens is enough to make you high, especially as it invokes the lifestyle of Tuscany and Provence, regions where mesclun greens have long been part of everyday fare.

"Cut-and-come-again" refers to a simple method of harvesting young salad greens, whereby they are cut back with a pair of scissors and left to regrow. This way several collections can be made from one sowing of seeds. Mesclun mixes are suitable for growing in the smallest garden, and *perfect* for raised bed or container gardening.

Here's how to grow a mesclun patch:

1. Blend a mix of suitable seeds, or buy a packet of prepared mix. Note: Mustard greens and arugula add heat to the salad blend. Dandelion, chicory and endive add a tangy bitterness to the mix.
2. Scatter seeds lightly over a prepared bed or filled planter.
3. Cover lightly and water.
4. Keep soil moist once the crop is growing.
5. Harvest the baby greens when they are four inches high, either by picking individual leaves or cutting to one inch above the ground with a pair of scissors.
6. Fertilize with liquid fish fertilizer and in two to three weeks another crop will be ready to harvest.
7. To keep your salad bowl full, broadcast mesclun seeds every three to four weeks, and your cut-and-come-again greens will just keep on coming!

Suitable seeds for a mix include arugula, beetroot, chard, chervil, chicory, corn salad, dandelion, endive, Italian parsley, kale, land cress, lettuces, mustard greens, onion greens, oriental greens, orach, sorrel, spinach and perpetual spinach.

For a winter mesclun mix, choose winter-hardy lettuces, oriental greens, mustard greens, kales, land cress, corn salad and spinach.

Four Season Food Gardens

Since discovering the incredible diversity of vegetables to harvest from the garden in winter, I've been promoting four season food harvesting with a vengeance. It's a blast (in more ways than one!) to go out in the middle of winter to see what's for dinner. Even during a snowfall we can pull leeks for a leek and potato soup, flavoured with celeriac root and frozen parsley if so desired.

Why leave garden beds empty once your early crops of peas, lettuce and garlic have been harvested, when you can plant a wide array of winter vegetables? There are more than forty varieties of cold-hardy vegetables to choose from.

The secret is getting the timing right, but once you factor a winter garden into your plans, it's easy. Allocate garden space specifically for winter crops, or follow early crops of favas, peas, lettuce, potatoes, garlic or shallots by seeding or transplanting winter vegetables in their place. When following an earlier crop, don't forget to feed the soil by adding organic soil amendments. Mixing compost, aged manure or leaves into the soil keeps fertility high for follow-on crops.

Plants to Grow in Your Food Garden

Lettuces: 'Brunia' (red oakleaf), 'Rouge d'Hiver' (romaine), 'Winter Density' (butterhead), 'Vulcan' (red leaf lettuce)

Salad Greens: Endive, corn salad, landcress, arugula

Greens: Chard, kale, collards, mustard greens, perpetual spinach, tatsoi, pac choi, 'Lutz' beet greens

Crucifers: Sprouting broccoli, cabbage, cauliflower

Onions: Leeks, garlic, French shallots, perennial bunching onions

Root crops: Turnips, beets, carrots, Jerusalem artichokes, New Zealand yams, celeriac

Herbs: Parsley, coriander, rosemary, bay, oregano, sweet marjoram, chives, sorrel, lovage

In beds saved for winter vegetables, sow buckwheat, a fast-growing, summer green manure crop that increases fertility. Dig buckwheat under before it sets seed, allowing three weeks before planting. Buckwheat adds nitrogen to the soil, which is of great value to the next crop of vegetables.

If sowing seeds directly in the garden, the best time is late June to early August, but don't forget the importance of daily watering during hot spells. Thin out seedlings, and help them establish more quickly with a few feedings of liquid fish fertilizer.

Transplants of cool-weather vegetables can be started outdoors as they germinate in cooler temperatures. Most take only seven to ten days to germinate and the only protection needed is from the sun. Transplant into the garden no later than mid-September to give time for plants to establish good roots before the onset of hard frosts.

Winter vegetables survive freezing temperatures by pumping sugars into their cells as antifreeze. That's why kales, collards and Brussels sprouts taste sweeter after a few hard frosts. Once harvested, sugars convert back to starch. This is why store-bought vegetables never match the flavour of fresh-picked ones.

Multiplier onions must be one of the best deals for gardeners! Each bunching onion establishes quickly into a new clump, giving a bunch in return for just one planted.

Growing a winter vegetable garden is a snap once the vegetables have been planted. There's no weeding, no insect problems to deal with, and no watering. All you have to do is put on gumboots to harvest them! (See *Squeaky Beans,* third week of February and *Grow The Best Garlic,* third week of October.)

Tips for Growing Winter Vegetables

- Grow a variety of your favourite vegetables.
- Follow early crops of peas, potatoes, lettuces and garlic.
- Direct seed winter vegetables in the garden from late June to early August.
- Start seeds from late June to mid-July.
- Transplant established seedlings into the garden no later than mid-September.
- Help transplants get established with feeds of liquid fish fertilizer.
- Add lime to brassicas to prevent club root.
- Remove older leaves regularly to prevent a build-up of flea beetles and eliminate cabbage worms.
- Harvest greens after hard frosts when they have become sweeter.

Walla Walla onions are an overwintering variety with large, pungent bulbs. Established transplants, tucked in by mid-September, grow into large cooking onions for harvesting the following June/July.

Second Week of July

Edible Flowers

You'd be surprised how many of your garden flowers make wonderful additions to recipes. Early eighteenth century cookbooks routinely offered recipes for soups and salads that called for marigold, cowslip and violet flowers. Roses have been used to add a note of fragrance and colour to dishes since well before Elizabethan times.

> Try layering rose petals in a fruit compote, using rosewater to flavour apple pie or blending rose petals and chives into cream cheese for a cracker spread.

There's no better way of livening up green salads than by sprinkling them with flower petals. A salad tossed with the orange petals of calendula, tangy nasturtium flowers and the colourful petals of *Viola tricolor* (Johnny jump-ups) is bound to attract admiring comments.

> Try floating bright blue borage flowers in a punchbowl of lemonade, or freeze some in individual ice cubes and float these in a punchbowl. This adds elegance, as well as a refreshing cucumber taste.

Gladioli and tulip blossoms don't have distinctive flavours but they do make lovely holding cups for sweet mousses, fruit sorbets and savoury spreads. Serving appetizers or desserts this way makes an impressive start or finish to any meal. Fuchsia, cornflower, and pineapple sage blossoms don't have distinctive flavours either, but will make colourful edible garnishes.

The blossoms of dianthus and scented geraniums can be used to add a subtle taste to sorbets and desserts. Dianthus adds a light nutmeg flavour; scented geraniums vary in flavour from rose to lemon to nutmeg.

The flowers of herbs also add intriguing flavours to dishes. Lavender blossoms add an appealing scent to custards, flans and sorbets. The leaves and flowers of lemon verbena can be steeped to make a lively lemony herb tea, and add lemon flavour to custards and flans. Chive blossoms add

Lynda Dowling serves her delicious edible flower salad for lunch, tossed with a light vinaigrette dressing.

an oniony touch to salads, omelettes and spreads, while pretty blue rosemary blossoms enhance any Mediterranean dish.

Carthamus tinctorius Mexican saffron, can be used as a substitute for expensive Spanish saffron.

Zucchini blossoms (use male flowers only) can be served in soups by adding them during the last five minutes of cooking. They can also be dipped in a light batter and deep fried. Stuffing squash blossoms with different fillings makes a stunning presentation.

Daylily blossoms are everyday fare in the Orient. Either the bud or the day-old spent blossom may be cooked. The flavour is crisp and mild, not unlike green beans. The daylily flower is a delicacy that most people like on first taste. Simply steam the flowers for five minutes, or stirfry them into an Asian-style dinner.

> Edible flowers are best picked around noon on a sunny, dry day. Only eat those grown without pesticides, and then only in moderation.

Mothers used to tell children to eat their vegetables, but modern-day mums tell their kids to eat their flowers!

A Visit to the *Sticky Wicket Wildlife Garden*

Where dips the rocky highland
Of sleuth wood in the lake
There lies a leafy island
Where flapping herons wake
The drowsy water-rats;
There we've hid our fairy vats,
Full of berries
And of stolen cherries.

Come away, O Human child!
To the waters and the wild,
With a fairy, hand in hand,
For the world's more full of weeping
Than you can understand.

From *The Stolen Child* by W.B. Yeats

The Sticky Wicket at Buckland Newton, UK, is a wildlife garden set in the heart of west Dorset's fertile Blackmore Vale. Here Pamela and Peter Lewis have created one of the finest examples of managed meadow gardens in the British Isles, with an inspiring two and a half acres of themed gardens. Each garden has a focus on different wildlife.

I enjoyed chatting with Pamela over a cup of tea in her teahouse. Her labour of love at the *Sticky Wicket* is fuelled by the knowledge that 98% of Britain's wildflower meadows have been destroyed in the last fifty years. This is mainly due to farming practices, which destroy the meadow flowers with the use of artificial fertilizers and pesticides.

The Sticky Wicket is managed organically, using no harmful chemicals. "We are experimenting with companion planting, peat-free composts and every aspect of gardening in tune with nature," Pamela explained. She has outlined the challenge of creating meadows on clay in her book, *Making Wildflower Meadows.*

The first themed garden, The Round Garden, was a blaze of highly decorative plants, with a focus on scent and aroma. The Round Garden is in an open, sunny site and provides a nectar paradise for butterflies, bees and beneficial insects. Plants in colour ranges from pastel-pinks to lavender-blues, violet, magenta and crimson are softly spun together in circular beds. The plants include alliums, nepeta, geraniums, agastache, scabious, lavender, thyme, fennel, aster and phlox. *Verbena bonariensis* oregano, echinacea, sedum, buddliea and eupatorium are selected for being in the greatest abundance at the height of the butterfly season in August and September.

The cooling Frog Garden has been planted in shades of blue and yellow, with a wildlife pond and a bog as a central feature, surrounded by grass lawns managed to encourage wildflowers. By the pond, the specimen tree *Cornus controversa variegata* mingles with *Rodgersia podophylla,* and is surrounded by a selection of moisture-loving plants – *Deschampsia* 'Gold Veil', hosta 'Honey Bells', *Iris sibirica* 'Papillon' and *Persicaria bistorta superba.*

Plants in the Round Garden at the Sticky Wicket provide a nectar paradise for butterflies, bees and beneficial insects.

The Bird Garden is designed to attract and observe an increasing number of bird species, and explores the potential of pink, red and plum-coloured plants. Some of Pamela's favourite plants here are *Prunus padus* 'Colorata', *Clematis viticella* 'Purpurea Plena Elegans', *Papaver* 'Pattie's Plum', *Cimicifuga ramosa* 'Atropurpurea', *Miscanthus sinensis* 'Kleine Fontaine', *Angelica gigas* and *Ligularia dentata* 'Desdemona'. Seed heads are left for the birds, and together with grasses provide insect winter habitat, as well as dramatic skeletal interest in winter.

In the White Wilderness Garden, a long border shimmered with plants, and encompassed all the seasons and aspects of wildlife gardening. *Veronicastrum virginicum album* Culver's root, is a plant whose showy white spires I admired in many gardens in England. White potentilla flowered alongside *Galega officinalis alba*, white phlox, yarrow, echinacea 'White Swan', *Lysimachia clethroides*, *Artemesia lactiflora* 'Guizhou', *Sedum spectabile* 'Iceberg' and *Nicotiana sylvestris*, with the wildflower *Epilobium angustifolium album* Rosebay willow herb in full glory at the back of the border.

Many plants that bear fruit, berries or hips have white flowers, and Pam has used examples of these – cherries, crabapples, hawthorns, amelanchier, black currant, red currant and roses – as foundation plants for the white wilderness garden. Fragrant winter flowers often occur on berry-bearing, white-flowered shrubs such as osmanthus and sarcococca.

The New Hay Meadow, beyond the white garden, has been rewardingly restored since 1997 to rich flower status. Over thirty meadow species have been sown, including ragged robin, dyer's greenweed, yellow rattle, birdsfoot, trefoil, betony, devil's bit, scabious and orchids.

Many dry stone walls and log piles with turf incorporated have been built around the meadow to attract a wide range of fungi and insects as they biodegraded. These provide habitat for a range of creatures from reptiles to field mice, hedgehogs, slow worms, toads, mason bees and bumblebees, all of which like to nest in cavities.

The dovecote, home to cooing white doves.

The vegetable garden was aglow with the hot colours of companion plants – tansy, fennel, achillea, agrimony, goldenrod, rudbeckias, pot marigolds, nasturtiums and red, orange and yellow daylilies – while tall sunflowers attracted pollinating bees and provided seed for birds.

Colour-coordinated recycled plastic bottles were hanging throughout the vegetable garden containing lacewing 'hotels' to provide a habitat for beneficial aphid predators. Some were used as traps for weevils, earwigs or slugs, while others rattled against canes to scare away pheasants and wood pigeons.

This wildlife garden opened my eyes to the myriad ways home gardeners can work to enhance, attract and protect the valuable wildlife that plays such a crucial part in the health of our gardens, yet is so often sorely overlooked and neglected.

Dry stone walls provide habitat for a range of creatures, who like to nest in the cavities.

Third Week of July

Lazy, Hazy, Crazy Days of Summer

I don't know about you, but it's all happening in my garden right now. So much for the lazy, hazy, crazy days of summer! The crazy part is about right. I'm collecting seeds like crazy, taking cuttings like crazy, harvesting fruit, veggies and herbs like crazy, seeding winter veggies like crazy, pricking out seedlings like crazy and cleaning up the garden like crazy!

Since I got an irrigation system installed in the main garden, there's one thing that's not driving me crazy anymore – and that's dragging hoses around.

Not only does an automatic sprinkler system allow me more time for gardening, but it also conserves water. Each station runs for a set time and comes on early in the morning to prevent wastage from evaporation.

Overwetting?

Overwatering wastes water. Many plants require no more water than Mother Nature supplies, so gardeners often lavish their gardens with regular waterings unnecessarily. Half the water we put on our lawns is lost to runoff, when really it takes only one inch of water per week to ensure deeper root systems, which fare best in periods of hot, dry weather.

Having said that, it's important to remember that there's no such thing as a drought-tolerant plant until it's become well established. All plants need regular watering from the time they are planted until they are well rooted, but most take just one growing season to establish.

Slow-growing trees and shrubs can take two or more seasons. Watering newly planted shrubs often and lightly encourages roots to grow close to the surface, making them vulnerable to drought. Deeper root systems mean plants become drought tolerant once they are established and can be weaned off watering to the point where natural rainfall satisfies their needs.

TIPS:

- Avoid excessive water loss from evaporation by watering in the early morning (ideally before 9 a.m.).

- Avoid windy days to prevent wastage from wind drift.

- Add organic soil mulches to increase the water-holding capacity of the soil and lock in moisture.

Water is not an infinite resource, so by using it sparingly we help ensure there's enough for us all. A brown lawn, which recovers in fall, is a small sacrifice to make to conserve water. (See *Dry Gardens,* first week of April.)

Softwood Cuttings

Now's a good time to multiply some of your favourite woody plants by taking softwood cuttings from the current year's growth. It's often surprising how readily these cuttings will root.

Rule of Thumb

Your cutting should have some flexibility and bend without breaking. If it snaps when bent, the cutting is too woody; if it is very flexible between the fingers, it is too young. Ideally a cutting should be a skinny pencil width in thickness and will not snap or bend too easily. The length of a cutting will vary, but generally it should not be over six inches long.

Take cuttings early in the day to reduce water loss, and place in a rooting mix as soon as possible, removing the lower leaves. If you don't have time to prepare the cuttings immediately, put them in water or seal them in a damp plastic bag, and keep them in the shade, or a fridge, until you are ready to insert them.

Rooting Mix

Mix equal parts by volume of the following:
Coarse washed sand : perlite : peat
Optional: granular rock phosphate (1/6 of total)

The key to success is to use clean containers, and to prepare cuttings in a sterile environment. For the best results use a clean, sharp knife to prepare the cuttings. Trim the stem just below a node at the base, and above a pair of leaves at the top, ensuring that the growing tip of the cutting is upright. Using a dibber, place your cuttings into the rooting mix; several cuttings can be placed in one pot. Firm the cutting in, with the bottom pair of leaves just above the surface of the rooting mix. Label the pot carefully and water in thoroughly.

TIP: Use willow water (*Salix* spp.) as a rooting hormone. Salicylic acid is a natural rooting compound. Simply cut up sections of *Salix* and soak them in a small amount of water. Leave the cuttings to soak in willow water for 24 hours before potting them up. Water cuttings in with the remaining willow water.

Place cuttings in a sheltered place where they receive light, but are out of direct sun. Photosynthesis is necessary for the cuttings to grow and produce roots, so an adequate amount of filtered light is essential. Prevent cuttings from wilting by keeping them moist at all times. A spray mister works well for this.

Any attempts at flowering should be 'nipped in the bud' by removing the flowers. When the cuttings begin to grow or when roots emerge from the bottom of the pot, you will know the cuttings have rooted. They should then be potted on into their own pots in a soil-based growing medium that contains nutrients to support new growth.

Most perennials root within three to four weeks if taken while the plants are actively growing. Rooted cuttings taken later in the year will need winter protection in a greenhouse or on a sunny windowsill. They can then be potted on into four-inch pots in early spring.

Go ahead and experiment. Take cuttings from silver-leaved species such as lavender, santolina, senecio, sage and helichrysum now. Then trim the plants to shape, shearing off all spent flower stems down to new leafy growth.

Be brave with established plants, and cut them back to six inches (15 cm) above the ground. A good trim encourages vigorous flowering next year, and if done now, fresh foliage will have time to grow, so that plants will retain interest in fall and winter.

In July, take softwood cuttings of abelia, azalea, berberis, calluna, camellia, choisya, cornus, erica, escallonia, euonymus, garrya, helianthemum, kerria, kolkwitzia, lonicera, penstemon, philadelphus, potentilla, ribes, sarcococca, weigela, willow, wisteria and vitis.

Bay laurel is slow to root. Placing cuttings on bottom heat facilitates rooting. This cutting, taken in October, and placed on a heated propagation table was well-rooted by the following April.

Fourth Week of July

In the Flower Garden

- Divide colchicums, autumn crocuses, once the foliage has died down. If they are left congested they do not flower as well. Introduce some bulbs to other areas of the garden for an extended splash of purple in fall.

Colchicum, autumn crocus, 'The Giant' flowers in early fall.

- Cut delphiniums down to the ground as soon as they finish flowering and feed them with granular seaweed so they will produce a second flush of flowers in fall.

- Irises (apart from *Iris foetidissima*, grown for its colourful seed heads) should be deadheaded, so they put their energy into beefing up the rhizome, rather than going to seed.

- Encourage continued displays in planters and hanging baskets by regularly deadheading and feeding them.

- Encourage pansies and violas to reflower by shearing off the stems to within one inch of the base and covering with a sprinkling of screened compost mixed with sand.

- July is the last opportunity to trim fast-growing evergreen hedges such as cypress, *Lonicera nitida* and privet.

Violas will reflower if sheared back and topdressed with compost.

In the Greenhouse

- Damp down the greenhouse floor every morning on hot days to increase humidity. Plants love this and it helps discourage spider mites.

- Check for pests. Sticky yellow cards catch flying insects and alert you to potential problems before they establish.

- Remove diseased foliage and sweep the floor periodically to maintain a good level of hygiene.

- Regularly pinch out tomato suckers and tie vines to their supports. Feeding container grown plants regularly with liquid seaweed encourages greater fruit set.

- Pinch the tips of cucumber sideshoots to a couple of leaves beyond developing fruits. Picking cucumbers regularly encourages greater production.

In the Vegetable Garden

- Direct seed vegetables that are fast maturing, such as kohlrabi, turnips, radishes, arugula and winter lettuces.

- Put ripening squashes onto a bed of straw or (unpainted) wood to lift them up from the wet ground and away from bugs.

- Hoe emerging weed seedlings regularly between the vegetable rows.

- Check to see if shallots planted in the spring are ready for harvest.

- Harvest garlic when the tops have died back by two thirds. Do not wait until the tops have completely died down, as when the bulbs mature the cloves start separating and the garlic does not store well. Hang up in small bunches, in a warm dry place away from direct sunlight for drying.

- Turn and mix the compost heap. Mixing in grass cuttings, ready compost or manure helps speed up the breakdown process. *TIP:* Keep the hose running the whole time you are turning the pile, as in summer accumulated materials will be very dry. Aim for the consistency of a wrung-out sponge throughout the turned pile.

In the Fruit and Berry Patch

- Don't harvest rhubarb after the middle of July, as leaves and stalks become toxic due to a build-up of oxalic acid.

- Prune gooseberries after harvest by cutting the main shoots and sideshoots to five leaves. Next year's fruit will develop on new, one-year-old wood.

- Following the summer crop of raspberries, remove any brown canes that have fruited, cutting them down to the ground. For everbearing varieties, leave newer canes to produce the fruit in fall.

Stripping in the Garden!

- Don't throw away ruined pantyhose. Pantyhose strips are perfect for tying up perennials, annual vines, grapes, wisteria, climbing roses, tomatoes, eggplants, peppers and what have you. Cut pantyhose into one-inch wide stretchy strips, which will grip and hold and not cut into soft plant tissues. If you don't wear pantyhose, no problem – you can buy bags of them from any thrift store.

- Strip diseased or discoloured leaves from the base of tomatoes, eggplants and peppers. Check the undersides of leaves for colonies of whiteflies or aphids. Removal now prevents infestations later. Remove older leaves of beet greens, chards and perpetual spinach that have not been harvested. Leafminer damage shows up as tunneling in the leaves; flea beetle damage appears as little round holes in the leaves. By stripping them now you will prevent a build-up of these pests in the garden.

So Many Weeds…So Little Time!

Everything is growing at a real pace now, especially those confounded weeds! Take up arms against weeds while they are easy to extract. Prevention is always better than cure. Good cultivation techniques – hoeing, mulching, mowing, digging and improving drainage on heavy soils – keeps weeds at bay.

Hilda's Polish Fruit Platz

Preheat oven to 375°F (190°C)

Base:
Sift together:
2 cups flour
2 tsp. baking powder
1/2 cup sugar

Cream:
1/2 cup oil
1/2 cup sour cream (leave 3 tsp. for topping)
2 eggs
1 tsp. vanilla
1 tsp. lemon zest (use orange zest for rhubarb)

Blend the wet and dry mixtures, and press lightly onto a 9" x 13" baking pan.

Add 4 cups fruit – apricots, blackberries, blueberries, plums, rhubarb (use orange zest), strawberries, raspberries, cherries. Sprinkle 1-2 Tbsp. cornstarch over fruit to set (how much depends on how juicy the fruit is).

Topping:
1/2 cup sugar
3/4 cup flour
1/4 cup butter, chilled and cut into pieces

Rub gently together with your fingertips into a coarse, crumbly texture. Add 3 tsp. sour cream and lightly bring the mixture together into larger 'clumps'.

Sprinkle the topping over the fruit. Bake for 25 minutes covered with foil, and 20 minutes uncovered, until the top is lightly browned. Serve warm or cold. (Freezes well too).

Annual weeds germinating in the border should be hoed up and left to dry, before being added to the compost pile. Do not add weeds that have already gone to seed unless you compost at high temperatures or have solarized them in black plastic bags.

Dandelions and docks, perennial weeds with deep tap roots, are much easier to deal with when small. Be sure to remove the entire root, as any segment left behind will produce a new plant.

Pernicious creeping weeds, such as bindweed or ground elder, have long underground roots. Watch out for new growth and dig it out as soon as possible. This work is back-breaking, but rewarding in the long run.

Taking the Work Out of Weeding

- If it has just rained, this is the time to weed! Instead of digging, tugging and cursing embedded weeds, they will now leap out of the soft, damp earth into your hand!

- If there's no rain in sight, watering deeply the day before pulling deep-rooted weeds will make the job easier.

- Never let weeds flower and go to seed! If you don't have time to pull them out, lop off the tops with a scythe, hedge clipper, rotary trimmer or mower. This will keep them in check until you have time to pull them out.

- Use a hoe or three-pronged cultivator a couple of times a week between rows in the vegetable bed to remove young weeds as they spring up.

- Mulch between plants to prevent weeds from establishing. Cardboard or newspapers (no coloured inks) held down with stones work well, or use layers of clean straw (no weed seeds).

- Kill weeds growing between cracks in the pavement and patio by pouring boiling water over them.

- Eradicate immature weeds by spraying them with undiluted vinegar. Acetic acid (4.5%) penetrates and kills roots. Several sprayings may be necessary if weeds have become more established.

Questions & Answers

Erin: I want to grow a vegetable garden in an area that is infested with morning glory. Can you suggest a good way I can get rid of this invasive weed? I cannot till the area until I do or I will be compounding my problem a thousandfold!

Answer: I've had past success getting rid of morning glory by sheet mulching. Lay folded cardboard boxes over the problem area and cover with a one-foot deep layer of leaves, compost or manure. After one growing season the boxes will have started to break down. Pull back the top layer to reveal the long white strands of fleshy morning glory roots, which will have surfaced to the cardboard in desperate search of air and light. Peel up the roots to eradicate them from the area. Rake the rest of the organic material back over the bed. Your problem will be solved and the area will be amended at the same time!

I used a similar method to fight back an area infested by *Equisetum* horsetail by laying jute-backed carpets over it. These prevented moisture, light and air from reaching the soil. The carpets lasted for two years before showing signs of disintegrating, by which time the horsetail was extremely stressed, and did not resurface. (Of course over time *Equisetum* will re-establish, but we are now using this area as a chicken run, so the 'girls' will take care of the horsetail, and we'll get mineral-rich eggs!)

The girls! Chickens make perfect cultivators and de-buggers, and provide manure and eggs to boot.

August

I think that I shall never see
A poem lovely as a tree.
A tree whose hungry mouth is pressed
Against the earth's sweet flowing breast;
A tree that looks at God all day,
And lifts her leafy arms to pray;
A tree that may in Summer wear
A nest of robins in her hair;
Upon whose bosom snow has lain
Who intimately lives with rain.
Poems are made by fools like me,
But only God can make a tree.

Joyce Kilmer

Fang Zhang

First Week of August

Too Dry?

- When planting during dry spells, if you dig down and find bone-dry soil, fill the planting hole with water and allow it to soak in before planting. Then soak again from the top after planting.

- If you find a plant in drought stress, give the poor blighter a jolly good root soak! Turn the hose on and leave it running gently over the root zone of the droughted plant so the water soaks in around the roots and does not just run off. This will perk up the plant and help it to survive for the rest of the season.

- It's very stressful for new plants to get established in hot, dry weather. Tempting as it may be, it's best to wait for fall before introducing new plants to your garden – especially shrubs and trees. Fall brings cooler weather with more humidity, which is much easier on bare root and container stock having to adapt to a new garden.

Busy Little Bees

The pollination of flowers enables plants to bear fruit and set seed for future generations. 75% of our food plants depend on being fertilized by pollination. Bees are the number one pollinators on earth, responsible for pollinating one third of the crops that feed us, so we should be concerned about protecting their well-being.

> 70-90% of the indigenous bee population in the US has been lost to urban sprawl and the widespread use of pesticides.
> *The Forgotten Pollinators* by Steve Buchman

There are tens of thousands of different bee species worldwide, which fall either into the category of social bees, such as the honey bees and bumble bees that live in hives, or solitary bees that live and nest alone. Solitary bees lay eggs in their own nests, from which young bees emerge in spring to feed on nectar, and pollinate flowers in the process.

> The number of bumble bee species in the UK has fallen from nineteen to six.
> Naomi Saville
> Cambridge University, Department Zoology

The blue orchard mason bee, *Osmia lignaria,* is a solitary, indigenous bee that nests in forested areas on both coasts of North America. This wood-dwelling bee emerges when the temperature reaches 14°C. It's no coincidence that this is also the temperature when fruit trees blossom. Where I live on Vancouver Island, blue orchard mason bees are very effective pollinators, visiting up to 2,000 blossoms a day. They are a shiny, blue-black colour, and are slightly smaller than a honey bee, making these non-aggressive bees easily mistakable for bluebottle flies.

Because bees are the principle source of pollination for flowers, fruits and vegetables, it's in the gardener's interest to provide a healthy, pesticide-free habitat for them. Here are ways to encourage pollinating bees in your garden:

- Blue orchard mason bees pollinate plants close to their nests as they have a limited foraging range of 100 yards. Provide them with nesting boxes, which are simple to make or can be purchased. Make sure the nesting cavities are in stackable layers (see photo), so they can be removed and cleaned out to prevent the spread of deadly bee mites.

A condominium of bee boxes

- Leave dead wood, branches and tree trunks in the garden for wood-dwelling bees to nest in.

- Leave areas of non-cultivated, undisturbed soil for bumble bees, which live in the ground.

- Grow single flowers in blue, yellow and purple, which attract native bees, that bloom in April to early June when bees are collecting nectar and building their nests.

- Provide a constant source of flowers for bumble and honey bees, which feed for the whole growing season. Short-tongued bees like the shallow flowers of the Umbelliferae, Brassica and Compositae family. Long-tongued bees are attracted to flowers with deep corollas, such as larkspur, columbine, snapdragon, mint and members of the Solanaceae family.

- Double flowers do not attract bees. They are showy, but produce less pollen.

- Native plants provide a good source of food for bees.

- Provide a shallow water source for bees to dip and sip in, and to make mud for nesting.

- Avoid pesticide use. Residues on flowers can be fatal to bees. If control is necessary, use the least toxic product, and spray late in the evening when bees are not flying.

Handy Harvesting Tips

Freezing corn - Freeze corn fresh. Fresh corn is the sweetest, as sugars convert to starch after it is picked. Peel off the outer wrapper layer, leaving the remaining light husk layer, and freeze the corn in a plastic bag. To cook, strip off the husk layer and drop the still-frozen corncob into boiling water for exactly ten minutes. The corn will taste as good as the day it was harvested!

Extend the life of lettuce - Remove damaged outer leaves and seal lettuce in a clean plastic bag without air holes; natural moisture keeps it fresher longer. Leaving the roots on when harvesting extends the life of lettuce when refrigerated.

Onions make you cry? - Keep tears away when preparing onions by chilling them before you

cut. Cold slows down the movement of volatile 'tear gas'. If you are already weeping, place your wrists together and run cold water over them, which immediately clears the air and stems the tears.

Storing half an onion - If you only need half an onion, use the half that sprouts. Store the root end because it will keep longer in the refrigerator. (Store in an airtight container to keep the strong smell from spreading.)

Prevent celery droop - Cut off the stalk ends and stand in a jug of cold water in the fridge until they get crispy again. Celery can be stored in airtight containers or plastic bags until eaten.

Get the gas out of beans - Soak the beans and throw the soaking water away (or water your houseplants with it), then cook the beans in fresh boiling water. Or purchase a bottle of Beano™. A drop of this in the first mouthful of your bean dish will help prevent any embarrassing after-effects!

For the tastiest beans - Use the freshest beans possible (avoid cracked and shriveled dried beans). Do not add salt to the water until they are cooked thoroughly, as it interferes with the tenderizing process.

For garlic lovers - Soak garlic cloves in boiling water for five minutes, so the skins will slip off easily. Mince peeled cloves into small chunks and spoon into a jar. Cover with olive oil, and refrigerate. Garlic in oil keeps refrigerated for up to three weeks.

Ripen green tomatoes - Seal green tomatoes in a brown paper bag with an apple. Apples release ethylene, which speeds up ripening.

Freeze tomatoes whole - Freeze cherry or smaller tomatoes whole in freezer bags. Larger tomatoes are best quartered. There's no need to thaw them before using; frozen tomatoes are best if added directly to the recipe.

Preserving 'speared' potatoes - If you accidentally spear potatoes when harvesting (and who doesn't?), clean them up and refrigerate in cold water in an airtight container. They'll keep this way quite a long time.

Second Week of August

Flowers for Special Occasions

Here's a list of garden flowers to make wonderful summer arrangements:
achillea 'The Pearl', crocosmia, dahlias, ferns for greenery, gladiola, gypsophila 'Baby's Breath', hydrangea 'Brussels Lace', Japanese anemones, lavatera 'Mont Blanc' or 'Silver Cup', leycesteria 'Himalayan Honeysuckle', lilies, matricaria 'Bridal Robe', oregano 'Hopley's Purple', phlox, salal for greenery, statice, sunflowers, verbena.

Recipes from the Garden

Summer Wine Bowl

Perfect for summer entertaining, offer this refreshing, light wine punch to your guests.

Makes 1.5 litres of punch:

2 Tbsp. granulated sugar
1/4 cup brandy
1/2 cup fresh mint sprigs
1 long strip orange rind
1 bottle (750 ml) dry white wine
1 tray ice cubes
1 orange, thinly sliced and seeded
1 1/2 cups (375ml) soda water

Several hours before serving (or the night before), stir together the brandy and sugar in a large bowl until the sugar has dissolved. Add the mint and orange rind, and press with the back of a wooden spoon to release the flavours. Stir in the wine. Cover and chill.

At serving time, remove the mint and orange rind with a slotted spoon. Stir in the ice, orange slices and soda water. Serve from a punch bowl garnished with fresh mint sprigs.

Eating outdoors in summer can be a nightmare because of wasps. Discover the power of cloves, which keep wasps away. Place several small dishes filled with ground or whole cloves (or a mix of both) around food tables – and watch wasps disappear!

Asparagus (or Broccoli) Ricotta Quiche

Preheat the oven to 375°F (190°C)

The 'You-Can't-Go-Wrong' Shortcrust Pastry Recipe:
2 1/2 cups unbleached white flour (or use 50% whole wheat pastry flour)
1/2 lb. chilled butter (or 1/4 lb. butter and 1/4 lb. vegetable shortening), cut into large pieces
Pinch of salt
1 large egg (or 2 small eggs) beaten, made up to 125 ml of liquid with cold water

In a mixing bowl blend the flour, salt and shortening with two knives or a pastry cutter, until it begins to form into clumps. Add the egg mix, using a fork to gently form the mixture into a ball. (Handle the pastry as little as possible). If too wet, dust with flour; if too dry, add a few drops of water.

Place the pastry on a lightly floured surface. Dust it with lightly with flour. Roll it into a circle of even thickness, until the circle is large enough to fit into the quiche dish, leaving a one-inch rim to flop over the edge of the dish. Tuck the excess rim under and crimp it between your fingers to make the decorative edge for the quiche. Put the dish lined with pastry in the fridge to chill.

Filling:
Layer the filling into the pastry-lined dish in the following order:

1 lb. asparagus (or broccoli), chopped, lightly steamed and cooled (or substitute 1lb. of spinach or 1 large cauliflower)
1 bunch of green onions, chopped
3 cloves garlic, minced
2 cups ricotta cheese
2 cups grated Swiss, Cheddar or Fontina cheese (your choice)

Custard:
5 eggs
1 1/2 cups light (half and half) cream
2 Tbsp. flour
1 tsp. salt
1 tsp. ground black pepper
2 tsp. fresh basil leaves, chopped (1 tsp. dried)
3 sprigs fresh parsley, chopped
Grated rind of one lemon
1/2 tsp. nutmeg (optional)

Mix above into a smooth custard in a blender. Pour over the filling. (Do not overfill or it will spill out and create burning smoke in the oven.)

Reduce oven to 350°F (175°C). Place the quiche on the middle shelf. Bake for 45 minutes, until the custard has set and the quiche is nicely browned. (Place foil over the top to stop it from browning if you need to bake for longer to set the custard.)

Leave to stand for 10 minutes before serving.

Serve hot or cold with a garden salad and/or new potatoes, boiled with a sprig of garden mint.

Salad Niçoise

Simple and Elegant!
(Serves one, so multiply for guests)
Preparation Time: 15 minutes

1 1/2 cups green leaf lettuce
   (buttercrunch is my favourite for
   this recipe)
1 can tuna (or smoked tofu, grated)
1 hard boiled egg, quartered
6 cooked tender green beans
4 cherry tomatoes, halved
6 black olives, pitted

Toss with a homemade vinaigrette and
serve with a warmed baguette.

Scott's Salsa Recipe

8 medium tomatoes, diced
1 onion, chopped
1 green pepper, diced
1 fresh jalapeno*, diced
2 cloves garlic, minced
2 tsp. salt
2 tsp. ground cumin powder
1 bunch fresh coriander, chopped
1 Tbsp. olive oil

*Broil jalapeno to loosen the skin, then
peel it off. If you like your salsa hot, leave
the seeds; if not, remove them now.

Sauté the onion and green pepper with
the spices (except fresh coriander) in a
little olive oil. When slightly soft add the
tomatoes. Allow to simmer until the sauce
begins to thicken, but the tomatoes are not
mushy. Add the coriander. Allow to cool.

Will keep refrigerated for up to a week.
The flavours will intensify the longer it sits.

Bruschetta

Preheat oven to 300°F (150°C)

Topping:
Diced tomatoes lightly drizzled with extra
   virgin olive oil
Finely minced red onions
Salt & pepper to taste
Fresh basil, chopped

Lightly toast slices of baguette or ciabatta
bread which have been lightly brushed
with olive oil and sprinkled with parmesan
cheese. Cover with the topping.

Place in oven for 5 minutes. Serve warm.

Roasted Tomatoes

Intensify the flavour of your homegrown
tomatoes!

(1 to 2 hours roasting time)
Preheat oven to 350°F (175°C)

5 lbs. whole washed roma tomatoes
2 Tbsp. extra virgin olive oil
2 tsp. salt
1 tsp. freshly ground pepper

Place tomatoes in a single layer in a large
roasting pan, lined with parchment paper.
Drizzle with olive oil and season with salt
and pepper.

Put the pan, uncovered, in the oven and
roast the tomatoes for 1 to 2 hours until
they have reduced in size by one-third and
are lightly browned on top. Let cool for 15
minutes. Add to a multiple of recipes, or
just eat on a cracker or with nacho chips.

Tomato Purée

Place the roasted tomatoes and juice into
a blender, and blend 'til smooth.

Freeze the purée in all sizes of containers,
from big batch sauce size right down to
ice cube trays (place the frozen cubes into
freezer bags). Use the purée as a base for
spaghetti, chili, soup...whatever.

Roasting tomatoes adds more 'Oomph'
to them!

Feature of the Month
Pick a Peck of Perfect Peppers

The greenhouse in August is full of dazzling rows of ripening peppers – a multicoloured spectacle of peppers changing to either red, orange, yellow or brown, depending on the variety. Normally grown as annuals on the west coast, peppers are actually tender perennials, needing maximum sunshine and warm sheltered sites to thrive.

For the best yields it's advisable to get an early start on the season. Start pepper seeds in late February, under grow lights indoors or on bottom heat in a greenhouse. They germinate best around 75°F (23°C), and can take anywhere from one to four weeks to germinate. Then they grow best at 70°F (21°C) during the day, and no lower than 60°F (15°C) at night.

Peppers don't like warm days followed by cool nights, so it's best to wait until the soil has really warmed up in early June before setting them out. Peppers belong to the Solanaceae family, so avoid blight by not planting them where tomatoes, eggplants, peppers and potatoes have grown before.

They grow best in moist warm soils, between 65-80°F (18-26°C), in a neutral pH around 6.5. Kelp meal and a handful of rock phosphate in the planting hole will provide the high levels of phosphorus and potash needed for fruit production. A handful of dolomite lime will prevent calcium deficiency, which causes blossom end rot, a common problem for peppers.

TIP: Create a mini-greenhouse around your pepper plants. Hammer a cedar stake into each corner of the pepper patch; wrap 6 ml plastic around the outside of the stakes, stapling it onto each stake to hold it tightly in place. A lightweight plastic roof can also be framed up and used for extra protection during cold nights.

Try growing peppers in black plastic two-gallon pots, one pepper plant in each pot. A length of sturdy bamboo or a tomato cage is enough to support the bushy plants. The pots can be placed in a greenhouse, or on a hot deck or patio, so you can enjoy your colourful peppers up close and personal and regularly pick a peck of perfect peppers.

TIP: Foliar feeding with liquid seaweed throughout the season encourages greater fruit set. Blossom end rot results from irregular watering, so consistent daily watering is very important.

Garden Path favourites:
(Heat scale sweet to hot 1-5)
Pimiento (1): thick-walled, very sweet, juicy slicer for salads, sandwiches, stuffing and baking.
Italian Sweet and **Red Bull's Horn** (1): thin-walled, slightly tapered, sweet red peppers good for roasting and stuffing.
California Wonder (1): thick-walled, blocky green bell peppers, good for salads, dips and baking.
Dainty Sweet and **Jingle Bells** (1): smaller, multicoloured ornamental peppers for sweet eating.
Gypsy (1): high yields of slightly tapered, yellow peppers which grow well in cooler conditions, good for fresh eating and stuffing.
Klari Baby Cheese (1): bell peppers, the shape of a baby gouda cheese, great for fresh eating, roasting and stuffing.
Chocolate Bell (1): thick-walled, juicy, dark bell peppers, good for eating fresh, dips and stuffing.
Tequila Sunrise (2): orange, carrot-shaped, thin-walled peppers with a slight kick, good for pickling, drying and roasting.
Ancho (2) (also called Poblano): dark green, tapered fruits with slightly hot, distinctive flavour in Mexican cuisine for stuffing and sauces.
Hungarian Black (3): extremely early, small pointy black fruits, good for eating fresh, drying and roasting.
Early Jalapeno (3): medium-hot peppers, ideal for salsas and pickling.
Starburst (4): smaller, tapered multicoloured ornamental peppers for hot eating and drying.
Habanero, Scotch Bonnet, Serrano (5): smaller peppers 'Hot enough to blow your head off!'

Take the heat out of peppers
The seeds and placenta contain capsaicinoids that give hot peppers their mouth-searing pungency. Use hot peppers with extreme caution. If your head is about to 'blow off', eat dairy products or starchy foods such as bread or rice. Do not drink cold water, which will actually increase the heat. Handle the seeds of hot peppers with respect. Don't rub your eyes or inhale too deeply around them, or you'll be sorry.

Growing peppers through black landscape fabric holds the warmth in the soil and gives peppers a good start when you first plant them out, which gives you better yields later on.

Stuffed Peppers

Preparation time: 30 minutes
Cooking time: 35 minutes
Preheat oven to 350°F (175°C)

6 large peppers or 8 medium peppers, cut
  in half, seeds removed
Steam peppers above boiling water for
5 minutes.

3 Tbsp. butter (or olive oil)
1 large, sweet onion, finely chopped
2 tsp. garlic, minced
1 cup frozen peas

Sauté for 5 minutes.

Mix with:
3 cups cooked rice (brown or white)
1 tsp. sunflower seeds
1 Tbsp. dried fruit (e.g. blueberries,
  cranberries or currants)
1 1/2 tsp. salt
1 tsp. ground black pepper
1 tsp. green peppercorns (optional)
Finely chopped fresh garden herbs (or
  dried). Choose from parsley, parcel, dill,
  oregano, sweet marjoram, or mint.
3 Tbsp. olive oil

Stuff the peppers with the rice mix and lay
on a baking sheet. Top with 4 oz. mozzarella
mixed with 4 oz. cheddar cheese (optional).
Cover with aluminum foil while baking for
30 minutes.

Remove the foil for the last 5 minutes to
brown the cheese.

Serve warm with a green or tomato salad.
Great for potlucks or picnics!

Tender Eggplants

When you see the beautiful, star-shaped purple blossoms of eggplants, you might decide to grow them for their flowers alone. Eggplants are a tender, warm-weather plant that produce best in long, hot summers, so it's important to get an early start on the growing season.

Start the seeds of eggplants at least eight to ten weeks before setting them out. They germinate in soil temperatures of 75-90°F (23-32°C). Providing seed trays with bottom heat or growing them under grow lights speeds up germination.

Plant eggplant seedlings out in early June, as soon as the soil has thoroughly warmed up, in fertile, well-drained garden loam with a pH around 6.0. The best place to plant seedlings is a south facing, sheltered location with reflected heat off a wall, or where they receive at least eight hours of hot sun a day. These tender beauties require average temperatures of between 70-85°F (21-29°C), as the fruit will not set if temperatures fall below 65°F (18°C).

I get around the fact that we don't get long, hot summers by growing eggplants in five-gallon pots in the greenhouse. The bushy plants grow about two to three feet tall, and only require a short stake or tomato cage for support. I fill the containers with screened compost mixed with a good scoop of balanced organic fertilizer, and plant one seedling per five-gallon container.

'Dusky' and 'Vernal' will produce large, eight-inch oval black fruits in cooler growing conditions. For reliable and early production, grow Japanese varieties with long, slender, purple fruits, such as 'Ichiban' – perfect for Oriental dishes. Choose a variety with days to maturity suited to your particular growing conditions.

Mini eggplants such as 'Apple Green' or 'Antigua' are extra-early and productive, setting smaller fruits that mature earlier than other types. The flavourful egg-shaped fruits are three to five inches long, with thin skin that does not need to be peeled.

Eggplants *(Solanum melongena esculentum)*, are in the nightshade family, Solanaceae, and are related to tomatoes, peppers and potatoes. They can be bothered by a number of pests ranging from aphids, Colorado potato beetles, cutworms, flea beetles and tomato hornworms. They can also be infected by fruit rot and verticillium wilt, especially in cooler climates.

Having said all this, the only problem I have ever had growing eggplants has been aphids, a problem easily remedied by spraying plants with insecticidal soap. So don't let this list of pests and diseases deter you from growing them.

TIP: To avoid potential problems, practise crop rotation by not planting eggplants where you have grown tomatoes, peppers or potatoes before.

Eggplants are ready to harvest when the skin is glossy and smooth. Dull skin is an indication that they are overripe, and will be tough and bitter as a result. They produce between three to five fruits per plant, depending on the variety, which will keep up for two weeks after harvest. The 'minis' with smaller fruits are a lot more productive.

Italians grow varieties with snow-white flesh, considered to have the best flavour of all. 'Casper' is a variety of white eggplant that can be found in seed catalogues. It is a compact plant producing six-inch, ivory-white fruits with mild flesh, and skin that does not require peeling. 'Ping Tung Long' is a variety from Taiwan, considered the most spectacular eggplant available to gardeners. The fruits are just over one inch in diameter, but grow up to twelve inches long, and the shiny, dark-lavender skin glows and radiates beauty in the garden. The traditional variety from Thailand, 'Thai Green', has gained a reputation for its distinctive taste. The slender twelve-inch fruits have tender, light green skin with tasty flesh that absorbs spicy flavours well.

Eggplants are so versatile they appear in many ethnic dishes. The French put them in ratatouille, the Greeks put them in moussaka, the Italians use them in eggplant parmigiana, grilled vegetable paninis and lasagnas, and in the Middle East they are used to prepare a delicious spread or dip called baba ganouji.

The best news of all is that eggplants are low in calories (only 27 per cup), high in fibre and also a good source of vitamin B2.

Although not always the easiest vegetable to grow, it's a rewarding and delicious experience preparing eggplants harvested from your garden, and I wouldn't be without the sight of those gorgeous purple flowers for anything!

Eggplant Parmigiana

Preheat oven to 400°F (200°C)
Preparation time: 15 minutes
(Serves 4 to 6 people)

1-2 large eggplants, sliced 3/4" thick
1 cup flour
1 egg, beaten with a little milk
Breadcrumbs
Olive oil
1/2 lb. Mozzarella cheese, sliced
6 oz. tomato paste
Dash of red wine
1 tsp. oregano
1 clove of garlic, minced
Salt & pepper to taste
1 cup grated parmesan cheese

Dip slices of eggplant in flour, then the egg mix and then into breadcrumbs until they are well coated. Heat olive oil in frying pan and sauté the coated slices until they are tender and browned on both sides. Add extra oil if needed.

Mix tomato paste with a little red wine, oregano, salt, pepper and minced garlic.

Arrange the browned eggplant slices in a single layer on a greased baking dish. Place a slice of mozzarella cheese on each one, spread with 2-3 tablespoons of the tomato sauce, and top with grated parmesan.

Bake for 15 minutes. Serve steaming hot with a side salad.

Third Week of August

Bring on the Biennials

A biennial is a plant that flowers and goes to seed in its second year, which means you need to plant them in fall to get a colourful show for the following spring. A lot of wonderful spring flowering plants fall into this category, and there are two characteristics that make them even more desirable to grow. One is that if you let some go to seed, you'll get lots of free volunteers the following spring. Two is that they grow well in full or part sun, so will grow just about anywhere in the garden.

Foxgloves

Foxglove seedlings should be planted out now. *TIP:* They are best planted in groups of threes. Try *Digitalis purpurea* 'Apricot Beauty' or *D. purpurea* 'Alba' for an elegant show that brightens up shady areas of the garden.

Digitalis purpurea *'Apricot Beauty'*

Sweet Williams

For gardeners who love fragrance, Sweet Williams are it! Lovely clusters of blooms will fill any room with their heady perfume. They grow happily in full to part sun and also work well in planters.

Forget-Me-Nots

The legend of how myosotis, a little blue flower, earned its name dates back to Adam's naming of all the plants and animals in the Garden of Eden. Adam overlooked the forget-me-not, and when it cried out, he pledged it would never be forgotten again!

Adam was right…once you introduce this pretty blue flower to the garden you'll never forget it, as it's a prolific self-seeder that pops up all over the place. It's particularly happy growing in part sun and moist soils, but grows easily anywhere. If you decide *enough already!* just pull it up after flowering, before it sets seed.

Wallflowers

Wallflowers, *Cheiranthus* spp., range in colour from maroon to golden yellow to orange-red. The will sweetly scent the April and May garden, and make wonderful fragrant spring bouquets. If you prune them before they set seed, you will get another season of bloom from them next spring.

Campanula

Campanula spp. are rampant self-seeders, with bell-shaped flowers that provide big blasts of colour from soft blue to deep blue. They sometimes have white or pink bells too. Campanulas make colourful long-lasting spring bouquets.

Clary Sage

Everyone marvels when *Salvia sclarea* clary sage, does its thing. This striking, aromatic plant wins admiration with silvery spikes of papery-purple bracts. It's almost impossible to find this plant at garden centres, so you'll have to grow it from seed in spring. Simply shake out a few seeds before cutting it down if you want to grow it again next year.

Sweet Rocket

Hesperis matronalis sweet rocket has got almost everything going for it. Its big clusters of phlox-like, purple or white scented flowers on three-foot plants are a mainstay in early spring borders. Sweet rocket is easy to grow, drought tolerant, grows in part-shade to full sun, has beautiful fragrant cut flowers and is a rampant self-seeder. What more could a gardener ask for?

Let's Hear it for Hydrangeas!

Appreciated for showy clusters of flowers in white, red, pink or blue, it's around this time that we can enjoy the free-flowering show from hydrangeas. Hydrangeas kick in with their colourful spectacle while other plants are fading. The name should tell you the most important thing about these plants – they are water-loving and need moisture to thrive. They grow best in fertile soil in light shade, with varying degrees of protection against frost.

Hydrangea macrophylla, bigleaf hydrangeas, are divided into the mopheads and the lacecaps. Mopheads have large ball-like flowers. The lacecaps are prettier, with smaller fertile flowers surrounded by a mass of larger sterile florets.

The colour of hydrangeas is affected by the amount of aluminum available to the plants. Aluminum is present in all soils, but its availability to plants depends on the acidity of the soil. With a change of half a point on the pH scale, the colour of the flowers can change from pink or red to blue.

To change the colour of hydrangeas to blue, lower the pH by adding aluminum sulfate at the rate of one pound to seven gallons of water. Soak the ground in the spring every two weeks as necessary to lower the pH half a point. To change colour to pink or red, raise the pH half a point by adding lime at the rate of five pounds per 100 square feet in spring or fall.

One of my favourites is the more temperamental *Hydrangea aspera,* an imposing sight with huge, ten-inch, porcelain-blue ringed with lilac-pink lacecap blooms against large, soft, woolly leaves. Unless given protection from wind and sun, these large soft leaves get raggedy or sun scorched fast, so find a sheltered location for them to thrive.

Hydrangea paniculata 'Grandiflora', or Pee Gee hydrangeas as they are commonly called, are tall shrubs bearing large, white cone-shaped flowers in August/September. A mature Pee Gee is so showy that it's worthy of a place of honour as a small specimen tree in the garden. The large flowering panicles turn from creamy white to deep pink as fall progresses, a colour change that becomes a real head-turner! This hydrangea will benefit from a hard pruning every year.

In my opinion, second only to this show are the white lacecap flowers of a mature specimen of *Hydrangea petiolaris,* a slow-growing, self-clinging climber. Patience is a virtue, but the spectacle of billowy-white lacecaps covering a wall or climbing up a tree is worth the wait.

Hydrangea quercifolia, oakleaf hydrangea is grown for stunning fall foliage and its long, cone-shaped, white flowers. The deeply lobed, oak-like leaves turn deep burgundy in fall, an even more brilliant show when grown in full sun.

The latest rage is *Hydrangea macrophylla* 'Lemon Wave', with marbled yellow, cream and green leaves, highlighted by gentian-blue lacecap flowers. This shrub provides an exquisite show of delicate flowers against striking foliage – a winning combination that's hard to beat.

Phormiums Add Drama

Dramatic is the best way to describe the impact phormiums have in the garden – those with bold coloured, wide sword leaves in particular. There are numerous phormium cultivars to choose from, and the colours range widely. Most were first grown in New Zealand by Duncan and Davis, who introduced them to Europe.

Phormiums are among the finest of architectural plants. I highly value the sight of the leathery, sword-like leaves when backlit by the sun. Heavy snowfalls may bend some of the leaves double

Phormium *'Maori Chief'* is very effective underplanted with Alchemilla mollis *lady's mantle.*

and crease them, but once the roots have found their way deep into the soil, plenty of new foliage will take their place.

Phormium tenax, New Zealand flax, may flower from time to time, but the best leaf forms hardly ever do. They are perfect in key positions, such as beside steps or at the end of walkways, but they also look snazzy in pots. Make sure to grow them in sturdy containers, as the roots have enough strength to crack terra cotta and even concrete! For the long term you may want to plant them in a wooden barrel girdled with iron bands!

Phormiums are best planted in early spring. Adding plenty of compost to the site encourages the fleshy roots to proliferate. Once established, they will thrive in difficult situations, but they prefer a moist soil that does not dry out in full sun, and in extreme conditions will benefit from some protection over the winter.

After a deep winter freeze, many gardeners lose phormiums, or the tops turn brown and look dead. If the roots survive, cut them back to the ground, and wait for new leaves to emerge from the centre. After a few years in good soil, *Phormium tenax* will be properly established, and some varieties can top six feet with a width of three feet across. If that doesn't add a touch of drama to your garden, nothing will!

Heritage Hollyhocks

There's no plant that typifies English cottage gardens more than hollyhocks. A stately perennial, *Althaea rosea* makes the finest of background plants in the border. It has the highest powers of attraction when grown as a showpiece against a south facing wall or along a fence, where it relishes the reflected heat. If seeds are sown early in the year blooms may appear the same year, but normally the hollyhock performs as a biennial in its second year. On the temperate west coast, hollyhocks often grow as perennials and over time you can expect many spires of blooms from one established plant. They also self-seed readily.

Ever since collecting seeds of the heritage Point Ellice House hollyhocks (1867-1914), I have been enamoured with the tenacity of these plants, whose seeds can lie dormant for decades.

The main drawback with hollyhocks is rust. Picking off the lower infected leaves as the plant grows stops the spread of this unsightly problem. Even if it's necessary to strip off all the leaves, it will not affect flowering.

Hollyhocks thrive best on neglect. Established plants growing in hot, dry sites without regular watering tend not to suffer as badly from rust. Humidity spreads fungal spores, so dry heat is a solution to this problem.

Althaea rosea *hollyhocks typify English cottage gardens.*

Fourth Week of August

Container Gardening

How can gardeners run out of space when containers offer so many creative gardening possibilities? Container planting expresses our unique personalities and reflects the feel of our gardens. Anything goes – you can be dramatic or subdued, the beauty being that it can all change from one year to another.

Basic considerations

- Plants in pots dry out quickly, especially on a concrete patio in full sun. Feel the soil in containers to be certain the plants are getting enough water.

- Water regularly, at least daily in hot weather, and apply water slowly until it runs out from the drainage holes.

- Make contingency plans if you're going away. Place your most valuable plants in shallow saucers in a shaded corner, and fill saucers with water. (Don't do this with succulents. Just give them a good drink before you go and set them out of full sun.)

- Clay pots breathe, allowing faster water loss through evaporation, so you may need to water plants in terra cotta pots more than those in plastic pots.

- Small pots dry out more quickly than large planters, so be sure to choose a container large enough to prevent plant roots from drying out too fast.

- Ensure that drainage is good. Any plant sitting in stagnant, saturated conditions will rot.

- Deadheading improves the quality and duration of the show.

- Topdress established planters with screened compost every year to provide ongoing feeding to plants throughout the season.

- Do not allow plants to become rootbound in their containers. At the first signs of stress, check the roots and if necessary move the plants into a larger container.

Container Vegetables

Many gardeners don't grow vegetables because they don't have a vegetable garden, but anyone can grow beans, peas, salad greens or herbs in a container, window box or half oak barrel. I grow bumper crops of cucumbers, peppers, eggplants, basil and tomatoes in large five-gallon containers.

Free-draining soil with adequate drainage is imperative, or the soil will dry out, compact and strangle the roots. An adequate level of fertility is needed to feed the plants throughout the season. This can be achieved by incorporating compost or granular organic fertilizer into the mix or liquid feeding on a regular basis. A regular watering routine is important, as once the roots fill the containers, they start to dry out fast.

Screened compost is rich in nutrients and light enough to sustain the healthiest of plant growth for a bumper crop of vegetables. A watering of liquid seaweed from time to time really boosts fruit production, and gives plants extra resistance to the stress of being grown in confined conditions.

North Country is a low-growing, compact bush that will yield 2-5 pounds of sweet blueberries when container grown.

How to Grow Lovely Leeks

Leeks are very slow to develop, so if you have not started them already, you have probably missed the boat for a fall and winter crop. For tender fall leeks, get the seeds started in late February or early March in a cold greenhouse. They can soon be hardened off to grow on outdoors, as they can handle cool weather. When leek seedlings are a skinny pencil thickness, transplant them into the garden, where they will grow on to provide leeks in fall and winter.

If leeks were seeded directly in the garden in March or April, then thin them out now and transplant them into tidy rows, where they will grow on to mature.

Here is the traditional way of planting leeks:

- Mark a straight line in the garden and water along it to soften the soil.

- Use a dibber to make planting holes six inches apart along this line. Make the holes about six inches deep.

- Drop one leek seedling into each hole, so the roots are snuggled into the bottom of the hole.

- Water seedlings in with a watering can or sprayshower so that the soil just settles over the roots.

- Keep them watered until they are well-established. Every time you water, soil fills into the hole and eventually creates leeks with six-inch long, white blanched stems, which are the best part of the leek.

Luscious Lettuces

There should be some room in the garden now for lettuces, as they make a great follow-on crop to peas, garlic, favas and early salad greens. Grow a row of luscious lettuces to provide scrumptious salads for the rest of the year.

TIP: Add winter-hardy varieties to the selection to provide salads longer into the cold season.

- Make a shallow furrow in the soil and thinly sow lettuce seeds directly into it. If the soil is dry water along the open furrow first.

- Rake along the length of the furrow to cover the seed, and use the back of the rake to press the seed into the soil. This ensures better and more even germination.

- Water in along the row with a watering can.

- When lettuce seedlings have grown two inches tall, thin them out to nine inches apart.

- As soon as hard frosts threaten, cover the lettuce patch with a cloche to prolong the season of harvest.

Tip the Tomatoes!

At the end of August all tomatoes need to be encouraged to ripen by removing the top of the plants with their trusses of immature fruit. These will not have time to develop or ripen now, so why leave them? At the same time, remove all the foliage to expose the tomatoes to the last ripening rays of the summer sun.

This may seem drastic, but it doesn't harm the plants, and it does prevent harvesting loads of green tomatoes!

TIP: If you do have green tomatoes at the end of the season, put them in a brown paper bag with an apple to speed up ripening. Check bag frequently and remove the ripe tomatoes.

Stripping all the leaves from tomato plants at the end of August helps the fruit ripen faster, and will not harm the plant.

Vine Weevils

Adult vine weevils, *Otiorhynchus sulcatus*, feed on the foliage of many herbaceous plants and shrubs, especially rhododendron, euonymus, hydrangea, primula, epimedium, bergenia, sedum and strawberry.

Leaf damage is unsightly (look for notches in leaf margins), but rarely affects the plant's growth. The adults are 9 mm long, dull black beetles with a pear-shaped body when viewed from above. Adult weevils may be seen on the foliage at night, but during the day they are hidden in dark places. They are slow-moving insects that cannot fly, but they are persistent crawlers.

Far more serious is the damage caused by the soil-dwelling vine weevil larvae; plump, white, legless grubs up to 10 mm long with pale brown heads. These feed on roots and bore into tubers and succulent stem bases, devastating many herbaceous plants, in particular those growing in pots. They also kill woody plants by gnawing the outer tissues of large roots and stem bases. Plants can wilt and die as a result of grubs devouring their roots.

The way to control vine weevils is to inspect damaged plants at night with a flashlight, picking off the adult weevils. *TIP:* Shaking the shrubs over an upturned umbrella will dislodge weevils making it easier to see and collect them. In the greenhouse, look under pots and surfaces, where the beetles may hide during the day.

Trap adults with sticky barriers, such as Tanglefoot™, which can be wrapped around pots and plant stems. Encourage predators such as birds, frogs and ground beetles, which eat vine weevils and their grubs. Nematodes are an effective biological control, which can be applied in August or early September when the soil is warm enough for the nematode to be effective, 55-68°F (12-20°C), and before weevil grubs have grown large enough to cause damage.

TIP: If you are experiencing problems with vine weevils, keep up your guard, because numbers can build up again even after the apparent disappearance of this pest.

September

While ripening corn grew thick and deep,
And here and there men stood to reap,
One morn I put my heart to sleep,
And to the meadows took my way.
The goldfinch on a thistle-head
Stood scattering seedlets as she fed,
The wrens their pretty gossip spread,
Or joined a random roundelay.

Jean Ingelow

First Week of September

Lawn Care

If it has started raining, now's the perfect time to feed the lawn. Use an organic fertilizer in fall, one higher in phosphorus and potassium to stimulate root development – not one high in nitrogen, which stimulates lush, leafy growth as we go into the dormant season.

Warm, moist soil activates myriad soil microorganisms, which break down natural source ingredients and slowly release them as nutrients to grass plants. Avoid synthetic lawn fertilizers with high NPK ratios, as they destroy the intricate web of soil life. Synthetic fertilizers also cause cause fast cellular plant growth, resulting in weak tissue more prone to insect and disease attack.

Think of the lawn as a monoculture of grass plants, which is exactly what it is. Monocultures are completely unnatural, which is why we have to work so hard to maintain lawns as those perfect 'green rugs'.

A community of happy plants keeps weeds, pests and diseases at bay, so consider the needs of the individual grass plant that makes up the lawn. Keep the pH neutral, around 6.5, by applying screened compost and dolomite lime to raise the alkalinity when necessary.

Practise a lawn maintenance program that includes regular aeration, dethatching if necessary, proper watering, seasonal fertilizing and mowing with sharp blades set at the correct height. All this goes a long way to creating a healthy green lawn.

When cutting, use a mulch mower that leaves grass clippings on the lawn. The clippings will break down to feed soil microbes. High populations of microbes breaking down organic matter should prevent a build-up of thatch.

Need a Lawn Restoration?

- About mid-fall, cut the grass really short.
- If there's a build-up of thatch (undecayed grass roots, etc.), dethatch the lawn.
- Aerate the lawn, leaving the core plugs to break down and feed the grass.
- Apply dolomite lime if your soil requires it. Lawns on the wet west coast where heavy rains tend to acidify soil usually need a yearly application.
- Wait two weeks after liming to fertilize. Use a 'winterwise' lawn food, such as a natural-source organic fertilizer high in phosphorus and potassium. Phosphorus (P) strengthens grass roots. Potassium (K) strengthens grass blades and promotes general good health.
- Topdress with screened compost or a sandy garden loam.
- Overseed with a grass mixture appropriate to the lawn's light and traffic conditions, and keep well watered until the grass seed has sprouted.
- Do not let a new lawn dry out at any time.
- Grass needs warmth and time to germinate. Some grasses take three weeks or more. Ideally, seed in time for a good root system to have developed before the first hard frosts.
- Apply a mycorrhizal inoculant or spray with compost tea. Effective microorganisms re-establish a proper microbial balance in the soil, if microbes have been decimated by chemical fertilizers, pesticides or herbicides. Microbes do not regenerate on their own, so they need to be re-introduced.
- When spraying the lawn with compost tea or adding a mycorrhizal inoculant, avoid chlorinated water, which destroys microbes. Use rain water, or fill buckets with city water and leave the chlorine to evaporate overnight before using. (See *Special-teas*, second week of April.)

How to Plant a Tree

The best time to plant trees in the fall is when it starts to rain again.

Make sure you choose an evergreen or deciduous tree that meets your needs. Fast forward to the full maturity of the tree to make sure it's going to survive the location you want to plant it in. Check for overhead wires, perimeter drains, roof lines, shade being cast, branches blocking neighbours' views – anything that means the tree may have to be cut down in the future!

- If you have natural gas, check where your gas main is before digging.

- Dig a hole four times wider, and a little deeper than the rootball.

- If dry, soak the hole with water before planting.

- If it's a ball and burlap tree, place it in the hole. Cut the twine at the top and gently pull the top part of the burlap away from the trunk, or remove it entirely, taking care not to break the soil ball about the roots. Handle by lifting from the bottom of the rootball, not by holding the weight with the tree trunk.

- Position the tree straight up in the centre of the hole.

- Attach the tree to strong stakes, one on each side. Pound them into the ground to prevent the tree from rocking back and forth during heavy winds. Use non-abrasive ties. Remember to remove stakes and ties after two years at the latest.

- Mix the soil dug from the hole with compost and mycorrhizal inoculant or aged manure. Use this mix to fill in around the roots. Make sure the trunk flare remains visible at the soil surface – do not bury it.

- Tamp down to remove airspaces, which encourage fungal diseases around roots.

- Water in well.

High Quality Trees

When buying a tree, check for:

- an adequately sized root ball, which has not circled in its container

- a trunk and bark free of wounds

- a strong form with well-spaced, firmly attached branches. Avoid a weak form, where multiple stems squeeze against each other, or where branches grow tight against the trunk.

Bare Root Stock:
The ends of the roots should be clean cut. If roots have been crushed or damaged, re-cut them and remove the injured parts.

Root Ball Stock:
Root balls should be flat on top. The diameter of the root ball should be at least ten times the diameter of the trunk, measured six inches above the trunk flare. (The basal trunk flare is the spreading trunk base that connects with the roots.)

Container Stock:
Roots should not have circled around the container. You should be able to see the basal trunk flare above the soil line for container-grown plants.

> ### Did You Know?
> Algae and lichens are primitive plants that grow anywhere there is adequate moisture. They are often found growing on tree trunks, but generally do not harm the tree. They often indicate stressful conditions for the tree, such as soil compaction, poor drainage or insufficient soil nutrients.

Grow a Hedge

There are many advantages to incorporating hedges into the landscape. Hedges provide privacy; protect from wind, dust and noise; define boundaries; emphasize elements within the landscape; and divide small gardens into garden 'rooms'.

Formal hedges are those kept regularly sheared into geometric shapes. The top should never be wider than the bottom. Formal hedges, such as yew, take a lot of work to keep looking neat and tidy. A sheared shrub or tree should have small leaves; never shear those that are large-leaved.

TIPS: While shearing, set up a plumb line to help you remain on course. Put a tarp or sheet down before shearing, so trimmings can be cleaned up speedily. Shears should be sharp and well oiled to avoid damaging the hedge.

Semi-formal hedges are those occasionally pruned to shape them or keep them in scale with the garden. English laurel hedges are usually grown as semi-formal hedges by pruning the branches, rather than shearing them into shape.

Informal hedges are never sheared and are rarely pruned, but are allowed to assume their natural form. This means it is important to choose plants that will be the right size when they mature.

Six-foot shrubs for informal hedges
Photinia fraserii, Abelia grandiflora, Ceanothus thyrsifolius California lilac, *Escallonia rubra, Forsythia intermedia, Pieris japonica* lily-of-the-valley shrub, and *Choisya ternata* Mexican orange.

Anenome japonica, *Japanese anemone, indispensible for fall colour in partial shade.*

Plants For Fall Interest

Annuals:
Begonia, calendula, cleome, cosmos, dahlia, fuschia, geranium (scented and zonal), impatiens, marigold, marguerite daisy, nicotiana, petunia, salpiglossis, tithonia, zinnia

Perennials:
Arundo donax, chelone, chrysanthemum, cordyline, eupatorium, fall aster, gaillardia, gentiana, grasses, helenium, heliopsis, Japanese anemone, knautia, phormium, physostegia, rudbeckia, salvia, sedum, verbena, zauschenaria

Shrubs:
Berberis, buddleia, cotinus, cotoneaster, euonymous, hardy fuschia, hydrangea, maple, phygelius, *rosa rugosa*, viburnum

Plant Phygelius capensis, *Cape fuchsia 'Moonraker' for a showy blast of fall colour in full sun.*

Apples Ready for Picking?

Lift the apple in your palm and give it a slight twist. If ripe, it should come away easily from the spur and drop into your hand. Apples on the sunniest side of the tree are usually the first to ripen. If you cut or bite into the apple and the pips are brown, this shows that the apple is ripe, and ready for eating.

Early apples can be eaten immediately. Apples harvested later will improve by being stored.

Second Week of September

Fall Cyclamens

The arrival of the fall flowers of *Cyclamen hederifolium* is like a miracle – their pretty flowers that resemble shooting stars appear so suddenly! One day, nothing...the next, the ground is dotted with tiny purple flowers. At first the flowers appear without leaves, but later their glistening silvery marked leaves spring up. Cyclamen flowers remain pristine for weeks, as they are unaffected by bad weather.

Cyclamen hederifolium is winter-hardy and tolerant of drought and shade, though it is equally happy in full sun. The corms multiply rapidly in dry conditions at the feet of conifers or under rhododendrons and other evergreen shrubs – sites where few other plants thrive.

TIP: Cyclamens relish a yearly covering of leaf mulch to replenish the soil.

Lovely Lilies

Schizostylis coccinea, the Kaffir lily, is a South African relative of gladiolus, with eye-catching flower spikes of scarlet, salmon-pink or pink in fall. It quickly establishes into generous clumps, which can highlight the front of borders, rockwalls or narrow beds along the side of the house.

TIP: To keep your Kaffir lilies flowering well, lift any crowded clumps of corms and replant only the fattest ones.

Nerine bowdenii are glowing pink lilies, bound to brighten up the diminishing days of fall. They are always appreciated for their clusters of deep pink, spidery petals, which appear anytime from September to October. Their glossy, strap-like foliage dies back in early summer before the blooms emerge.

TIP: Let the area go dry between then and the time the flowers appear, since nerines need to stay dry during the summer months. Full sun and well-drained soils are essential for success with these beauties.

If your nerines perform poorly in fall, divide any overcrowded clumps in spring, but do not replant the neck of bulbs below the surface of the soil or the nerines will not flower.

TIP: When thinning out in spring, plant some nerines in pots, which can be protected from summer moisture and placed around the garden for instant fall colour.

Colchicum autumnale are also lilies, but look like giant crocuses. At first you think you've got the seasons confused, but when you realize the magnificent purple flowers are commonly called autumn crocuses, you know you haven't. One bulb is all you need to get going, as they naturalize so fast into colonies, but it's best to start with at least three bulbs.

Colchicums spread easily in sunny, sheltered spots under trees or shrubs, but plant them where the flowers can be seen to full advantage.

TIP: Colchicums go dormant in summer, with their fleshy spring foliage dying down in June. If you pull up the foliage, mark the position of the bulbs so they are not accidentally dug up. At this time if colonies have become overcrowded, transplant some bulbs elsewhere to spread these pretty fall flowers around your garden.

Feature of the Month
Ten Things You Should Know About Roundup®

1. **Roundup® contains glyphosate, which can be persistent.** In tests conducted by Monsanto, manufacturer of the herbicide Roundup®, up to 140 days were required for half of the applied glyphosate to break down or disappear from agricultural soils. At harvest, residues of glyphosate were found in lettuce, carrots and barley planted one year after glyphosate treatment.

2. **Glyphosate can drift.** Tests conducted by the University of California found that glyphosate drifted up to 400 metres during ground applications, and 800 metres during aerial applications.

3. **Glyphosate is acutely toxic to humans.** Ingesting three-quarters of a cup can be lethal. Symptoms include eye and skin irritation, lung congestion and erosion of the intestinal tract. In California between 1984 and 1990, glyphosate was the third most frequently reported cause of illness related to agricultural pesticide use.

4. **Glyphosate shows a wide spectrum of chronic toxicity in laboratory tests.** The National Toxicology Program found that chronic feeding of glyphosate caused salivary gland lesions, reduced sperm counts and lengthened the estrous cycle. Other chronic effects found in laboratory tests included an increase in the frequency of lethal mutations in fruit flies; an increase in the frequency of pancreas and liver tumours in male rats, along with an increase in the frequency of thyroid tumours in females; and cataracts.

5. **Roundup® contains toxic trade secret ingredients.** These include polyethoxylated tallowamines, which can cause nausea and diarrhea, and isopropylamine, which can cause chemical pneumonia, laryngitis, headache and burns.

6. **Roundup® kills beneficial insects.** Tests conducted by the International Organization for Biological Control show that Roundup® caused mortality of live beneficial species when tested on predatory mites, lacewings, ladybugs and predatory beetles.

7. **Glyphosate is hazardous to earthworms.** Tests using New Zealand's most common earthworm show that glyphosate, in amounts as low as 1/20th of standard application rates, reduced the earthworm's growth and slowed development.

8. **Roundup® inhibits mycorrhizal fungi.** Canadian studies have shown that as little as one part per million of Roundup® can reduce the growth or colonization of mycorrhizal fungi.

9. **Glyphosate reduces nitrogen fixation.** Nitrogen-fixing bacteria, shown to be impacted by glyphosate, include a species found on soybeans and several species of bacteria found on clover. Amounts as small as two parts per million had significant effects. Effects were measured up to 120 days after treatment.

10. **Roundup® can increase the spread or severity of plant diseases.** Treatment with Roundup® increased the severity of Rhizoctonia root rot in barley, increased growth of Take-all fungus (a wheat disease), and reduced the ability of bean plants to defend themselves against Anthracnose.

From: www.guarding-our earth.com/aggrand/roundup.htm

A study published April 1, 2005 by a University of Pittsburgh researcher, Rick Relyea, examining a pond's entire community, found that Roundup® caused a 70 per cent decline in amphibian biodiversity and an 86 per cent decline in the total mass of tadpoles.

"The most shocking insight was that Roundup® (the second most commonly applied herbicide in the United States) was extremely lethal to amphibians," said Relyea, who initially conducted the experiment to see whether Roundup® would have an indirect effect on frogs by killing their food source, the algae. Instead he found that Roundup® actually increased the amount of algae in the pond, because it killed most of the frogs.

Previous experiments had found that the lethal ingredient in Roundup® was the surfactant, polyethoxylated tallowamine, which allows the herbicide to penetrate the waxy surfaces of plants.

Third Week of September

Putting the Garden to Bed

This is the time of year most gardeners look forward to with relief. All the watering, weeding, planting and gardening chores are behind them, and it's time to think about indoor activities. But not so fast! Before you hit that cozy chair by the fire, there are still a few gardening essentials that need to be done.

Putting your garden to bed for the winter begins with the fall clean-up, which should start by sharpening (or changing) the blades, and cleaning and lubricating secateurs and loppers.

After cleaning, sterilize pruning implements to avoid spreading disease from one plant to another. This is particularly important for roses and fruit trees, which are prone to a number of diseases that are easily spread.

TIP: Mist pruning tools with rubbing alcohol before moving from one plant to another. Lubricate pruning equipment by wiping the blades with an oily rag, putting a couple of drops of oil between them.

Cut back and tidy up mixed borders. Some herbaceous perennials, such as sedums, can be left for winter interest, and some grasses, such as miscanthus, for their seedheads. Leave the berries on cotoneaster and other shrubs to feed the birds in winter. *TIP:* Chop tall stalks into smaller pieces before composting so they break down more quickly.

Prune back rose canes that may break from wind damage. At this time of year, take only one third off roses if necessary, leaving another third to take off in early spring.

Remove foliage infected with powdery mildew and blackspot from roses. Mulch under roses for extra winter protection, and to cover any spores on the soil.

Remove dead or diseased branches on woody ornamentals to prevent disease from setting in.

Rake beds to remove diseased leaves or plant material, such as scab on fruit trees or rust on hollyhock leaves.

TIP: Do not compost diseased plant matter unless you can hot compost. Instead, dig a hole in the garden and bury diseased material there, since there are over 50,000 different species of microorganisms in the soil that will go to work on destroying plant pathogens.

There's suddenly going to be a lot of material from the fall clean-up, so be prepared by organizing your composting area. Empty bins with ready-to-use compost and mulch the garden with it. Screen some compost and topdress planter boxes or half oak barrels with it.

If the compost bin is full, turn it to aerate and mix the contents, moistening while turning. By next spring you'll have a binful of fabulous 'black gold' to start the gardening year with. *TIPS:* Leaving the hose running over the pile while it's being turned facilitates speedier breakdown. Covering the compost pile against winter rains with a tarp or unpainted wood prevents valuable nutrients from leaching out.

Go routinely around the garden collecting spent plant matter. Lift annuals from garden beds and remove all spent vegetables in the food garden. Compost them.

Tidy up conifers and evergreen hedges with a light pre-winter trim, but remember to taper the cut in toward the top. *TIP:* Hedge clippings take a while to break down. Put them in a plastic bag, and solarize before adding them to the compost. They will rot faster. Running the mower over leaves shreds them into smaller pieces, which break down faster.

Lift any boards, remove debris and old plant pots, and clean areas in which slugs and caterpillar cocoons may overwinter.

Have a good clear-out in the greenhouse. Clean algae build-up off glass using a 10% bleach solution, scrub shelving and benches, and hose off ledges, nooks and crannies. Sweep or rake the greenhouse floor.

Fourth Week of September

What To Do in the Garden

Take stock of your borders before the herbaceous plants die back completely. Which plants need lifting and dividing? Which should be removed? Which do you want to add more of?

This is a perfect time to redesign the garden, putting all those mental notes gathered throughout the year into action. Move plants, get rid of hideous colour clashes, and change plants that dwarf or hide others. Add exciting new plants to discover in next year's garden. Colourful spring bulbs and flowers, such as forget-me-nots, wallflowers, primulas, pansies, sweet williams and bellis daisies provide lots of cheery spring blooms. *TIP:* Buy spring bulbs early for the best selection.

Herbaceous perennials should be divided every three to five years to keep plants the right size in the border and flowering well. This is best done while the soil is warm and moist. Lift the plant, avoiding root loss, and chop the clump into smaller sections with a spade, axe or two forks placed back to back. Keep only healthy sections with good roots for replanting. *TIP:* Perennials that flower in the fall are best divided in spring (e.g. sedums, rudbeckias). Those that flower in spring and early summer are best divided in the fall (e.g. peonies, irises). Do not replant them too deeply, or they will not flower next year.

Save leaves from large trees such as maples, oaks and chestnuts. A covering of leaf mulch insulates roots, feeds the soil, helps retain moisture, and improves soil structure. Mulch also provides an extra layer of protection to half-hardy, tender plants such as gaura, penstemons and vegetables, such as artichokes, beets and carrots. (See *Lots of Lovely Leaves,* second week of October.)

Wrap frost-sensitive plants such as bananas or echium with burlap sacking.

Protect container plants from freezing by moving them closer to the house, under the eaves or a deck, into a sheltered corner, into a cool greenhouse or inside a brightly lit entranceway or garage. *TIP:* Give outdoor pot plants extra protection by placing one pot inside a larger one, and insulating the layer in between with burlap bags, straw or shredded newspapers.

Dig up and dry out begonia tubers and gladioli corms, which will not overwinter without rotting.

Wait until after the first hard frost, when the foliage turns black, to dig up tubers of dahlias and cannas.

Tie up cypress and cedar trees so the weight of heavy snow won't break or damage them.

Fasten climbing plants to supports to protect them against damage from high winds.

Cut back ornamental grasses discriminately. *Calamagrostis acutiflora* 'Karl Foerster' and *Spartina pectinoides* hold their shape through winter, providing interest for winter months. Herbaceous grasses become brittle and are more easily cut back in spring.

TIP: Shred leaves first by running a lawn mower on a high setting over them.

Sow fall cover crops such as fall rye, winter wheat, barley or field pea on empty beds from now until early November. They will be dug under as green manure crops in the spring. (See *Green Manures,* first week of November.)

Gather herbs such as rosemary, thyme and sage for drying. Cut stems about six inches (15 cm) long. Bunch and tie them. Put them in paper bags and hang in a warm, dry place. After about ten days, the herbs should be ready to be stored in darkened, airtight jars.

Saving Seeds

Check your garden for ripe seeds and collect them by shaking into clean, dry buckets or placing into brown paper bags. To clean them, remove the chaff from around the seeds, and carefully blow away any debris and dust, which may contaminate stored seeds. Spread cleaned seeds out on plates or trays, and allow to dry thoroughly before storing in labelled envelopes or airtight yogurt containers. (See *Saving Seeds Successfully,* third week of June.)

In the Fruit and Berry Patch

When the last crops of raspberries have been harvested, cut the woody fruited canes down to soil level. This helps prevent pests and diseases from developing, and lets in light to promote new cane growth.

Prune out the fruited canes of blackberries and hybrid berries such as boysenberry, tayberry and loganberry. Tie the remaining canes onto their supports to prevent winter damage.

The wingless, female winter moth walks up fruit trees from September on to lay her eggs on the branches. The resulting green caterpillars feed on foliage and blossoms the following spring. Tie grease bands around fruit tree trunks to keep the moth out of the tree. Use one or two six-inch, removable wraps (such as burlap sacking tied around the tree with twine), and coat them with a sticky product such as Tanglefoot™. *TIP:* Press the bands firmly around the trunk to prevent the moth from crawling under them.

Due to the prevalence of bacterial canker on the wet west coast, cherry trees and all stone fruits (peaches, apricots, etc.) should be pruned in late summer or early fall after the fruit has been harvested. After harvest, the flow of sap slows down dramatically and the leaves start to turn a month later. When the wood is drier, pruning cuts heal more quickly, making it less likely that bacterial canker will enter the cuts in winter.

Annual pruning is not required other than to help keep a balanced canopy or restricted form. Cut into clean wood, remove any diseased material that could infect the tree, and make sure you disinfect all pruning tools between trees.

October

Count your garden by the flowers
Never by the leaves that fall,
Count your days by golden hours
Don't remember clouds at all.
Count your nights by stars not shadows
Count your years with smiles not tears,
Count your blessings not your sorrows
Count your age by friends not years.

Anonymous

First Week of October

Light Up with Bulbs

Daffodils and tulips – so many choices, so many prices! Buyer beware, the inexpensive bulbs are low grade. They will produce a flower stalk, but may or may not produce a flower. Only top quality bulbs produce flowers and last for many years. Size often indicates better quality bulbs.

When Buying:

- Make sure bulbs are firm, not spongy. Avoid ones that are mouldy.
- Check for bloom times. You may or may not want all the bulbs blooming at the same time.
- Naturalizing bulbs multiply year after year. (Most tulips have been hybridized to the point that they only provide a good show for one year.)
- Deer? Forget tulips! Choose narcissi, snowdrops, chionodoxa, reticulate irises, alliums or fritillarias instead.
- For the rock garden, six-inch dwarf varieties of flowering bulbs work well.

When Planting:

- Plant bulbs in well-drained soil. Bulbs will rot in wet, cold, heavy soil.
- Plant the bulbs at a depth three times the size of the bulb.
- Sprinkle wood ashes in the planting hole as a bulb fertilizer for a better show.
  TIP: A handful of compost in the planting hole, or a topdressing with seaweed also enhances flowering.
- Avoid planting bulbs in straight rows, like soldiers. To achieve a more natural effect, simply throw the bulbs down and plant them where they land.

The Lasagna Technique

For a show-stopping spring display, plant layers of bulbs on top of one another. They'll find their way to the light bending around each other. *TIP:* To get the best effect, choose bulbs that flower in the same season, e.g. all mid-season or all late-season.

To plant the lasagna:

- Put five to seven narcissi, the biggest bulbs, on the bottom layer. Cover with potting soil.
- Put five to seven tulips on the next layer. Cover.
- Place five to seven hyacinths on the next layer. Cover.
- Place 10 to 20 crocuses on the next layer. Cover.
- Place violas, pansies, bellis daisies, forget-me-nots or primroses on the very top layer.

Alternatively, try this for your lasagna:

- Use all tulips. Choose one early-season, one mid-season and one late-season variety, to prolong the season of show, leaving the foliage to die back as the next variety begins to flower. You can still place violas or wallflowers on the top level if you wish.

Plantaholics Unite

It's very satisfying, as the days get colder and nights draw in, to review the past year in the garden. "So many plants...so little time," is what I seem to recollect. In reflection I might question my sanity, but instead I've concluded that I need to join the ranks of 'Plantaholics Anonymous'!

I know I'm not alone in the need for such a society. It's easy to recognize fellow plantaholics by their irresistible urge to possess that 'must-have' plant. The recommendation "it's best not to buy when you don't know where to plant," is always ignored. "Don't worry, I'll find somewhere!" How many of us have 'waiting areas' for plants needing to find homes in our gardens?

If you're not sure you belong to the rank and file of such an organization, the following plantaholic comments may help you to identify your standing. (If nothing else, they'll brighten the gloomy days of fall.)

"My garden beds are totally full... so I'm taking up more lawn!"

"There's no lawn left in the garden, and the beds are all full. What have you got that grows in containers?"

"I've run out of space...so I'm taking over my neighbour's garden! I'll take these three please."

In response to "Beware, this plant is very invasive!" a shrug and, "I like plants that spread fast." Plantaholics are thrilled by 'takeover' plants such as *Centaurea montana, Centranthus ruber,* aegopodium, crocosmia, shastas, euphorbias, ajuga, pachysandra and sweet woodruff.

At "This is a plant that needs space in full sun," the comment, "I'll try it in a container on my north-facing balcony anyway."

To "Don't let fennel go to seed, you'll have hundreds of them," the response, "No problem... I think it's *such* a great plant!"

Only plantaholics would complain, "The deer are eating everything in my garden! I hope they won't like all these new plants!"

It's a plant SALE! "What a deal! I'll buy twenty!"

It's only due to my plantaholic tendencies that I now maintain a two-acre garden. At this time of year, as I struggle to accomplish a never-ending list of chores, I am of two minds as to whether this is an enviable position to be in or not. Will I get the bulbs in? The beds mulched? Tender plants under cover? Window boxes changed? The garlic planted? The apples picked? The tomatoes harvested in time?

It's natural for a plantaholic to feel complete empathy with the seasons. Fall is the time to wind down; winter is the time to go dormant. Spring and summer are times to come fully alive again – bursting with new vitality and enthusiasm, totally oblivious to any need for restraint in one's gardening ambitions.

My exhausted self holds onto this encouraging thought as I prepare to tackle myriad gardening chores. Meanwhile I'll reach for the phone directory and see if there's an organization for one so hopelessly a slave to their garden as I.

Are you a potential member?

Second Week of October

Lots of Lovely Leaves!

Some gardeners love them and some gardeners curse them, but many don't realize what a wonderful resource leaves are. Piles of wet leaves may damage lawns and smother plants, but when added to the compost or left to rot down in the garden, they add organic matter and nutrients to soil. Leaves provide a source of nitrogen and phosphorus as they break down.

Leafy Tips

- Large trees such as oaks, maples, sycamores and chestnuts are wonderful sources of nutrient-rich leaves.

- Store leaves in fall for layering into compost throughout the year. *TIP:* A circular cage of fencing wire, or four posts wrapped with chicken wire, is a simple space-saving way to store leaves.

- A heap of leaves will break down into a pile of rich, crumbly leaf mulch in one year (faster if you turn the pile). Shallow-rooted plants such as rhododendrons, azaleas, camellias, hydrangeas, pieris, skimmia and heathers just LOVE leaf mulch.

- Don't position leaf piles under trees or hedges where fibrous roots will grow into the pile. *TIP:* If you must, put landscape fabric down first as a barrier.

- To reduce a pile of leaves, spread them out on a driveway and run a lawn mower over the pile. It will reduce to a tenth of its volume, and can then be sprinkled onto beds, where leaves will quickly break down into the soil.

- If you have pine trees, compost the pine needles separately. They take up to three years to rot down, but produce an acidic leaf mould that is excellent for ericaceous (acid-loving) plants such as azaleas, rhododendrons, pieris, hydrangeas, blueberries, heathers and camellias.

- Don't save leaves showing signs of disease, such as rust, black spot or mildew, since pathogens present may survive. Dig a hole and bury them in the garden, where microbes will get to work destroying them.

- Avoid shiny, waxy leaves, such as arbutus. They are slow to break down due to a waxy cuticle.

Thanksgiving Garden Sandwich

Take 2 pieces of multigrain bread.

Spread one with avocado.

Spread the other with your favourite cheese (Ricotta, goat's, bocconcini, tofurella – whatever!)

Layer your sandwich with whatever takes your fancy in the garden:
- Leaves of lettuce, coriander, arugula, parcel, chives or basil
- Slices of sweet pepper
- Slices of crispy cucumber
- Slices of chin-dripping tomatoes

Close your eyes...Take a bite!
Sheer Heaven!

With a little help from my friends, this huge pile of leaves got spread over the garden as a great soil-building mulch.

Gourmet Winter Meals

Over the winter months, "What's for dinner?" in our house means "What shall we harvest from the garden?" So many vegetables thrive in the winter food garden that we plan lots of menus around them. Here's a sample of some of the meals we enjoy from October to April, months in which food gardens are usually considered unproductive.

A typical winter salad consists of a little bit of many things growing in the garden. I tear up young leaves of Red Russian kale, Dutch curled kale, perpetual spinach, chard, arugula and corn salad, toss in some finely shredded tender baby leeks, and add chopped parsley, cilantro and Welsh bunching onions (scallions). I finish the salad by throwing in some mixed seeds or nuts, toss it with a tangy vinaigrette dressing, and garnish it with calendula flower petals. Who could resist the appeal of such a vibrant salad?

Collards, perpetual spinach, beet greens and green curled kale are sweetest after hard frosts. We use them for steamed greens in lasagnas and 'cabbage roll' type dishes, or add them shredded to casseroles, soups and rice dishes.

The patch of arugula, which self-seeded from a spring sowing, means we have tasty greens, mild and nutty when young, hot and spicy when mature, for sandwiches and salads. Arugula is also great sautéed with goat cheese and sundried tomatoes, the way Italians prepare it.

Corn salad provides mild greens, perfect for adding to sandwiches and salads. Individual leaves can be picked or the whole central rosette cut. Corn salad seeds freely around the garden, providing lots of fresh salad greens throughout the winter.

The strong celery flavour of celeriac root enhances casseroles and soups. Celeriac is much easier to grow than celery, and is sweet and crunchy raw for veggie dips. When added with the potatoes, it adds exceptional flavour to a hearty leek and potato soup.

Lutz beets are large, sweet when baked, and perfect for pickling. There's the added bonus of nutritious beet greens. Beets overwinter in mild winters, but may need a protective mulch in colder climates. Top your winter salads with grated beets followed by a handful of mixed seeds or nuts.

Parsley grows close to the ground in winter, so the flavour is concentrated, and enhances many winter dishes. Winter-hardy lettuces fare best under a protective cloche or cold frame. 'Winter Density' and 'Valdor' are hardy green lettuces; 'Rouge d'Hiver' and 'Brunia' are hardy red lettuces. Leafy Chinese coriander, or cilantro, will overwinter and even survive snow dumps with no protective covering. It adds a unique note to stirfries, salsas and omelettes.

The milder kale varieties, 'Red Russian' and 'Dutch green curled', are tender enough to eat in salads. Coarser kales, such as 'Lacinato' and 'Winterbor', provide greens with a stronger flavour. 'Redbor' kale is as worth growing for a stunning purple accent in the garden, as for tender steamed greens.

Nothing beats Swiss chard for succulent greens; 'Fordhook Swiss giant' is reliably winter hardy. Steam or sauté the succulent stalks and you will hardly be able to tell the difference between these and celery.

If you plant leeks in May, you'll be harvesting tender leeks from fall through winter. Even when there's snow on the ground, leeks can be pulled from the garden for dinner. The same goes for Jerusalem artichokes, which can be dug as needed, and are wonderful raw in vegetable dips as well as sweet and nutty when drizzled with olive oil and roasted for 25 minutes.

We look forward to spring for the tasty shoots of purple sprouting broccoli, and the succulent greens of 'First Early Market' cabbage. Cauliflowers, broccoli and cabbages take root and establish over winter, and burst into growth when the soil warms up in spring.

The pleasure of harvesting nutritious winter vegetables from your own backyard will make the effort of planting from July to September more than worthwhile.

Third Week of October

Grow the Best Garlic

Garlic has been revered for centuries for promoting good health and fighting infection, as well as for its many culinary uses. It contains selenium, an essential trace element often lacking in our diets. In these times of increasing stress, adding garlic to one's diet boosts the immune system and helps combat infections and illness.

Most garlic from the supermarket has been fumigated with methyl bromide, an anti-sprouting chemical, so it's best to start with bulbs of organic seed garlic from a reputable garlic grower. Make sure the garlic is free from white rot, a fungal disease that can wipe out your harvest for years to come.

Garlic falls into two distinctive sub-species. Hardneck (Rocambole) varieties, *Allium ophioscorodon,* produce a flower spike and have large, easy-peeling cloves, which will store from six to eight months. Rocambole garlics should be planted in October.

Softneck (or braiding) varieties, *Allium sativum,* have smaller cloves with no central stalk, as they do not produce flower spikes. They are generally more spicy, with cloves that will store for a year. Softneck garlics can be planted in October, but some varieties, such as 'Silverskin,' are best planted in early spring.

Elephant garlic, *Allium ampeloprasum,* is actually a perennial leek, and has a much milder flavour. Its cloves split up when it is dried, so elephant garlic does not store for very long.

Twelve Tips For the Best Garlic

1. Planting in October is best for hard-necked and most soft-necked garlic varieties. Plant cloves about six weeks before the first hard frost, as they need a month of near-freezing temperatures and at least one hundred days to mature. Spring-planted hardneck garlic does not grow into full-sized bulbs.

2. Chose a sunny site with rich, well-drained sandy loam – not too rich or the tops will overdevelop. Garlic does not do well in light, sandy soils, heavy clay soils, or soils lacking in organic matter. If your soil is poor, amend it with compost and aged manure and add wood ash to aid in bulb formation.

3. Replanting the largest cloves gives you the largest bulbs. Practise crop rotation yearly to avoid problems with white rot.

4. If garlic is spaced close or has competition from weeds, it will result in smaller bulbs. Space cloves six inches apart in the row, and the rows one foot apart.

5. Plant individual cloves with the pointy end up, about two inches deep below the soil surface.

6. Mulch with straw in spring, once the ground has warmed up, to cut down on weeding and watering. Doing this allows you to pull garlic by hand rather than forking it out, which may injure the bulb.

7. Stop watering about three weeks before harvesting to allow the bulbs to cure.

Garlic scapes are delicious raw, lightly steamed, or used in stir fries.

8. For hardneck garlic, cut the flower spikes (scapes) off when they appear. The energy used to go to seed takes away from bulb size.

9. Harvest bulbs of garlic in July, when about two-thirds of the leaves have turned yellow. Don't wait until all the leaves have yellowed, as the cloves separate in an over-mature bulb and will not store well.

10. Dry the bulbs by leaving them in the sun for two or three days, unless it is really hot, which may cause them to brown, or threatening to rain, which would cause them to rot.

11. Remove surface soil from bulbs but preserve the protective skin layers. Hang to dry in bunches of six to seven bulbs in a warm, dark, airy place. Garlic needs four to six weeks to cure thoroughly.

12. Storing garlic in a cool, dark place with ventilation provides the longest storage life.

White Rot in Garlic

White rot is an aggressive fungus that first hit California in 1939. Fruiting bodies, sclerotia, wake up in cold wet weather, activated by chemicals released by garlic. It only takes one sclerotium per 10 kg of soil to set off the white rot disease, which spreads rapidly through root systems, and is deadly to garlic. This fungal pathogen can survive in soil for 8 to 15 years once established, and is almost impossible to eradicate.

Prevention:
- Make sure any garlic you purchase is free from this deadly disease.
- Avoid spreading contamination by way of footwear or harvesting equipment.
- Destroy any infected plants immediately and do not compost.

Balsamic Roast Potatoes

(Makes 4-6 servings)

Preheat oven to 400°F (200°C)

4 large russet potatoes
1/2 tsp salt
1 Tbsp. extra virgin olive oil
1/2 cup crumbled feta cheese
1/2 cup coarsely chopped mint
Fresh ground pepper to taste

Vinaigrette:
1 tsp. Dijon mustard
1/2 tsp salt
1 clove garlic, minced
4 Tbsp. balsamic vinegar
1/2 cup extra virgin olive oil

Whisk Dijon, salt, garlic and balsamic vinegar together. Slowly beat in 1/2 cup olive oil.

Cut potatoes into six wedges lengthwise. Toss with 1/2 tsp. salt and 1 Tbsp. olive oil. Spread out, cut sides down, on a baking sheet. Bake for 15 minutes. Turn over and bake for 15 minutes more, until browned and cooked. Remove from oven and toss with vinaigrette, feta, mint and pepper.

Good as a potato salad at room temperature too!

It's All About the Foliage!

Picture this as a perfect recipe for fall colour (as well as a spectacular photo)! Glistening, bright purple beauty berries of *Callicarpa bodinieri* 'Profusion' backlit in the afternoon sun against the red, orange and gold foliage of *Viburnum opulus* snowball tree.

Many shrubs and trees glow in the fall, just when perennials and annuals are starting to fade into distant summer memories. *Nandina domestica* heavenly bamboo, provides year-round interest, but is particularly spectacular in fall, covered in clusters of tiny, orange-red berries. Take stock of colour in your garden now, and if "dull" is what you come up with, plant some fall colour.

I steer clear of prickly plants in my garden, but make an exception for *Berberis thunbergii* 'Atropurpurea'. This barberry bush covered in dark bronze-red leaves and tiny red berries looks spectacular on a sunny day underneath *Cotinus coggygria* 'Grace', the red-leaved smoke bush. But if it's red you're after, nothing beats cork-winged *Euonymus alatus,* the burning bush, for its vermilion-red leaves.

Each year around this time, I have a heyday planting for fall colour. "It's all about the foliage," I remind myself, while digging a hole for *Ginkgo biloba,* the maidenhair tree, whose fan-shaped, golden leaves will light up the garden. In the case of *Acer palmatum* 'Sango Kaku' it's not just about exquisite foliage from spring onwards, but also striking coral-red bark that glows all winter.

I just had to have *Cornus* 'Eddie's White Wonder', with leaves that change slowly from green to orange to deep red as the weather cools down. Eddie has the added attraction of masses of white dogwood blooms in mid-spring, and a habit of sublime elegance.

I've made one more exception to my 'prickly' rule by planting an evergreen variegated English holly, *Ilex aquifolium,* in the lawn as a specimen tree. I prune it to shape just before the holiday season, so I can bring sprigs of glossy, variegated foliage with red berries inside for decoration.

Dogwood shrubs are showy in full leaf – *Cornus alba* 'Elegantissima' with its green and white-edged leaves, and *Cornus alba* 'Aurea' with its dazzling chartreuse leaves. As winter approaches, colourful bark on eye-catching stems becomes the main feature. *TIP*: Prune these shrubs just above the ground in March to encourage clusters of colourful new stems to grow.

Virginia creeper lives up to its name, spreading quickly up anything it can cling to. The most colourful of all the Virginia creepers is *Parthenocissus henryana,* the 'Silvervein Creeper' with leaves that start purple, turn dark bronze-green with silver veins and then turn rich red in the fall.

The choices of great fall foliage plants are many, but one that gets a lot of attention is *Hydrangea quercifolia,* oakleaf hydrangea. This most handsome of shrubs has eye-catching, deeply lobed leaves that turn spectacular crimson-bronze in fall. It also makes a distinguished container plant.

Go on, don't be shy....light up your garden by adding more drama, texture, contrast, interest and colour to it.

Great Fall Foliage Plants:
Acer palmatum 'Sango Kaku' - Japanese maple
Berberis thunbergii 'Atropurpurea' - Japanese barberry
Callicarpa bodinieri 'Profusion' - beautyberry
Cornus 'Eddie's White Wonder' - dogwood tree
Cornus alba 'Aurea' - shrubby dogwood
Cornus alba 'Elegantissima'- shrubby dogwood
Cotinus coggygria - smoke bush
Euonymus alatus - burning bush
Ginkgo biloba - maidenhair tree
Hydrangea quercifolia - oakleaf hydrangea
Ilex aquifolium - English holly
Nandina domestica - heavenly bamboo
Parthenocissus henryana - Virginia creeper
Viburnum opulus - snowball tree

Cotinus coggygria *'Grace' sparkles with fall dew.*

Fourth Week of October

Dazzling Dahlias (Part Two)

- Decide which tubers to dig up and which to leave in the ground. Those in heavy clay soils are prone to rotting, so dig them up. If you have well-drained soil, or your dahlias are planted under an overhang, you may choose to leave them in the ground and cover them with a protective layer of mulch.

- After the first hard frosts when dahlias go black, cut down the stalks and lift the tubers.

- Leave the soil around the dahlia tubers and dry off the clumps. Store them with the dried earth around them as an insulating layer, in a burlap bag or lined box. Leave them in a cool, dry garage for the winter. (See *Dazzling Dahlias (Part One)*, second week in April.)

Keep Your Roses Rosy

> The rose is a rose,
> and was always a rose,
> but, the theory now goes
> that the apple's a rose,
> and the pear is, and so's
> the plum I suppose.
> What next will prove a rose?
>
> *Robert Frost, 'The Rose Family'*

Reduce the effects of wind and snow damage by pruning hybrid tea and floribunda roses back by a third. The rest of the pruning is then left until spring. Strip all the leaves off any remaining canes. Don't compost the leaves, as they may harbour spores of black spot, mildew or rust. Bury them in the garden instead.

Prune climbing and rambling roses by removing dead, damaged or diseased and spindly growth first. The aim is to maintain a vigorous framework of healthy canes. Ramblers tend to be more vigorous than climbers, so more wood can be removed. Prune all side shoots back to three buds.

Select strong laterals to form new main shoots, training them horizontally to encourage new lateral growth on which flowers are produced. If your roses are spindly, strengthen the laterals by tip pruning them. Strip off all remaining leaves.

To keep your roses healthy, rake fallen rose leaves from below them. Mulch under the roses with aged manure, compost or leaf mulch to protect roots over winter and cover any spores that may be overwintering there.

In the Flower Garden

- One or two-year-old rosemary or bay trees may not overwinter successfully, so bring young plants under protection. Planting them out once the roots have fully developed gives them a better chance of survival.

- October is the best time to plant heathers. Plant them in full sun, incorporating leaf mulch to improve soil structure. Heathers like poor soils, so there's no need to add other nutrients.

- Mulch around shrubs using composted manure, leaf mulch or garden compost (or all three!). Mushroom compost is a good soil conditioner but contains lime, so avoid it for ericaceous (acid-loving) plants such as rhododendrons and camellias. Try coir bricks instead, a by-product of the coconut industry, which slightly acidify the soil.

- Several species of soil-inhabiting fungi are responsible for circles of fairy rings that sometimes appear in lawns during fall wet weather. There are no chemical remedies available, so rake them up as they appear, and dispose of them to prevent new infections. In a severe situation you may need to dig out the topsoil to a depth of at least 12 inches (30 cm), and to an area extending 12 inches (30 cm) beyond the edge of the ring to help control the problem. Remove this soil and replace with fresh topsoil.

In the Vegetable Garden

- Fava beans can be planted in late October or November for an early harvest in May or June, but be prepared that some may rot in cold, wet winters.

- As the fern-like asparagus foliage yellows and dies, cut it down to an inch (2.5 cm) above the ground and compost it. Then spread mulch over the asparagus patch. Asparagus is a heavy feeder and relishes a feed with aged manure, compost or what-have-you!

- Cut back stalks of Jerusalem artichokes. The tubers, which are sweeter after a few hard frosts, can be harvested from the garden now and throughout the winter.

In the Greenhouse

- *The best way to prevent disease is to remove disease.* Go through all the plants in the greenhouse and remove any mouldy plant parts on leaves, stems or fruit. Keep a check throughout the winter for infections and remove such material on a regular basis. The damp, confined environment of a greenhouse is a perfect breeding ground for fungal spores and disease.

> Insulate greenhouses with bubblewrap as a cheap, effective way to provide double glazing. Tape sheets of wrap inside onto the panes of glass so that light comes through but warmth stays in.

- If heating the greenhouse, check that heaters are working properly and efficiently. For kerosene stoves, check the wick. Many plants will overwinter successfully in an unheated greenhouse, saving the expense of heating. The trick is to allow plants to dry out (especially succulents), and to water sparingly ONLY when needed. Once a month is usually sufficient, depending on how many warm, sunny days there are during winter.

In Your Pond

- Cut back dying marginal plants, and remove leaves that have fallen into the water before they sink, as they will break down at the bottom of the pond and cause algae to bloom. *TIP:* If there are lots of leaves falling into your pond, save time by covering the surface with netting to catch them.

- Remove and compost annual floaters, such as water hyacinth and water lettuce, before they rot.

Courtesy of the Barton Leier Gallery Garden

In the Fruit Garden

- If your rhubarb did not produce well, it may need to be divided. Now is a good time, as rhubarb needs a period of cold before it starts to grow again. Choose an open site with moist, free-draining soil, and plant sections of divided root about 30 inches apart. Topdress with heaps of aged manure – rhubarb is a heavy feeder!

- To protect fruit trees against fungal diseases, dormant spray all surfaces of the tree with 2 Tbsp. wettable copper to a gallon of water.

...eason dessert apples keep best if stored ...ised and unblemished, ideally on waxed cardboard trays. This allows you to inspect for signs of rot, and stop it from spreading, by keeping the fruit apart. Store trays in a vermin and frost-free place, away from strong-smelling substances. Store where the temperature is cool and constant, with good air circulation. *TIP:* Place apples with stalks down so fruit won't roll and bruise. Don't store apples in plastic bags. They'll sweat, and the build-up of ethylene and carbon dioxide will hasten ripening and core rot.

Apple and Dried Cranberry Crisp

Serves 8
Preheat oven to 375°F (190°C)

Topping:
1 cup all purpose flour
3/4 cup brown sugar, tightly packed
1 tsp. cinnamon
1 Tbsp. grated orange zest
1/2 cup unsalted butter, chilled
1/2 cup rolled oats

Combine ingredients. Rub in the butter with fingers, to get a coarse crumbly mix.

Add:
1/2 cup pecans (or walnuts), toasted for
　5 minutes, then chopped

Filling:
6 apples (approx. 2 lbs. peeled,
　cored and sliced)
1 Tbsp. white sugar
1/2 cup dried or 1 cup fresh or frozen
　cranberries

Place filling in an 8" square greased baking dish, level and cover evenly with topping. Cover with foil and bake for 25 minutes. Remove foil and bake for another 20 minutes or until the topping is crisp and lightly browned.

Simply divine with a dollop of yoghurt, ice cream or whipped cream!

Questions & Answers

Melanie: This year was a fine fig year. Now I have lots of immature figs left on my tree that won't ripen. Should I take them off, or will they continue to mature for next year's crop?

Answer: Remove all small, unripe fruit except for the tiny embryos that form close to the end of the shoots. Unless these are killed off in winter, they will grow to become next year's crop. *TIP:* Providing fig trees with protective barriers against frost, such as Remay spun polyester, can protect the future crop.

The secret to getting figs to ripen is to stress the tree by restricting its root growth. If given room to spread, fig trees grow quickly, and vegetative growth thrives at the expense of fruit production. When I visited the Lost Gardens of Heligan in Cornwall, UK, I noticed figs were grown in half oak barrels, which were moved into a greenhouse for winter protection. The five-foot tall, bushy fig trees were covered in ripening figs in July.

In their native habitat in the Mediterranean, figs thrive in dry, rocky conditions where they are not fussy about soil or fertility. What figs need most is hot sun and good drainage – they cannot tolerate wet soils. *TIP:* If you have heavy soil, put a layer of drainage rocks in the bottom of the planting hole.

The best time to introduce a fig tree to the garden is in spring, when it has a better chance to establish. Being softwood trees, figs are a pleasure to prune. In spring, after all danger of heavy frost, prune off any dead, diseased or damaged wood and ingrowing branches. If you want your tree to bush out, cut a third off the branch, so it will produce two branches.

November

Hush the rush • Hike and bike
Don't go far with your car
Explore your core • Less is more
Act with care • Try to be fair
Remember to share • Life is a prayer
Let's think globally and eat locally
Be content with no event
Don't be tired • Get unwired
Read a book • Learn to cook
Take your time • You will shine
Plant a tree • Embrace mystery
Toss the TV and your CV
Try to be clear • Let go of fear
Stay close to home • Grow your own
Conversation • Preservation
Check out quiet • Why not try it?
Take a walk • Forget the clock
Follow your heart • Forget being smart

Nina Raginsky

First Week of November

Gardening with Green Manures

Green manures are plants grown specifically to add organic matter and/or nitrogen to the soil, unlike cover crops, which are grown to prevent nutrients from being leached out of the soil, especially over winter. Hundreds of years ago during the feudal system of agriculture, farmers used four-year crop rotations, where one quarter of the land was left fallow every year. Farmers found the land maintained productivity when a fallow crop, which replenished the soil, was grown one year in every four. Growing green manures, and turning under the crop increases soil vitality, which results in healthier plants.

Green manure crops are seeded in fall. They are allowed to grow to a certain stage and then are dug into the soil in spring. This decayed matter provides food for the soil web of life – worms, microorganisms and other soil-borne organisms – which break down nutrients and make them available to plants. Green manures thereby increase soil fertility and improve plant health.

How else do green manures benefit soil?
Roots of green manure crops improve soil structure by breaking up heavy clay-based soils to allow better air circulation and drainage. Alternatively, the decomposed matter adds bulk to sandy soils, allowing them to hold more water.

When the availability of animal manures is limited, green manures play an important role. Seeds are inexpensive and easy to grow, and a small bag of seeds is a lot easier to lug around than a heavy sack of animal waste!

Why bother with green manures?
By putting down roots that hold soil structure together, green manure plants prevent erosion. Bare soils are vulnerable to being leached out or eroded by heavy winter rains. By storing valuable plant nutrients in their roots, green

Fall rye is cut back and then turned under in early spring.

manures hold plant food in the soil. Green manures that are legumes, such as field peas and favas, have the additional benefit of having bacteria on their roots that fix nitrogen from the air and add it to the soil.

Soil covered by a green manure crop is not susceptible to weed infestation. You know how nature abhors a vacuum! Better to plant a crop that benefits the soil than allow a weed infestation, which robs soil of valuable nutrients.

When can you sow green manures?
You can sow green manure crops in summer or winter, by choosing plants that flourish in these seasons. Manures can be sown in rows (best for larger seeds such as beans and lupins), or broadcast over the ground and raked in (for phacelia, rye and clovers).

In fall, a winter-hardy crop, such as fall rye, winter wheat, winter barley or field peas (leguminous) will germinate while the soil is still warm. Over the winter months, the soil will be covered with a low mat of green, and as it warms up in spring this will flourish. The lush top growth can then be cut back, and the rest of the plant dug or tilled under. In three to four weeks it will break down enough to begin spring planting in the enriched soil.

In summer, the choice could be buckwheat, alfalfa, fenugreek, phacelia or white clover – all of which grow fast in warm soils. These seeds can also be sown as an underplanting with another crop, as long as the two crops do not compete. The main crop can be harvested and the green manure dug under at the same time.

What kind of plants work as green manures?

- **Alfalfa** - winter-hardy, deep-rooting perennial, whose foliage contains an excellent range of plant foods. Sow April to July. If grown for a year or more, cut down two to three times to encourage new growth.

- **Bell beans** - winter-hardy, nitrogen fixers, related to broad beans. Sow September to November. Can be cut down and left to regrow once.

- **Buckwheat** - tender annual, related to polygonum, that tolerates poor soils. Sow April to August. Dig under when the first white flowers appear.

- **White clover** - vigorous, fast-growing annual that fixes nitrogen. Sow March to August. Prefers sandy soils.

- **Mustards** - fast-growing, winter-hardy annuals with yellow crucifer flowers. Sow March to September. Cut back after six to eight weeks, or any time up to flowering, when mustards get tough quickly. Note: Mustards are susceptible to club root.

- **Phacelia** - fast-growing annual. Direct sow March to September. Dig in before the pretty blue flowers open. Phacelia makes a good weed control.

- **Fall rye** - winter-hardy annual. Sow September to November. Grows fast in early spring. One of the most effective green manures. Note: Do not leave until the plants get well established, as they become well rooted and hard to dig under.

- **Vetch** - rapid-growing, winter-hardy annual, and a nitrogen-fixer. Sow March to September. Dig in after two to three months in summer, or leave to overwinter. Dig in before flowering. Good for weed control.

When's the best time to dig it in?

Just before maturity is the best time to dig in, before the plants set seed or get old and tough, which means the plant matter will break down less readily. The younger the green manure crop, the easier it is to incorporate into the soil, which means the sooner you'll be planting.

How hard are green manures to turn under?

Cut down the tops first. Using a weedeater is fastest, but cutting manually with hedge trimmers works just as well. Take a fork and up-end the whole plant, forking it under lightly and leaving it to breakdown. If you need to break up hard, compacted soil, a rototiller will make this job easier. No more than two passes does the trick. Overtilling soil destroys soil structure.

Do not overtill the soil or you will destroy soil structure.

A Farmer's Feedback

Bernie Martin-Wood: Last year I started using certified organic hen scratch as a green manure. I bought a 20 kg bag for $11.49. It consisted of 50% wheat and 50% barley seed. Some say that barley is not winter-hardy, but it certainly is at Two Wings Farm, as I have used it for many years instead of fall rye, which I find requires excessive tilling in the spring. I have also used winter wheat with success (but I don't know if the wheat in the hen scratch is winter wheat). It probably isn't, but it still does fine over the winter at our farm in Metchosin, Victoria. I usually mow the tops twice in early spring before I till my cover crop.

Second Week of November

The Miracle of Mulch

Mulch is a funny sounding word for a practice and product that provides such value. What exactly is it? Basically, it's the term used for layers of organic material added to soil. It's only since the 1970s that the practice of mulching began to catch on. Now it's de rigueur for conscientious gardeners, who endlessly expound its virtues.

The major benefits of mulch are:

- It reduces water loss from the soil.
- Suppression of weed growth.
- Protection from soil temperature extremes.
- Soil building and feeding, achieved by layers of organic matter that break down over time to form humus, which provides a source of nitrogen and phosphorus, as well as many trace elements.
- It lightens clay soils and bulks up sandy soils.
- It protects soil from wind erosion and provides an extra blanket of protection to plants in winter.

Apply ready compost in fall for a wonderful mulch.

What kind of mulching materials are there?

Materials range from compost, grass clippings, manure, leaves, wood chips, pine needles, straw, hay, coffee grounds, and even weeds (with no seeds!). Technically, non-organic materials such as landscape fabric, gravel and rocks can provide a mulch, but avoid materials that may break down and contaminate the soil, such as black plastic, and cedar or treated wood chips.

How much mulch do you need?

A three-inch (7.5 cm) layer of mulch is usually applied. If you wanted to add a three-inch layer of organic material to a 200 square foot garden, you would need two cubic yards of material. (Two cubic yards is the amount that would fill a square bin four-feet high and four-feet wide, which happens to be the ideal holding capacity of a compost bin!).

So if you calculate the square footage of your garden beds, you will know how many full compost bins you need in order to be able to spread three inches of compost over them every year. How simple can that be?

When do you apply mulch for maximum benefit?

Mulch garden beds every fall, immediately after the final weeding, cut-back and clean-up is done. It's the last thing to do in the garden before 'putting it to bed for the winter'.

In addition to increasing biological activity in the soil and feeding plants, mulch covers weed seeds so they will not germinate. Surveying tidy beds covered in a cozy layer of mulch is very satisfying. *TIP:* Before covering beds with mulch, replace plant labels while you know what and where the plants are. Tomato cages work well for marking where bulbs, peonies and dahlia tubers are. Place cages over any areas you want left undisturbed.

In hot weather, mulch acts as an insulating barrier, preventing evaporation and locking moisture into the soil. The only time not to mulch is when the ground is cold or waterlogged.

Are there any problems with mulching?
Wood-based mulches, such as sawdust or wood chips, and carbon mulches such as hay, straw and leaves can temporarily tie up nitrogen as they start to decompose. Supplementing with additional nitrogen may be necessary if plants show signs of stress from nitrogen deficiency, such as yellowing.

Some gardeners fear that damp layers of mulch provide breeding grounds for bugs and slugs. It's true that bug populations will increase due to the decomposition of the mulch, but these are for the most part the 'good bugs', busy at work assisting in breakdown and not damaging your plants. Slugs can be attracted to mulch in wet spring conditions, and for this reason it's best to wait until spring rains are over and the soil has warmed up before mulching. Usually by spring, mulch spread in fall has broken down to the point that it does not present problems.

TIP: If fungal problems occur, spread mulch out more thinly or remove it from under plants to increase air circulation.

Hardwood Cuttings
Hardwood cuttings are easy to start propagating in late fall or early winter, after leaf fall when the wood is dormant. Deciduous trees and shrubs such as cotinus, dogwood, willow, poplar and buddleia are good bets. Take heel or stem cuttings about a pencil in thickness from wood that grew the same season.

Heel cuttings. These are desirable for material that is harder to propagate. Pull the twig off an older branch, leaving a 'heel' at the base of the cutting.

Stem cuttings. Cut these six to twelve inches (15-30 cm) long, cleanly above a bud, with a sloping cut. Over the winter the cut surface will callous; it is from here that the roots will grow in spring.

Before inserting cuttings into rooting mix (see page 36) remove any soft tips.

Some species root better on bottom heat, because warmth is needed to encourage callous formation. (I experience the greatest success by placing cuttings in pots of rooting mix on a heated propagation bench, with bottom heat provided by thermostatically controlled heater cables).

Cuttings can be heeled into moist sand in a cold frame until spring. Insert bundles of ten cuttings into the sand with two-thirds of the cuttings buried. A few buds should remain above ground, from which the plants should regrow in spring.

Plant the sprouted overwintered cuttings outside in early April, before the buds break. Make a trench six inches deep and line it with a layer of sand. Plant the cuttings 6 inches (15 cm) apart at the same depth they were in the coldframe (two-thirds buried) and firm the soil from the trench around the cuttings. For more than one row, space the rows 12 inches (30 cm) apart.

Leave the cuttings growing in the trench until fall, ensuring that they do not dry out. They will root along the buried stem. They can then be potted up in their own pots into screened compost.

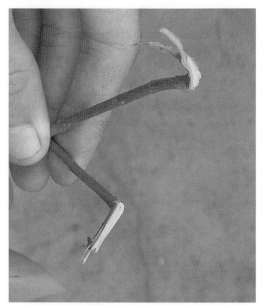
Heel cuttings

Pressure-Treated Wood

Billions of cubic feet of lumber, pressure treated with chromated copper arsenate (CCA), are sold in North America each year. CCA is an EPA-registered pesticide containing inorganic arsenic, which protects wood from termite attack and decay. Inorganic arsenic penetrates deeply into and remains in pressure-treated wood for a long time. However, it may migrate from treated wood into surrounding soil over time, and may also be dislodged from the wood surface. Exposure to inorganic arsenic presents certain hazards.

What is CCA and why is it harmful?
Chromated Copper Arsenate (CCA) consists of three principal compounds: arsenic in the form of arsenic pentoxide; chromium in the form of both hexavalent chromium and trivalent chromium; and copper in the form of copper oxide. Arsenic and hexavalent chromium have notorious reputations as toxins, carcinogens and teratogens.

CCA originated in 1938, but the concern over CCA in pressure-treated wood products only began a few years ago, when researchers discovered that fly ash from incinerators contained high levels of arsenic. CCA-treated wood scrap, burned as fuel, released deadly arsenic as arsine gas, and left arsenic and chromium in ashes. One tablespoon of arsenic-tainted CCA wood ash is considered lethal to humans.

Laboratory animals exposed to arsenic produced offspring with many different kinds of malformations, including cleft lip, cleft palate, open eye, limb defects, ear deformities, exencephaly and protruding organs. This was true for several different species of laboratory animals; the resultant malformations were dependent on dosage and timing.

Until 2004, no warning labels or literature were available for consumers, even though the industry was well aware of the health hazards of CCA. They were aware that the public, including children and pregnant women, were handling and being unknowingly exposed to potentially hazardous compounds, but they continued to drag their feet on solving the problem by switching to safer chemicals, such as alkaline copper quartenary (ACQ), a CCA alternative.

Finally, in 2205, CCA treated lumber was banned due to its toxicity. However, with an average life span of fifteen years or more, pressure-treated wood will pose a problem for years to come.

Alternatives to pressure-treated lumber for edging vegetable and ornamental beds and children's play areas include rough cedar, recycled untreated wood, driftwood, and recycled plastic lumber.

Precautions:
- Avoid frequent or prolonged inhalation of sawdust from CCA-treated wood. When sawing, sanding or machining, wear a mask. Such operations should be performed outdoors to prevent indoor accumulations of airborne sawdust. All sawdust and debris should be cleaned up and disposed of after construction.

- Wear gloves when working with treated wood. After any contact with the wood, wash thoroughly before eating, drinking, smoking or using the toilet.

- Because preservatives may accumulate on clothes, launder work clothes before reuse. Wash them separately from other clothing.

- Do not use treated wood for construction of beehives, due to the contact with honey.

- Treated wood should not be used anywhere it comes into contact with drinking water.

- Treated wood should not be burned in open fires, stoves, fireplaces or residential boilers, because toxic chemicals may be produced in smoke and ashes.

Summarized from www.mindfully.org/Pesticide/CCA-Pressure-Treated-Wood.htm
October 11th, 2004

Third Week of November

Questions & Answers

Diane: I would like to plant a kiwi. Of course I have to build a strong arbour first! When is the best time to plant this vine?

Answer: Kiwis take several years to establish and produce fruit. Young vines may be prone to damage in severe winters, so plant kiwis in spring after all danger of frost is over. It's best to provide young vines with winter protection for the first year or two, or make sure the kiwi's roots are well established before planting out.

Marion: We have just moved into a new house and half the lawn is infested with morning glory. We intend to turn much of the lawn into a native plant garden, but I hesitate to do anything until I get the morning glory under control. I've been told Roundup® is the only way. What are my alternatives?

Answer: This lawn has to go! For such a weed-infested lawn a sod stripper works wonders. You can rent one inexpensively. Set the sod stripper down to a depth that will peel off the sod with the roots of the morning glory in it. Remove the sod from the garden. Topdress the area with good garden loam, and reseed it. (See *Golf Green Lawn,* second week of March and *Lawn Care,* first week of September.)

Keep on top of any morning glory that may try to re-establish in the new lawn. Continue weed prevention by practising good turf management (aerating, proper cutting, watering, feeding etc.), keeping the grass happy but not the weeds.

Tineke: I do not understand the pruning of my two hydrangeas. #1, I pruned all the bare and dead-looking stems down to maybe a foot after the winter. Result: No flowers, but lots of new foliage! #2, I did the same, but only a few flowers. When is the proper time to prune hydrangeas?

Answer: Some hydrangeas flower on the previous year's growth and some on the new season's growth. #1 will therefore bloom for you next year, as it represents the former. #2 represents the latter. For pruning correctly, you need to establish which type of flowering hydrangea you have in the garden. Complicated, isn't it?

Wendy: My dad and I are frustrated with quack grass. He has dug up the bed twice, pulled all the grass, vinegared anything that has come back, tried landscape fabric, and has now decided to put the perennials in the bed into pots, give up the battle and use decorative gravel around the pots. Is there another way to defeat this nefarious grass?

Answer: Quack grass (or couchgrass) and morning glory are two pernicious weeds that run amok from rootstocks that creep under the soil surface and send up new plants as they travel. If broken, each section can become a new plant! The more you try to get these weeds out, the more likely you'll break the roots, which will double your trouble. For this reason, under no circumstances should an area invaded by such weeds be rototilled.

I have successfully dug out a large garden bed infested with quack grass, using a spading fork, carefully peeling back and removing every section of root I could find, and disposing of it. Never put pernicious weeds in the compost pile. Put them in black plastic bags and leave them in the hot sun to solarize them. You can then compost them. (Also see *Questions & Answers,* fourth week of July.)

After the initial attack, every time you spot quack grass, remove it immediately before it can re-establish. Eventually, persistence and effort will pay off and you will be on top of the problem.

Suzanne: We have a substantial area of ancient rockery covered in ivy. I've been ignoring it for years but can't do that any longer; it's scaring me! Apart from pulling it out, which would be impossible as the roots go way down beneath the rock, how can I get rid of it in a biologically friendly way? Or can I?

Answer: Ivy climbs, spreads, penetrates and clings to any surface it comes into contact with. Anyone who plants or inherits an invasive ivy should be prepared to control it when it gets out of hand. This may mean several cutbacks a year because as ivy matures it spreads even faster.

The best approach is to trace it as far back to its roots as possible, and cut it (or saw it) down. Keep on doing this as it attempts to come back. As the top growth dies back, the challenge will be to remove the dead, brown matter. Cut, cut and cut again, until the ivy is so weakened it struggles to grow back.

Sawing the woody 'trunk' off ivy at the base stopped top growth, but it was too late for this tree, which was suffocated by ivy left to its own devices for years.

Joanne: Your information about Roundup® (second week of September) has me thinking you will be interested in this. I was told by a farmer that he uses it to fell the potato foliage, and to make tubers develop firmer skins for harvest. In previous years I have seen the crop turn brown overnight. When I asked if it was blight, I was told about the Roundup®. I still find this hard to believe.

Answer: I went on the Internet to check this out. I did a Google search on glyphosate + potatoes. Roundup application pre-harvest, during the growth cycle and even before planting is just the tip of the iceberg! Read a summary of recommendations for industrial potato farming at www.wsu.edu/~potatoes/ipm.htm. I will never eat conventionally grown potatoes again!

Frank: My Brussels sprouts are about six-feet tall, loaded with sprouts from the bottom to the top. The problem is they are not tight knobs but loose clusters of leaves. Could it be something to do with soil texture? My soil is quite sandy.

Answer: It's all about experimenting until you find a variety suited to your garden. I experienced leafy sprouts a few years back growing a heritage variety called Long Island Improved ('Catskill'). Now I grow 'Vancouver', a four-foot tall plant, which grows loaded with tight buds of great Brussels sprouts.

Brussels sprouts 'Vancouver'

Fourth Week of November

The Greens and the Browns

For our two-acre garden, we built two three-bin compost systems using free recycled wooden pallets. In preparation for filling a bin, I stockpile ingredients such as the following:

- moss scraped off the roof (green and brown)
- fallen leaves from big-leaf maples (brown)
- spoiled hay from our neighbour's horses (brown)
- herbaceous prunings from the fall cleanup and seedless weeds (green)
- leftover nursery plants, potted in screened compost (green and brown)

I also don my gumboots to fetch a trailerload of fresh steamy horse manure.

TIP: Make gumboots super cozy by using a felt liner and wearing a pair of thick woollen socks.

The above materials will make some great compost. When building or turning a compost pile, incorporate layers of manure because it's rich in bacteria and microbes, which are activators for decomposition.

The quality of the finished compost and the speed of breakdown is contingent on the layering of materials, so pay particular attention to how you build the pile. At this time of year, when materials are damp, there may be no need to moisten the pile as you build.

The best ratio of carbon materials (the browns) to nitrogen matter (the greens) in your pile has been determined to be 30:1. This means that most of the materials you add should be browns (carbon). Too many browns – a pile with too much sawdust, woodchips or leaves – would take years to break down. Too many greens – grass clippings – will release excess nitrogen as ammonia gas, and you'll get a slimy, smelly mess!

To build a compost pile

Use materials you have at hand, identify them as greens or browns, and start to build. Begin with a layer of herbaceous prunings, because woody stalks provide a well-aerated layer for the foundation of the pile. Make each layer no more than six inches deep, and alternate greens and browns as you build.

Our compost 'sandwich' looks something like this: leaves followed by potted plants, a layer of manure followed by spoiled hay, followed by moss, followed by herbaceous prunings, and leaves. These layers are repeated until the bin is full (ideally two cubic yards in capacity, four feet x four feet x four feet). This is not an exact science; guesstimating works fine.

Insulate the top layer with leaves to lock in heat generated by thermophilic (heat-loving) bacteria, which are responsible for speedy breakdown. In winter, cover the entire pile with a tarp or wood (unpainted), to prevent rain from leaching out valuable nutrients.

Just think of a green and brown lasagna that will feed your plants when you are making compost – it will make the task much more fun!

December

A naked house, a naked moor,
A shivering pool before the door,
A garden bare of flowers or fruit
And poplars at the garden foot.
Such is the place that I live in,
Bleak without and bare within.

Yet shall your ragged moor receive
The incomparable pomp of eve,
And the gold glories of the dawn
Behind your shivering trees be drawn;
And when the wind from place to place,
Doth the unmoored cloud-galleons chase,
Your garden gloom and gleam again
With leaping sun, with glancing rain.

Here shall the wizard moon ascend
The heavens, in the crimson end
Of day's declining splendour; here
The army of the stars appear:
The neighbouring hollows dry and wet
Spring shall with tender flowers beset,
And oft the morning muses see
Larks rising from the broomy lea;
And every fairy wheel and thread
Of cobweb dew-bediamonded.

When daisies go, shall winter time
Silver the simple grass with rime.
Autumnal frost enchant the pool
And make the cart-ruts beautiful;
And when snow-bright the moor expands
How shall your children clap their hands:
To make this Earth our hermitage
A cheerful and a changeful plage
God's bright and intricate device
Of days and seasons doth suffice.

R.L. Stevenson

First Week of December

Weeds and What They're Good For!

Weed seeds arrive with birds, on the wind, on our shoes and clothing, and on pet fur. They are persistent, lying dormant until conditions are just right for germination. Digging soil brings weed seeds up to the surface, which helps them germinate. Perennial weeds can spread quickly by division, when each little piece roots into a new plant. These are two more good reasons to practise no-dig gardening and regular mulching. *TIP:* Hoe weeds before they set seed and multiply your problem!

> 'A weed is a wild herb springing where it is not wanted'.   Concise Oxford Dictionary

A garden will always have weeds, but there's a great deal to be learned from observing them. There's always a good reason why weeds spring up in the first place. An infestation points to an imbalance in the soil, such as poor drainage, lack of aeration, low fertility or a mineral deficiency. Weeds often thrive in poor soils, which indicates that the soil is deficient in the essentials for healthy plant growth.

> To acquire knowledge, one must study; but to acquire wisdom, one must observe.
> *Marilyn vos Savant*

Many perennial weeds are deep rooted, penetrating into the sub-soil where they access trace elements and minerals. When they decompose, their leaves and stems enrich the soil with these valuable elements, which may not otherwise be available to shallow-rooted plants. It's important to return weeds to the soil for this reason, either by composting them or turning them under to decay in the garden. Deep roots also penetrate to aerate soil, helping with drainage. Dandelions, which thrive on heavy clay soils, do a great job of this.

Weeds can be used as indicators of general problems, and can even correct imbalances and deficiencies. Weeds disappear when these conditions are corrected and soil conditions favour the growth of other plants (hopefully not other weeds!). The solution to a weed infestation is therefore to improve soil fertility, not to zap the area with soil-destroying herbicides.

> "What is a weed? A plant whose virtues have not yet been discovered."
> *Ralph Waldo Emerson*

What Weeds Can Tell Us

- Daisies, rich in calcium, thrive on lawns lacking in lime. (When daisies decompose, they add calcium to correct this deficiency.)
- *Equisetum,* horsetail, indicates an acid, clay soil in need of drainage. If the soil is drained and fertility rises, horsetail will disappear.
- Docks, sorrel and thistles indicate heavy, badly drained and acid soils.
- Dandelions indicate that the soil lacks essential minerals and elements.
- Clovers, medicks, vetches and wild peas (legumes) indicate a nitrogen deficiency, and can correct this condition in the soil.
- Creeping buttercup thrives in heavy, poorly drained soils.
- Bindweed generally thrives in sandy soils.
- Stinging nettles prefer light, sandy soils. (High in nitrogen, nettles stimulate the growth of plants nearby.)
- Chickweed, groundsel, chicory, and lambsquarters are shallow-rooted weeds that grow in fertile conditions. They indicate an improvement in fertility.

Comfrey and stinging nettles make high-quality liquid fertilizers (see *Special-teas,* second week of April). By extracting minerals from the sub-soil and storing them in their leaves, nettles and comfrey become rich in nitrogen, potassium and calcium. Nettles are also high in iron. When nettle leaves are steeped in rainwater, the resulting concentrate can be used as a feed, releasing nutrients to plants.

Nature never leaves the ground uncovered. In winter, weeds give protection from rains and roots penetrate to aid with drainage. They also provide a store of food for soil bacteria, which can then remain active to build a store of plant food for spring. Where groundcovers remain and flourish in winter, the result is an increase in soil fertility.

Weeds That Feed
- *Asclepias* (milkweed) - butterflies
- *Cirsium* spp. (thistles) - butterflies, goldfinches
- *Chenopodium* spp. (lambsquarters) - songbirds
- *Melilotus* spp. (sweet clover) - butterflies
- *Stellaria media* (chickweed) - songbirds
- *Taraxacum* spp. (dandelions) - goldfinches, pine siskins
- *Trifolium* spp. (clover) - butterflies
- *Urtica dioica* (nettles) - butterflies

Asclepias tuberosa *butterfly weed - bright orange flowers attract butterflies in mid-summer.*

Red Wigglers
Eisenia foetida, commonly known as red wigglers, live in piles of garden waste, manure and compost piles – anywhere they can find a good source of food. They have two stomachs and eat all the time, one worm eating half its weight in a day!

Red wigglers need to be kept moist at all times because they breathe through their skin. They are at home in organic material, but do not like bright light or high temperatures, preferring to burrow underground, where it is dark and cool. That's why, when you turn compost and it heats up, worms crawl out or move to the edges where it is cooler.

Vermicomposting is a way of turning food waste under controlled conditions into rich, fertile worm castings. Two pounds of red wigglers (about 2,000 worms) will consume one pound of waste a day. Vermicomposting can be done year-round, inside and outside, by apartment dwellers and homeowners. The resulting worm compost is excellent for houseplants and soil conditioning. All you need is a container, some wiggler worms, bedding such as shredded newspaper, and your fruit and vegetable waste.

Save the Worms!
The real tiller and fructifier of the soil is *Lumbricus terrestris,* the earthworm. As earthworms move through soil, they mix and keep it in motion, creating aeration which improves drainage. During digestion they humify organic matter, combining it with ingested clay colloids to form nutrient-rich worm castings. Their castings aid bacteria, actinomycetes and other organisms that dwell in the soil. Earthworms continuously excrete $CaCo_3$ as slime as they move through the earth, which helps maintain a soil pH within the range plants prefer.

> Over half a million earthworms can live in just one hectare of soil. Together they can eat nine tonnes of leaves, stems and dead roots a year, and turn over 36 tonnes of soil. They are the engineers of the ecosystem.

Excessive tilling, and the use of pesticides, herbicides, fungicides, and chemical fertilizers will harm or destroy earthworms. Reducing their populations creates a loss of humus, a collapse of soil structure, and negative effects on soil aeration, nutrition, pH and water holding capacity.

> "It may be doubted whether there are many other animals which have played so important a role in the history of the world as have these lowly organized creatures. All the vegetable mold of England passed through, and will again pass many times through the intestinal canals of worms." *Charles Darwin (1881)*

Earthworms starve in sterile soils; they need organic matter derived from compost, manures, mulch or green manure crops to feed on. So feed your soil and SAVE THE WORMS!

Getting to the Root of the Vegetable

I consider many root crops to be winter staples; cold-hardy plants that see us through the coldest months, whether harvested from the garden as required or from storage. Early North American settlers depended on root crops to get them through the winter. Beets, carrots, parsnips, turnips, rutabagas and salsify have been grown as reliable winter staples for hundreds of years.

Growing Tips

- When direct seeding, mix seeds with sand to prevent overseeding and overcrowding.

- To avoid disease, practise crop rotation by not planting where root crops were grown the previous year.

- Avoid planting in heavy soils, where roots will become stunted or forked. Well-worked soil with a friable tilth is best.

- Add potash in the form of kelp meal or wood ashes, and phosphorus in the form of rock phosphate for the best root development.

- Thin root crops to give them space to grow, or they will become misshapen.

- Root crops do not need as much sun as above-ground plants, so can be interplanted amongst rows of other vegetables.

Harvest root crops in the afternoon. Plants gather their vital life force from photosynthesis during sunlight hours. At the end of the day, plants move this life force down from the leaves to be stored in the roots. Root crops harvested in the afternoon have been shown to have better keeping qualities.

Beets *Beta vulgaris*
Direct sowings of beets can be made in succession from late March until early August. Plant seeds one inch apart, and when the seedlings are two inches tall, thin them to four inches apart. Beet seedlings can be transplanted, so one row can turn into two or more. Eat the tender thinnings, followed by the tasty baby beets, and leave some mature beets for fall storage or for succulent beet greens, (even sweeter after hard frosts). Beets store better than any other root crop, and may be mulched to get them through the winter in the garden. My favourite variety for large sweet beets and prolific greens is 'Lutz'.

'Lutz' beets - for large sweet beets and lots of nutritious beet greens.

TIP: If beets are not tender and sweet it may be due to a lack of boron in the soil. Boron can be supplied by sprinkling borax very *lightly* over the soil.

Carrots *Daucus carota*
Carrots originally hailed from Afghanistan, where they were purple, red or white. The first orange carrots came from Holland in the 17th century. Seed of members of the Umbelliferae family, such as dill, celeriac, carrots, sweet cicely and parsnips is slow to germinate, and must be absolutely fresh for good germination. Direct seed in May, as soon as the soil has warmed up. Carrots need a sandy loam, so heavy or clay soils must be lightened with organic matter, which should be added the fall before, as newly manured ground results in forked roots.

To avoid thinning, which attracts the carrot rust fly, seedlings can be left crowded in small groups, when they will grow into small bunches of carrots. Try the nifty carrot trick (See *A Nifty Trick for Carrots,* first week of May) or mulch your carrot patch with coffee grounds, which confuses the female fly as she hunts for foliage to lay her eggs on.

Many gardeners agree that Nantes carrots, which have blunt rather than tapered roots, are the best flavoured. Unfortunately Nantes carrots are seldom grown commercially, so they are not usually found in supermarkets. In my clay soil, which has been amended, I grow Danvers carrots successfully. *TIP:* Carrots are high in beta carotene and loaded with minerals, but try not to peel them, as many of the nutrients are in the peel or just under it.

Celeriac (Celery Root) *Apium graveolens*
Much easier to grow than celery, celeriac is often overlooked as a tasty root vegetable that can be harvested throughout winter. Seeds are slow to germinate and can be started indoors in late February/March. Transplant seedlings into the garden in May, ten inches apart, where they will grow to baseball-sized roots by fall. The best sized roots require rich, moist soil. Use peeled celeriac whenever you want a hit of celery, without the hassle of growing it.

Celeriac - celery root

Jerusalem artichokes (Sunroot)
Helianthus tuberosus
A perennial vegetable, that once planted will become a permanent fixture in the garden. Jerusalem artichokes spread rapidly by underground shoots that grow into tubers. There are many varieties, with either red or white tubers, some producing showy yellow 'sunflowers' in October. The red varieties tend to be more prolific than the white ones.

One of the easiest plants to grow, Jerusalem artichokes thrive in any garden soil, but the best tubers are grown in good soil in full sun. Tubers should be planted early in the year in March or April, before they have rooted, and can be left to grow until harvested in late fall. They are sweetest if left until after hard frosts, and can be harvested as needed throughout the winter. Try eating them peeled and sliced with a veggie dip (crunchy and refreshing), or drizzled with olive oil and roasted for 25 minutes (sweet and nutty).

Jerusalem artichokes can be dug as needed from the winter garden.

Pickled Sunroots (sweet and crunchy)

6 large sunroots, washed but unpeeled
1 1/4 Tbsp. coarse salt
3/4 cup white vinegar
6 Tbsp. sugar
1/4 teaspoon hot red pepper flakes

Thinly slice the sunroots and transfer to a stainless steel or ceramic (non-reactive) bowl. Add 1 Tbsp. of salt. Using your fingers, rub each piece with salt. Let stand for 15 minutes at room temperature, then rinse under cold running water.

Add vinegar, sugar, red pepper flakes, and the remaining 1/4 Tbsp. salt. Toss to combine. Refrigerate for a week before eating. Will keep refrigerated up to six months.

Onions *Allium cepa*
Onions need heat and sun for bulbing, but it is the amount of daylight that determines the time it takes to form a mature bulb. 'Yellow Globe', which requires less daylight, matures in 100 days, but 'Red Wethersfield' which requires 14 hours of daylight, will take longer to mature. It's important for northern gardeners to choose the variety they grow with care. Yellow types store well and can last until spring.

Onions are actually easier to grow from seed than sets, as they won't bolt as fast. Sow seed indoors in late February/March or direct seed outdoors in April. Onions can be grown in double or triple rows to save garden space, as they only need to be planted the width of the bulb apart. *TIP*: Allow the soil to dry out two weeks before harvesting in fall, and cure the onions well in warm, dry conditions for improved storage life.

Parsnips *Pastinaca sativa*
The trick to growing good parsnips is to direct seed them in time for the roots to mature by winter, so get them in no later than May. Parsnips can freeze solid without losing any of their flavour, in fact, a hard freeze will improve them.

Try boiling parsnips until tender and tossing them with butter and cinnamon, which complement their sweet flavour. For a delicious side vegetable, try drizzling them with olive oil and roasting them in the oven for 30 minutes.

Potatoes *Solanum tuberosum*
One of the most diverse food crops in the world, potatoes have been grown for thousands of years, originating from the Andes, South America, but only arriving in North America with the Irish settlers.

Although potatoes like a well-fed and manured soil, do not over-manure, as this can lead to potato scab. Do not lime soil where potatoes are to grow, as they prefer an acidic pH below 6.

Potatoes are usually planted in April. It's best to plant an entire medium-sized tuber, as cutting the seed potatoes leaves them susceptible to rot in cold, wet soils. Plant potatoes by making a shallow furrow and lining it with layers of grass clippings and leaves. Grown this way, potatoes will be cleaner and easier to 'pluck' out. When potato plants reach six inches tall, hill earth up onto the stems to exclude light, but make sure the tubers are not buried too deeply, as this adversely affects the yield.

TIP: To get the longest season of harvest, plant one early-season variety ('Epicure','Caribe'), one mid-season variety ('Yukon Gold','Red Pontiac'), and one late-season variety ('Russet', 'Yellow Banana').

Rutabagas *Brassica napus*
In England, where I grew up, the big yellow roots of rutabagas are called Swedes, and are often eaten mashed with potatoes, nutmeg, salt, pepper and butter to make them more palatable.

Rutabagas originated back in the 1600s from an accidental cross between a cabbage and a turnip, and many people find the strong flavour not to their liking. Mashing them with another root crop makes all the difference. Rutabagas are extremely winter-hardy and can be dug from the garden throughout the winter.

Turnips *Brassica napus*
Native to Scandinavia and northern Russia, turnips have a short growing season, which makes it easy to grow a good harvest of them for winter. They are as easy to grow as beets, and like beets, their nutritious, tasty greens are often overlooked. If protected under a six-inch layer of mulch, turnips can be harvested throughout the winter.

Winter varieties of squash when properly stored will keep throughout the winter for use in many delicious recipes.

Luke's Roasted Vegetables

Preheat oven 375°F (190°C)

Cut the following into thick strips:
6 large carrots
6 medium yams (or substitute squash)
1 red pepper

Add:
1 large red onion, quartered into chunks
1 garlic bulb with tips of cloves sliced off
1 small piece of fresh ginger root, diced
1 sprig fresh rosemary

Toss the above together in a marinade of:
1/3 cup olive oil
2 Tbsp. balsamic vinegar
2 Tbsp. maple syrup
3/4 Tbsp. soy sauce
1/2 tsp. coriander seeds, heated in an
   iron skillet and crushed
1 tsp. Madras curry powder
1 tsp. salt
1/2 tsp. pepper

Whisk until well blended.

Roast uncovered on a baking sheet for 30 minutes. Turn the vegetables to baste and add 1/4 cup of whole almonds. Turn heat down to 350°F (175°C) and roast for another 30 minutes.

Adapted version - first seen in Helen Chesnut's column, Times Colonist.

Second Week of December

Greenery for the Festive Season

Make your own seasonal decorations using greenery from nature. You can make festive wall swags, table settings, wreaths or arrangements in vases, using an abundance of available natural materials. Have fun being creative, and don't forget the ribbon!

Festive Greenery

- Salal (pretty pink berries, glossy green foliage)
- Swordferns (dramatic foliage, colourful spores)
- Mahonia (dark green, handsome foliage)
- *Sarcococca* sweet box (dark green, glossy foliage, black berries)
- *Nandina domestica* heavenly bamboo (red-tinged foliage, shiny red berries)
- *Callicarpa* beauty berry (profusion of bright purple berries)
- *Ilex* spp. holly (berries and colourful foliage)
- Trailing ivy (colourful foliage)
- Cedar, fir, balsam and hemlock boughs (the mainstay of arrangements)
- Assorted cones (have fun looking for different shapes and sizes)
- *Cornus* spp. dogwood (colourful red stems)
- Rosehips (red, red, red!)
- *Cotoneaster* spp. (red berries)
- *Vaccinium* spp. huckleberries (more red!)

Never wildcraft from nature with a 'clearcut' mentality. Take only what you need in consideration of the impact on the remaining ecosystem.

Gift Ideas for Gardeners

- Bird feeders (squirrel proof!)
- Bags of bird food
- Suet or peanut blocks
- Great gardening books...so many to choose from!
- A trug or basket to put a selection of gifts in
- Almond biscotti, for gardening tea breaks (see recipe page 160)
- A bulb planter (with a bag of bulbs, too?)
- A dibber - great for planting bulbs, garlic, peas, onions and leeks
- Garden stakes, tied with ribbon or raffia
- Bamboo poles - as above
- Gardening gloves, rubberized or leatherized for thorny plants!
- A woolly gardening hat
- Ear muffs - warm ears are a must!
- Felt liners for boots - cozy feet are another must!
- Gumboots to go with liners
- Garden clogs - great for slipping in and out of the house
- Balls of green jute twine
- Hedge trimmer
- Hose reel
- A Korean hoe - a most useful hand tool
- Kneeling pads
- Gardener's hand cream or soap
- Relaxing bath salts for aching muscles!
- Gift certificate for a massage (even better!)
- Loppers
- Plant pots
- A lightweight wheelbarrow (gift wrapping could be a problem!)
- Secateurs – only the best quality will do
- Seeds
- Hand tools or gardening gadgets
- Tool hooks
- Outdoor thermometer and/or barometer
- Watering cans or spray wand
- A partridge and pears to hang in a tree
- Next year's garden calendar (or make one with pictures from your own garden)
- Aluminum plant tags, which last forever!
- A magazine subscription
- Membership to a gardening club
- Gift certificate from a local garden centre
- Season ticket to a local botanic garden
- Glass bowls filled with pebbles and paperwhites
- Pots of planted *Iris reticulata,* grape hyacinths, cyclamen or hyacinths
- An amaryllis bulb
- A gift certificate from you or the kids for gardening work that says "I'll turn the compost, rake the leaves or cut the lawn for one month"
- A mug, apron or T-shirt that says: "Gardening Forever – Housework Whenever!"
- A fridge magnet or coaster that says: "I Live in the Garden, I Only Sleep in the House!"

Ten Reasons to Eat Organic Food

1. Organic farming is better for wildlife

A report by Britain's Soil Association shows that wildlife is richer and more varied on organic farms. A typical organic field has five times as many wild plants, 57% more insect and animal species, and 44% more birds in cultivated areas than a conventional field.

2. Organic farming is better for the soil

Other British Soil Association studies show that organic fields have deeper vegetation and more weed cover. The soil in organically cultivated fields contains 88% more 'epigeal arthropods' and more diverse and abundant populations of earthworms and soil insects, including pest-eating spiders and beetles.

A new Swiss study demonstrates that organic soils house more microbes and mycorrhizae (fungi that attach themselves to plant roots and help plants absorb nutrients).

3. Organic food is better for reproduction

Ten out of fourteen animal studies show that animals fare better when fed organic food over conventional food. Chickens fed on organic food have a 28% higher rate of egg production. There were half as many perinatal deaths, and other deaths prior to weaning, for baby rabbits and mice whose mothers ate organic food.

4. Organic food may fight cancer, stroke and heart problems

Plants produce salicylic acid as a defence against stress and disease. If plants never have to resist bugs, because of pesticide use, they generate less salicylic acid. Scottish scientists found that organic vegetable soups contained almost six times as much salicylic acid as non-organic vegetable soups. Salicylic acid has been shown to help fight hardening of the arteries and bowel cancer.

5. Organic food contains more nutrients

According to a *Globe and Mail* study done in Canada in 2002, today's fruit and vegetables contain dramatically less vitamins and minerals compared to fifty years ago. The average potato has lost 100% of its vitamin A, 57% of its vitamin C and iron, 28% of its calcium, 50% of its riboflavin and 18% of its thiamin. Similar results have been found in Britain and the US.

In a review of thirty studies comparing the nutrient content of organic versus conventional crops, organic crops had higher nutrient content 40% of the time, while conventional crops were higher 15% of the time.

For twelve foods studied, a cancer specialist in France found that organic food showed higher amounts of vitamins A, C, E and B, and increased levels of zinc and calcium. On average, organic food contains higher levels of vitamin C and essential minerals such as calcium, magnesium, iron and chromium, as well as cancer-fighting antioxidants. Top chefs prefer organic food, because they say it tastes better, and prefer using local and organic ingredients.

6. Debunk the myth – organic farming CAN feed the world!

In 1998 the Rodale Institute in Pennsylvania published the results of a 15-year study comparing three ways of growing maize and soybeans: a conventional method using chemical fertilizers and pesticides, an organic crop rotation system using legume crops, and an organic system using manure as fertilizer. The average yields were similar for all three systems.

In Britain, a 150-year-old experiment by the Rothamsted Experimental Station shows that organic yields measure up: wheat yields on manured plots average 3.45 tonnes per hectare, compared to 3.40 tonnes on chemically fertilized plots. An eight-year study at the U of C, Davis, California, shows similar yields for conventional and organic tomatoes, safflower, corn and beans.

7. Organic food contains no GMOs

Genetically modified crops, food ingredients and inputs are not allowed under organic standards.

8. The reliance on drugs is removed

There is growing concern about the high use of antibiotics on farm animals, and the possible associated effects on human health. Animal welfare is taken very seriously under organic standards. The benefits of the organic approach are acknowledged by animal welfare organizations worldwide.

9. Organic farming produces higher yields under drought conditions

Organic soils hold more water. Studies of grain and soybean production in the US Midwest showed that organic growers produced higher yields than conventional farmers during droughts, while they had similar yields during regular conditions.

10. Organic food and farming is safer

Farmers in Canada and the US who use the pesticide 2,4-D suffer a higher rate of non-Hodgkin's lymphoma cancer. In Sweden, exposure to phenoxy herbicides has been shown to increase the risk of contracting lymphomas sixfold. Migrant farmworkers suffer abnormally high rates of multiple myeloma, stomach, prostate and testicular cancers.

Organic farming is safer for wildlife and the environment, causing less pollution from spray drifts and runoff and less toxic residues and waste.

Thanks to Guy Dauncey for help in compiling this list: www.earthfuture.com.

A study conducted by the UK's Soil Association found that organic milk has higher levels of nutrients and antioxidants than conventional milk. Dairy cows raised on an organic diet produced milk with 50% more Vitamin E and 75% more beta carotene than conventionally farmed dairy. The organic milk was two to three times higher in zeaxanthine and lutein, both powerful antioxidants.

www.organicconsumers.org

Third Week of December

The Wonder of Walnuts

There's a lot more to walnuts than their tasty crunch! Walnuts have many health benefits. They are rich in antioxidants, vitamins and omega-3 fatty acids. In 2004 the US Food and Drug Administration even touted a handful of walnuts a day as reducing the risk of coronary heart disease. Chinese herbalists take advantage of the walnut's insecticidal properties by using them as a vermifuge to get rid of internal parasites such as tapeworms.

Dyes are made from walnut husks and used for furniture stains, hair dyes and inks, and we all know walnut wood makes beautiful furniture. Crushed walnut shells have a range of uses, from industrial-strength abrasive cleaners and high-powered insulation material, to cosmetic exfoliating face masks. Walnut kernels are pressed to make walnut oil, used long ago by the ancient Egyptians for embalming mummies.

Although often planted as shade trees (with the bonus of edible nuts), walnut trees (genus Juglans) have a darker side. They are toxic to a number of plant species, emitting a chemical called juglone (5-hydroxy-1,4-naphthoquinone) from their roots, which leaches into the soil and causes nearby plants to turn yellow and die. The most potent of all is the black walnut, a fast-growing tree to 100 feet! Don't plant walnut trees anywhere near flower, shrub or vegetable gardens, as they can affect plants within a 50-foot range.

Keep Your Christmas Tree Happy

- Start right! When choosing a tree, make sure it's fresh by shaking it vigorously to ensure the needles do not drop.

- When you get your tree home, saw off about half an inch from the base to open up water-conducting channels.

- If possible, leave the tree outside with its base standing in water until you're ready to bring it indoors.

- Indoors, secure your tree in a water-holding stand or use a large bucket, and wedge the tree in firmly with stones or soil.

- Avoid placing your tree in a warm spot close to a fire or radiator, where its life will be considerably shortened.

- Christmas trees need water, whether rooted or not. Trees can drink up to a litre of water a day. Place the tree trunk in a reservoir of water and top it up each day. If Christmas trees are regularly watered you won't need to spray them with an anti-desiccant chemical spray.

Almond Biscotti   Preheat oven to 300°F (150°C)

Beat together:
2 1/2 cups sugar
2 cups cake flour
1 3/4 cups plus 3 Tbsp. all-purpose flour
1/8 tsp. baking soda
1/8 tsp. salt

Combine:
4 large eggs
2 tsp. unsalted butter at room temperature
1 tsp. vanilla essence
1/4 tsp. almond essence

Stir in:
1 1/2 cups whole almonds, toasted
  and chopped

Grease a large cookie sheet and line with parchment paper. Put dough on a floured surface and form into two 4" wide by 12" long logs. Place these 2 1/2" apart on the parchment paper.

Bake one hour until golden brown.

Logs will spread and flatten. Cut them into strips 1/2" wide and place the biscotti strips on parchment paper again, flat side down. Bake for another 30 minutes.

Jose Cuervo Christmas Cake

1 cup water
1 tsp. baking soda
1 cup sugar
1 tsp. salt
1 cup brown sugar
1 cup lemon juice
4 large eggs
1 cup nuts
2 cups dried fruit

1 bottle Jose Cuervo Tequila

- Take a large bowl and check the Jose Cuervo Tequila to be sure it is of the highest quality. Pour one level cup and drink.

- Turn on the electric mixer. Beat one cup of butter in a large fluffy bowl.

- Add one teaspoon of sugar. Beat again. At this point it's best to make sure the Cuervo is still O.K. Try another cup... just in case!

- Turn off the mixerer thingy. Break 2 leggs and add to the bowl and chuck in the cup of dried fruit. Pick the frigging fruit off the floor. Mix on the turner! If the fried druit gets stuck in the beaterers, just pry it loose with a drewscriver. Sample the Cuervo to check for tonsisticity.

- Next, sift two cups of salt, or something. Who giveshz a sheet. Check the Jose Cuervo.

- Now shift the lemon juice and strain your nuts. Add one table.

- Add a spoon of sugar, or somefink. Whatever you can find.

- Greash the oven. Turn the cake tin 360 degrees and try not to fall over. Don't forget to beat off the turner!

- Finally, throw the bowl through the window. Finish the Cose Juervo and make sure to put the stove in the dishwasher.

CHERRY MISTMAS!!!

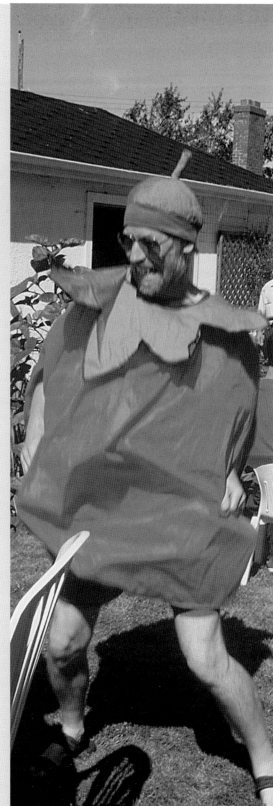

Fourth Week of December

Peat-Free Gardening

Peat is a fast-disappearing resource that provides a rich habitat for rare flowers, insects and birds. Peat is found in damp habitats covered with reeds, rushes, mosses and other bog plants. Once a peat bog is drained, the environmental impact is devastating and irreversible.

Over three million cubic metres of peat is used for horticulture in the UK every year, and only 6% of the UK's original lowland peat remains. Of the remaining peat extraction sites, twelve include sites of special scientific interest. Peat bogs are paying too high a price.

As a growing medium, coir-based products have received mixed reviews from traditionalists. A frequent complaint is that coir dries out much faster than peat. In fact, coir retains water well, but gardeners are taken in by the surface appearance, which seems dry. Unlike peat, which is almost impossible to rehydrate once it dries out, coir-based mediums respond well to rehydration. Most problems with coir are actually caused by overwatering, which results in nutrients being washed out.

Trials are now under way to assess peat-free growing mediums that contain a combination of composted wood fibre, bark and loam, with added nutrients. These are being used for tests on perennials, bedding plants and a range of shrubs.

A trial at Sissinghurst, which began in March 2000, has yielded positive results. Peat-free mediums were found to be no more difficult to use, and though slightly more expensive than conventional peat-based growing mediums, went further. They are not suitable for seed-sowing, because the nutrient level is too strong; nor for rhododendrons or other acid-lovers, which respond better to other formulas.

Of course the best solution is not having to use peat in the first place by making your own compost. (See *Composting Is Not Rocket Science!,* first week of March and *The Greens and the Browns,* fourth week of November.)

Questions & Answers

Pauline: Could you advise what brand of heating coils you use for bottom heat? You obviously think coils are better than mats, or is it just the scale of your operation that determines your choice?

Answer: I use commercially available heating cables, which are thermostatically controlled. The thermostat keeps the heat regulated at 70°F (21°C). (Your local garden centre should stock these.) Mats work fine too, but are more expensive to purchase. I use a 25-foot long cable in a 6' x 4' wooden propagation box, the cable 'snaked' and laid four inches apart along the entire length of the box. The cable is simply held in place by nailed U-shaped tacks, and is then covered with two inches of sand. Pots of cuttings and tender plants are placed on top of the warm sand.

You could also fill the box with several inches of rooting mix and root cuttings or start seeds right into this. Propagation mediums on bottom heat stay warm throughout the winter, and seeds germinate and cuttings root very successfully this way. Tender plants survive deep freezes that may otherwise kill them when provided with this energy-efficient means of heating.

Marion: We are going to have a subdivision built behind our beautiful, forested back yard. Help! We need a barrier to go up quick! Do you think Leylandii cypress would be a wise choice, if we maintain it once a year?

Answer: I see your dilemma and I agree that Leylandii cypress would be a fast-growing screen for you. After all, they grow fifteen to twenty feet in five years! In fact, so fast-growing that in the UK they have caused court cases between neighbours. Leylandii cypress block views and sunlight, and hedge people in when they don't want to be. Some borough councils are putting "anti-social" bylaws in place to forbid the planting of these trees. If you feel Leylandii cypress will not cause problems to your potential neighbours, go ahead and stand back while they take off!

Carol: This fall I collected seeds from columbine and nodding onion. Do I need to freeze these seeds to store them before planting in early spring?

Answer: Low moisture and temperatures slow the seeds' metabolism so that their food reserves stay high for longer. Seeds achieve their longest potential viability if stored in a refrigerator or freezer.

TIP: It's important to allow frozen seeds to reach room temperature before opening the container to prevent moisture from condensing on the cold seeds. Take what you need and return the rest to the freezer.

Without freezing, seeds should be stored in cool, dry, dark places in paper envelopes (recommended for large seeds such as beans and peas) or airtight containers.

Seeds must be thoroughly dried before storing, which can be done in a number of ways. They can be simply air-dried on plates (see *Saving Seeds Successfully,* third week of June and fourth week of September). A food dehydrator can be used, but make sure the temperature does not exceed 95°F (35°C).

Seeds can also be dried using silica, available from florists. While dry silica particles are blue, they turn pink as they absorb moisture. Place an equal weight of dry silica in an airtight container, with your seeds separated from the

silica by cloth or paper. Seeds should be thoroughly dry no longer than one week later. The silica can then be removed and dried. Spread it on a tray and dry in the oven at 200°F (93°C) until the particles turn blue again. It can then be reused.

Let's Speak Latin

Plant Origin:
Canadian origin – *canadensis*
Japanese origin – *japonica*
Of the Southern hemisphere – *australis*
Eastern – *orientalis*
Mountainous – *montanus*

Plant Colour:
White – *albus*
Grey-blue – *glaucous*
Green – *viridis*
Red – *rubus*
Purple – *purpureus*
Yellow – *luteus*
Golden yellow – *aureus*
Sky blue – *azureus*

Plant Habit:
Creeping – *repens*
Hanging – *pendulus*
Tall, upright – *erecta*
Tree-like – *arboreus*

Plant Habitat:
Wild, common – *vulgaris*
Growing in fields – *campestris*
Of woods or forest – *sylvestris*
Of the sea – *maritima*

Plant Description:
Broad-leaved – *latifolius*
Narrow-leaved – *angustifolius*
Oak-leaved – *quercifolius*
Fragrant – *odoratus*
Musk scent – *moschatus*
Lovely – *amabilis*
Medicinal – *officinalis*

Before a Brand New Gardening Year

- Rake leaves and debris off the lawn.

- Remove decaying plants and fallen leaves from the pond to prevent methane and hydrogen sulfide gas build-up. (These gases are poisonous to fish if levels build up in pond water.)

- Check tree ties, so that strong winds won't uproot newly planted trees.

- Prune grape vines while they are dormant. Left until the sap starts to flow again, the sap will bleed from every cut. Prune back lateral stems to leave one or two strong buds on each stem.

- Clean underneath the rider mower or lawn mower. Protect metal surfaces from rust by spraying with WD40.

- If not done already, drain gas from weedeaters and lawn mowers, and run them dry. This will prevent gas lines from deteriorating over winter.

- Have your mower and weedeater serviced so they are ready for the next season.

- Keep on mulching – especially newly planted trees, bushes and semi-hardy perennials. *TIP:* Avoid contact between mulch and stems to prevent rotting.

- Sow seeds of berries. Hawthorns, species roses, cotoneaster, mountain ash and pyracantha can be propagated by squashing berries to extract their seeds. Clean off the seed pulp before sowing. Sow in pots filled with a sandy propagation mix and cover with a layer of coarse grit. Water. Leave outdoors in a cold frame over winter so the seed gets its period of chilling. Germination should take place in spring.

- Check greenhouse plants regularly. Remove dead or decaying leaves and any plants infected with botrytis.

- Water greenhouse plants sparingly *only* as needed, preferably in the morning or early part of the day so they don't sit wet and cold at night.

- If a shrub or tree has outgrown its allotted space, or you want to shape it to create a more pleasing aesthetic, prune it during the dormant season. *TIP:* Never use the word 'HACK' when referring to your pruning technique!

- Keep bird feeders filled on a regular basis. Once you start feeding birds, they come to rely on you for food. Cold snaps leave them vulnerable. Nuts, seeds, fatty scraps and fruit will attract a diversity of birds to your garden all winter.

- Pat yourself on the back! You have worked hard and performed miracles in your garden this past year. It's time to look forward to a brand new gardening year, working in co-creation with Mother Nature.

Index

A

Alfalfa, 142
Amaranth, 25
Anise hyssop *Agastache foeniculum*, 79
Aphids, 49, 61, 65, 75, **76-77**, 78
Apples, 63, 121, 138
Apricots, 126
Artichokes
- globe *Cynara scolymus*, **80**, 86
- Jerusalem *Helianthus tuberosus*, 25, 53, 62, 132, 137, **154**
Arugula, 54, 60, 91
Asparagus, 86, 137
Autumn crocus *Colchicum autumnale*, 98, **122**
Azaleas, 13, 50, **69-70**, 131

B

Bamboo, **40**, 67
Basil, 44, 78, 114
Bay, 44, 97, 136
Beans, 104
- fava, **22-23**, 32, 61, 137, **142**
- green, 25, 61, 81
Beautyberry *Callicarpa bodinieri*, 145
Bees, 94, 95, **103-104**
- Blue orchard mason (*Osmia lignaria*), 103
Bee friend *Phacelia tanecetifolia*, 79
Beer traps, 56
Beets, 60, 82, 92, 99, 132, **153**
Beneficial insects, 75-79, 94, 123
Berries, 53, 63, 87, 99, 126
Biennial flowers, 7, 85, **111**
Bindweed, **100**, 151
Birds, **5-6**, 88, 152
- bird feeders, **5**, 164
Black spot, 49, 51, 77, 131
Blackberries, 53, 87, 126
Blueberries, 10, 114
Borage *Borago officinalis*, 44, 62, **79**, 93
Botrytis, **14**, 26, 41
Brussels sprouts, 60, 82, 92, 147
Bt (*Bacillus thuriengensis*), 76
Buckwheat, 32, 61, 87, 92, 142
Bulbs, **19**, 49, **65**, 85, 125, **129**
Burning bush *Euonymus alatus*, 145

C

Cabbage, 14, 25, 78, 82, 92, 132
Camellias, **19-20**, 50, 56, 97, 131
Campanulas, 85, **111**
Canker, **20**, 126

Cardoon...

Cardoon *Cynara cardunculus*, 80, 86
Carrots, 26, 28, **60-61**, **82**, 87, 153-154
Caterpillars, 76
CCA - Chromated copper arsenate, 145
Celeriac, 60, 62, 132, **154**
Cherries, 126
Chickweed, **151-152**
Christmas tree care, 160
Clary sage *Salvia sclarea*, 111
Clematis, **39**, 55, 84
Cloches, **28**, 132
Clover, 141, 142, **151**
Club root, 14, 59, 142
Codling moth (*Cydia Pomonella*), 63
Coffee grounds, 61, 65, 87, 143, 153
Coir (coconut fibre), 68, 136, **162**
Collards, 82, 92, 132
Comfrey, **52**, 151
- comfrey tea, **51-52**
Companion planting, 28, **78**
Composting, **33**, 124
- three bin systems, 34
- compost tea, **51**, 119
Container gardening, **67**, 91, **114**
Copper
- barriers, 56
- sprays, 20, 137
Coriander (Chinese cilantro), 25, 79, 132
Corn, 25, 26, 28, 61, 104
Corn Salad (mache), **53-54**, 91-92, 132
Cornflower *Centaurea cyanus*, 79
Cotyledons, 41
Couchgrass, 35, **146**
Cover crops, 22, 126, **141-142**
Colchicum, see Autumn Crocus
Creeping buttercup, 151
Crop rotation, 25, **59-60**, 141
Cross pollination, 81-82
Cut flowers, 64
Cyclamen, 28, 55
- *C. hederifolium*, 122

D

Dahlias, **50**, 65, **136**
Daisies, 151
Damping off (*Pythium*), 27, **41**
Deerproof plants, 56
Delphiniums, 49, 56, 98
Dianthus, **86**, 93
Dill, 25, 26, **44**, 79
Disease resistance, 7

...

Division, **35-36**, 125
Dogwood *Cornus* spp., 18, 97, 145
Dolomite lime, 10, **14**, 37, 59, 119
Dormant sprays, **20**, 137

E

Earthworms (*Lumbricus terrestris*), 24, 123, **152**
Earwigs, 50, 65, 76
Eggplant, 26, 86, **109-110**, 114 *↦mid march indoors.*
English cowslip *Primula veris*, 69
English holly *Ilex aquifolium*, 135
Epsom salts, 43, 50
Euphorbias, 55, 56, **65**, 84
Evergreen huckleberry *Vaccinium ovatum*, 88

F

Fairy rings, 136
Fall cleanup, 124
Fall interest plants, 121, **135**
Fall rye, 13, 32, 53, 126, **141-142**
Favas, see Beans
Fennel *Foeniculum vulgare*, 44, 79
Fertilizers, **2**, 31, 119, 152, 159
Festive greenery, 156
Figs, 138
Fish fertilizer, 27, 28, 41, 92
Flea beetles, **14**, 78, 92, 99, 109
Foliage interest, 135
Forget-Me-Nots *Myosotis sylvestris*, 66, 85, 111, 125
Foxgloves *Digitalis purpurea*, 26, 55, 85, 111
Fruit trees, **20**, 137
Fungicide, 6, **63**, 77
Fungus gnats, 27, 77

G

Garlic, 53, 77, 98, 104, **133-134**
- scapes, 62, 87
- white rot, 134
Genetic modification (GMO), 2, 6, 32, 159
Germander, 50
Germination, 7, **26**, **28**, **41**, 64
Gift ideas for gardeners, 157
Glyphosate, 123
Golden marguerite *Anthemis tinctoria*, 79
Grapes, 164
Grasses, 36, 40, 79, 125
Grease bands, 126
Green manures, 13, 22, **32**, **141-142**

Carolyn Herriot has been operating *The Garden Path Nursery* in Victoria since 1989 (certified organic - IOPA 1406), from which grew her organic seed business, *Seeds of Victoria.*

Carolyn shares her passion for gardening in public lectures and workshops, and as a garden writer. Her garden has been featured in many magazines: *Better Homes and Gardens, The BC Gardener* and *The Complete Canadian Gardener.* Following the success of her gardening show, *The Garden Path,* on CJVI AM900 radio, she now appears as co-host on *Get Up and Grow* on Global TV and the *GO* show on CHTV.

Carolyn introduced Seedy Saturday to Victoria in 1993, and has helped establish Seedy Saturday shows in many other communities. She was awarded the White Oak trophy for her contribution to the Victoria Horticultural Society in 1994, and was recognized by *Focus on Women* magazine for her work as Head Gardener at Point Ellice House in 1996. In 2000 she was awarded the YM-YWCA Women of Distinction award for her unique contribution to the community.

In 2001 Carolyn helped to found SOUL, The Society For Organic Urban Landcare, for which she currently serves as Director, and as Chair of the SOUL Organic Garden Club.

Carolyn lives and gardens in Victoria BC, Canada. Her number one passion is still talking about plants and getting down and dirty in her beloved garden!

Take a cyber visit to *The Garden Path* at www.earthfuture.com/gardenpath.

Want to order more copies, or a copy for a friend?

A Year on The Garden Path:
A 52-Week Organic Gardening Guide
by Carolyn Herriot

A Year On The Garden Path provides invaluable gardening advice any time of the year. Simply turn to any week in the book to get seasonally relevant, practical advice, solutions to problems, and lots of organic gardening tips.

An Organic Gardening Guide That Never Goes Out of Date!

'Thanks for all that wonderful information and entertainment you have sent via your newsletters. I am glad to hear you are putting them into a book, it's a good idea. You are an excellent writer and all that effort should be somewhere in permanent form. Yes, I would like a copy!' — Marilyn Pollard, B.C.

'Thank you very much for all the newsletters I received in 2004. They are informative and fun and most helpful when dealing with pests and problems. I have enjoyed your recipes, poetry and humour.' — Pat Battles, B.C.

A Year on the Garden Path (per copy)	$24.95 Cdn, $19.95 US	$ _____
Postage and handling (per copy)	$4.00 ($8.00 to the US)	$ _____
Taxable Subtotal		$ _____
Add 7% GST on taxable subtotal		$ _____
Total		$ _____

Name: _____

Address: _____

City: _____ Postal Code/Zip: _____

E-mail: _____

Phone: (____) _____ Fax: (____) _____

PAYMENT METHOD:
❏ Cheque (Made Payable to The Garden Path)
❏ VISA
❏ Mastercard

Name on Card: _____

Card Number: _____ Expiry: _____

Signature: _____

You can order by:
Faxing this form to: (250) 881-1304
Phone (have credit card number handy): (250) 881-1555
Online from our website: www.earthfuture.com/gardenpath
By mailing to: The Garden Path, 395 Conway Road
Victoria, BC V9E 2B9

~ Thank You for Your Order ~

Reviews

'Carolyn Herriot's book is a gardener's best friend, a complete chronological guide of when to and how to; good organic and hard-to-find formulas for feeding and pest control; reminders on when to start food crops, perennials, annuals and herbs, with good information on small fruits, fruit trees and ornamental shrubs. I love her care and concern over our garden allies – birds, bugs, worms and frogs. Carolyn's book is a keeper because we will all need it as a constant reference and companion.'
–*Brian Minter (gardening expert and owner of Minter Gardens)*

'Written in an easy to follow style, 'A Year on the Garden Path' is jammed full of sensible and practical ideas. Many gardeners re-locate and find west coast gardening a whole new ball game; they are amazed they can grow winter vegetables, which is just the tip of the iceberg! Read this book and be inspired to have a garden 52 weeks of the year.'
–*David Tarrant (television host, international lecturer, writer and horticulturist)*

'This is an immensely good-hearted gardening guide compiled by someone who knows her stuff. Packed with practical advice, it excels because its wealth of information is provided within the context of our deepening environmental crisis. The Garden Path doesn't lead towards gloomy hopelessness, but rather to an empowering realization that the gardener's seminal work is to embody the major course correction required for humankind to begin treating Planet Earth with respect and affection.'
–*Des Kennedy (journalist, broadcaster, author)*

'Here is a week-by-week guide to growing the best possible vegetables, fruits, flowers and ornamentals while taking advantage of Nature's own aids to plant health and nurturing a robust, life-giving soil. Full of practical tips and toothsome recipes, 'A Year on the Garden Path' is a detailed map to environmentally friendly gardening.'
–*Helen Chesnut (gardening columnist, Times Colonist)*

'Carolyn Herriot has written and published a fantastic new gardening book. Every page of 'A Year on the Garden Path' is a feast of Carolyn's brilliant observations, earthy common sense and her wonderful wit and wisdom.'
–*Dan Jason (author and owner of Salt Spring Seeds)*

'Experienced and novice gardeners alike will enjoy this book. For those of us who resolve to keep a gardening journal and don't, this book is a great substitute, filled with weekly reminders of what is happening in most gardens. Easy to read, very practical and a must-have for gardeners new to this gardening zone. Herriot's enthusiasm for her garden is infectious. She leaves the reader feeling encouraged and inspired.'
–*Susan Ramsey (The Artful Gardener, Times Colonist)*